HUDDLED MASSES AND UNCERTAIN SHORES

Refugees and Human Rights

Volume 2

The *Refugees and Human Rights* Series aims to meet the increasing need for literature which probes the nature and causes of forced migration, the modalities and procedures employed when refugees present themselves, and the manner in which the human rights of refugees are, or should be, promoted and protected.

The Centre for Refugee Studies at York University has been an Organized Research Unit since 1988. It was designated a Centre of Excellence by the Canadian International Development Agency in 1991. In addition to affiliated York University faculty members from many different disciplines and professions, the Centre supports visiting scholars, postdoctoral fellows, and graduate students. Centre activities include an active Seminar Series, a Newsletter, international conference workshops, as well as offering Graduate Diploma and undergraduate General Certificate Programmes in Refugee and Migration Studies.

HUDDLED MASSES AND UNCERTAIN SHORES

INSIGHTS INTO IRREGULAR MIGRATION

by

BIMAL GHOSH

IOM International Organization for Migration

MARTINUS NIJHOFF PUBLISHERS
THE HAGUE / BOSTON / LONDON

A C.I.P. Catalogue record for this book is available from the Library of Congress.

ISBN 90-411-0531-X

Published by Kluwer Law International,
P.O. Box 85889, 2508 CN The Hague, The Netherlands

Sold and distributed in North, Central and South America
by Kluwer Law International,
675 Massachusetts Avenue, Cambridge, MA 02139, U.S.A.

In all other countries, sold and distributed
by Kluwer Law International, Distribution Centre
P.O. Box 322, 3300 AH Dordrecht, The Netherlands

Printed on acid-free paper

Printed in Great Britain.

Table of Contents

Acknowledgements

I am indebted to James N. Purcell, Director-General of the International Organization for Migration for his foreword to the book and to several officials of the organisation, notably Robert Paiva, Reinhard Lohrmann, and Regina Boucault, for their enthusiastic support and assistance in carrying out the study. I am particularly thankful to Atish Rex Ghosh of the International Monetary Fund for his help in completing the appendices to the book and to Swati Reina Ghosh of the World Bank who took an active interest in the study and promptly made available several latest documents of relevance to it.

Sincere thanks are also due to Sarita Sehgal for her valuable assistance in preparing the index, revising the text and making it ready for publication.

The views expressed, including the recommendations made, in the book are my own and the responsibility for any errors of omission or commission rest with me alone.

This study has been prepared with the financial support of the International Organization for Migration. The opinions expressed herein are those of the author and do not necessarily reflect the views of IOM or its member states.

Abbreviations

AFDC	Aid to Families with Dependent Children
CIREFI	Centre for Information, Discussion and Exchange on the Crossing of Frontiers and Immigration (EU)
CIS	Commonwealth of Independent States
EC/EU	European Community/European Union
ECOSOC	Economic and Social Council (United Nations)
FDI	Foreign Direct Investment
GAO	General Accounting Office (US Government)
GATT	General Agreement on Tariffs and Trade
GATS	General Agreement on Trade in Services
ICFTU	International Confederation of Free Trade Unions
ICMPD	International Centre for Migration Policy Development
ICRC	International Committee for the Red Cross
IGC	Intergovernmental Consultations on Asylum, Refugee and Migration Policy in Europe, North America and Australia
ILO	International Labour Organisation
IMF	International Monetary Fund
IIRIRA	Illegal Immigration Reform and Immigrant Responsibility Act (US)
INS	Immigration and Naturalization Service (US)
IOM	International Organization for Migration
IRCA	Immigration Reform and Control Act (US)
LDCs	Least Developed Countries
MFN	Most Favoured Nation Treatment
NAFTA	North American Free Trade Agreement
NICs	Newly Industrialising Countries
OAU	Organisation of African Unity
OECD	Organisation for Economic Cooperation and Development
OSCE	Organisation for Security and Cooperation in Europe
RCA	Revealed Comparative Advantage
SAVE	Systematic Alien Verification for Entitlement (US)
STEP	Special Targetted Enforcement Programme (US)
UN	United Nations
UNCTAD	United Nations Conference on Trade and Development

UNDP	United Nations Development Programme
UNEP	UN Environment Programme
UNHCR	UN High Commissioner for Refugees
World Bank	International Bank for Reconstruction and Development including International Finance Corporation and International Development Association
WHO	World Health Organisation
WTO	World Trade Organisation

Notes

- Dollar ($) refers to United States dollars, unless otherwise indicated.
- Billion is 1,000 million
- Purchasing Power Parity (PPP) is the actual power of a unit of local currency to buy goods and services in its country of issue. This may be more or less than what a unit of the same currency will buy of equivalent foreign goods and services at current market exchange rates.
- Country groups: Economies are divided into three groups using World Bank figures for GNP per capita. The groups are: low-income (GNP per capita of $695 or less in 1993); middle-income (GNP per capita of between $696 and $8,625 in 1993); and high-income (GNP per capita of $8,626 or more in 1993). Unless otherwise indicated, developed or industrial countries refer to high-income economies, while the term 'developing countries' is used generically for the remaining countries/economies.

The designations of country groups are used solely for statistical or analytical convenience and do not necessarily reflect a judgment about the stage of development reached by a particular country or area.

List of Tables, Boxes, Figures and Appendices

TABLES

BOXES

FIGURES

APPENDICES

Foreword

Irregular migration, including human trafficking, has emerged in recent years as a major international challenge. Both sending and receiving countries are affected by this alarming phenomenon. Worse still, the situation, from all indications, seems to be deteriorating fast. Yearly irregular immigration now equals around one-third of the legal inflow in the United States and half in Europe. Just as disturbing, the illicit trafficking of migrants consumes an estimated US$7 billion a year, constituting an enormous diversion of resources to unproductive and anti-social activities. The close ties between human trafficking, forced prostitution and smuggling of illegal arms and drugs makes irregular migration a multi-faceted menace. It cries out for an early and effective solution.

This book by Professor Bimal Ghosh is one of the most complete and penetrating studies of irregular migration to date. The analysis masterfully unveils the complexities of contemporary irregular migration and the various issues relevant to it. Using a broad canvas and an unbiased approach, the book clarifies the nature and root causes of irregular movements, unravels their immediate and far-reaching consequences and lays down possible remedies.

In choosing the title of the book *Huddled Masses and Uncertain Shores* – Professor Ghosh aptly captures the deep sense of anguish and insecurity from which large numbers of irregular migrants suffer before and during the journey to the destination country – and indeed for long thereafter. The book's comprehensive discussion of the social and economic causes and consequences in both sending and receiving countries sharpens the reader's awareness about the truth of irregular migration.

As the author notes, when there are powerful push factors in sending countries or pull factors in receiving countries and especially when the two converge, restrictive measures alone cannot arrest migratory flows; they are simply diverted to irregular channels. The analysis also makes it easy to understand why and how less competitive industries and marginal firms in receiving countries often welcome irregular immigration as a source of cheap and docile labour. This and the related discussion of the circumstances surrounding irregular movements will hopefully help remove the current, and seemingly widely held, belief that all irregular migrants are criminals and enhance the awareness of the need to protect irregular migrants from exploitation – as much for curbing irregular flows as on compelling ethical grounds.

From a policy-making perspective, the final chapters of the book are of exceptional importance. As he analyses current national measures against irregular migration, the author shows his incisiveness in drawing on the discussion in the first half of the study which enables him to convincingly reveal the reasons for their relative inadequacies. The need for close and continuing cooperation between governments of sending and receiving countries, international organisations and non-governmental bodies is highlighted with great specificity as Professor Ghosh moves on to delineate a comprehensive strategy to combat irregular migration, taking the analyses in the previous chapters to their logical conclusion. The pro-active strategy is demonstrated to be as important for fighting irregular migration as for ensuring better management of international movements of people. The two, as the author underlines, are closely inter-twined.

The three technical appendices to the book are an additional attraction for those readers who would like to delve a little further into such specific issues as the links between economic stagnation and pressures for irregular migration or those between unmet labour demand, immigration restrictions and irregular migration.

The IOM itself has stepped up its efforts, in cooperation with other international and regional organisations concerned, to overcome and prevent irregular migration, especially human trafficking. Clearly, however, the international organisations cannot fulfill this task on their own. Enhanced public awareness and understanding and imaginative government action are vital for this purpose. I see this book as a potential trigger in sensitizing national and international policy-makers and the general public about the realities of irregular migration in its diverse ramifications. Improved information about this complex problem would hopefully generate a more effective and comprehensive response, making it possible for current, often restrictive, policies against irregular movements to be complemented by a new set of coherent and forward-looking measures.

I envision Professor Ghosh's study to be of wide interest among governments, international organisations, universities and research institutions, migrant-serving associations and other non-governmental organisations. The lucidity of style and clarity of arguments should make this timely book equally valuable for the general reader who is interested to learn more about an issue which is poised to assume increasingly critical importance at both national and international levels.

James N. Purcell Jr.
Director-General,
International Organization for Migration

Preface

Irregular migration – or inter-country movements that take place in defiance of national laws and regulations – is not new. But over the past few years such movements, especially in the form of human trafficking, have seen an unprecedented increase just as they have become closely linked to international crime and violence. The mass media is now replete with ghastly stories about exploitation, extortion and other abusive practices that human trafficking often entails. Increasing publicity about these incidents has not however necessarily meant an enhanced awareness among the public or the policy-makers about the realities of irregular migration. National and international measures to curb irregular migration are being stepped up, but the harsh events on the ground, including the seemingly unstoppable irregular flows, clearly demonstrate that they are proving inadequate and largely ineffective.

True, a number of recent econometric and similar analytical studies in the United States and Western Europe have provided valuable insights into specific aspects of irregular migration. In most cases, however, they are too narrowly focused to capture all the ramifications of contemporary irregular migration as it affects sending, receiving and transit countries. Nor do they adequately deal with the multiple causes and varied consequences of such movements. And yet such an analysis is essential for formulating an effective and coherent strategy to remove the root causes of irregular and disorderly movements.

The present book is an attempt to fill this vacuum. It seeks to provide within a single framework a reasonably comprehensive analysis of irregular migration in its different aspects and dimensions: its nature, characteristics and magnitude; its causes, conditions and consequences; and the inadequacies of existing policies and measures. Against the backdrop of this analysis, the study in its last chapter puts forward a set of specific proposals which can be woven into a coherent and comprehensive strategy to combat irregular migration.

The fast-evolving situation, including rapid changes in national policies and legal measures, tends to turn the subject of irregular migration into a moving target, making it difficult to bring the reader right up to date with the latest developments. Although March 1997 served as the cut-off date for the preparation of the book, special efforts were made to incorporate some of the more recent information before the text finally went to press.

If the book stimulates some pro-active thinking in addressing irregular migration, the author will be more than content.

CHAPTER ONE

Discerning irregular migration: Complex configuration of movements

1.1. What is irregular migration? Definition, types and characteristics

The concern over irregular migration, though not new, is increasing. In Western Europe, as in North America, it is receiving wider attention as stricter measures are being adopted to combat it. New initiatives are also being taken to supplement or reinforce existing regional and international instruments dealing with different aspects of the issue.[1] And yet, there is still no clear or universally accepted definition of irregular migration.

An important reason for this is that irregularity or illegality in migratory movements can be viewed from different perspectives. This also at least partly accounts for the divergent terminology used to specify such movements. The panoply of terms used include: 'illegal migration', 'clandestine migration', 'undocumented migration' and 'irregular migration', emphasizing, at least implicitly, different forms or characteristics of irregular movements. A discussion of these characteristics, as attempted below, is important for a better understanding of the problems involved, for a clearer definition of irregular migration (the term generically used in this study) and, above all, for the formulation of effective policy responses.

Irregularity not an exclusive concern of the destination country

Irregular migration is generally viewed from the perspective of the destination country, but illegality or irregularity in migratory movements may occur either in the sending or the receiving country or both. For example, when a person travels across borders without a valid passport or an equivalent document required by national laws, the non-compliance of the legal requirement places him/her in an irregular situation in the country of origin. The non-possession of a valid national travel document should also normally make the entry irregular in the destination country even in cases where no visas are required. But this apart, there are several situations in which the irregularity of the movement arises from non-compliance of the laws and regulations concerning departure or exit from the country of origin, but not necessarily in the destina-

[1] For a discussion of the major international instruments see Chapter 4.

tion country. Irregular movements also affect a transit country: it faces problems which are similar to those of the country of origin or the country of destination or both, depending on whether the infringement of regulations relates to the entry, stay or departure of the migrant or to all three stages.

Irregularity from the perspective of the country of origin Although the practice is less common today, several countries in the past had restricted, on political, economic or ideological grounds, travel by its nationals to certain specified countries; the issuance of a valid passport did not automatically imply that travel to these countries was authorised. Without a proper 'endorsement' in the passport or a special exit visa, travel to such countries would be considered irregular in the country of origin, even if the person is legally admitted in the destination country.

Under the communist regime in Central and Eastern European countries, for example, a person was considered an 'illegal' emigrant if his/her stay abroad lasted more than 12 months without official authorisation from the home country. An overstaying person was a national who extended the duration of a stay abroad beyond the limit fixed by the authorities and indicated in the exit visa. Often an overstaying person was subsequently considered 'illegal'.[2]

A similar, though not identical, situation arises when there is non-compliance with the restrictions that may be imposed by the country of origin to regulate the level and/or composition of migratory outflows. Such measures were introduced, for example, by several Arab countries in order to restrain or regulate emigration on a selective basis in different periods of time (e.g. Egypt in the mid-1950s and during the 1960s and early 1970s; Algeria during 1965–1971 and especially in September 1973 and Syria in the mid 1970s). Some South Asian countries, for example, Bangladesh and Pakistan, prohibit the emigration of females below a minimum age to be employed as housemaids or nannies. (See Table 1.1 for a list of restrictions on female worker migration in selected Asian countries.) Emigration in defiance of these restrictions or in contravention of the conditions attaching to special authorisation would be considered illegal by the countries of origin, but not necessarily by the receiving states.

From the perspective of the country of origin, there could be a third type of irregularity in intercountry movements. This occurs when the emigrant fails to complete all the administrative formalities required by the national authorities (even if the movement may otherwise be legal). To illustrate, several South Asian countries (e.g. Pakistan and Sri Lanka), require all labour migrants to register themselves with the official agency specially set up for purposes of monitoring employment-related migration, and the failure to do so *ipso facto* makes a labour migrant irregular (or undocumented) in these countries, although the person may otherwise be in possession of all valid travel documents such as the passport and the entry visa for the destination country.

---

[2] OECD, *Trends in International Migration (SOPEMI)*, 1992, Paris, 1993, Appendix, p. 121.

Table 1.1. Restrictions on female worker migration in selected Asian countries

Country	Restrictions
Bangladesh	Women must be at least 21 years old to work as domestic workers. Ban on recruitment of entertainers.
Burma	Ban on recruitment of female workers, except in the case of professionals.
India	Women must be at least 30 years old to work as domestic workers in Western Asia or Northern Africa, with exceptions made on a case by case basis.
Indonesia	Women must be at least 22 years old. Restrictions regarding country of destination for household workers and male/female ratios recruited by authorised agents may be lifted under certain conditions.
Malaysia	None
Nepal	Women must be at least 18 years old. Selective ban on employment according to the country of destination.
Pakistan	Women must be at least 35 years old to work as domestic workers. Ban on recruitment of nurses.
Philippines	Domestic workers: women must be at least 25 years old; selective ban on employment according to the country of destination. Entertainers: women must be at least 23 years old; selective ban on employment according to the country of destination; must complete required academic and skills testings, possess Artist Record Book, undergo pre-departure showcase preview. Nurses: women must be at least 23 years old; must possess Bachelor of Science degree in Nursing and one year work experience in the Philippines.
Sri Lanka	Women must be 20 years old to work as domestic workers. Ban on recruitment of entertainers.
Thailand	Ban on recruitment of women except for the case of selected countries of destination. Entertainers must hold a diploma from school of arts and a license, and must not perform in night clubs.

Sources: Ministries or Departments of Labour responding to Abella in 1990 (Abella, 1995) and to the authors in September 1995. ILO: Lin Lean Lim and Nana Oishi, *International Labour Migration of Asian Women: Distinctive Characteristics and Policy Concerns, 1996* (mimeo). Based on information provided by the Ministries/Departments of Labour in 1990 and 1995.

Mexican law requires that Mexican nationals exit through official inspection stations. Thus, those who move, for example, to the USA through other exit points along the border automatically violate Mexican laws.

Paying attention to irregularities as they affect the sending countries, and not just the receiving ones, helps in formulating a comprehensive definition of irregular movements. This is also politically important in fostering cooperation between sending and receiving countries in order to combat irregular migration.

Irregularity from the perspective of the country of destination. From the point of view of the destination country, it is easier to discern the main characteristics of irregular immigration – or at least it is seemingly so. Non-nationals are generally considered to be in an irregular situation (i) when they have not complied with the required formalities, or have not obtained the authorisation required by law, for admission or stay or for their activity during such stay in a country; or (ii) when they cease to meet the conditions to which their stay or activity is subject. Three main elements of this definition need to be clearly discerned.

Irregular entry can take the form of clandestine entry or entry without (or with incomplete) travel documents required under immigration regulations of the country. *Irregular residence* relates to situations where a non-national within a country has not complied with the requisite formalities or obtained authorisation required by law for stay in the country. The stay will also be considered irregular if after having completed the formalities or obtained the authorisation a non-national subsequently ceases to meet the stipulated conditions. A non-national overstaying in the country beyond the period for which the residence permit or visa was issued is a typical example of such irregularity.

Irregular activity or employment refers to the pursuit of activities by a non-national within a country which are either unlawful or for which the person does not have, or has ceased to have, the necessary authorisation. Such cases of irregular employment arise when, for example, a non-national entering the country on a tourist visa subsequently takes on a job without the necessary authorisation, or a seasonal worker with a short-term work permit is employed beyond the period of his/her work permit.

Intertwining of irregularity: immigrant's entry, stay and activity

Differences in definition and measurement of irregular migration also arise because of the complex interlinkages between the three elements mentioned above, namely entry, residence and activity of the irregular immigrants. It is useful to distinguish between these three elements, although, as discussed below, in many cases they become closely intertwined.

Irregular employment does not necessarily imply or constitute irregular immigration. A non-national may be holding an irregular job (without the authorisation required under the relevant regulations or clandestine employment in contravention of labour laws), but his/her entry and residence in the receiving country may continue to be legal. All clandestine workers (e.g. employed in contravention of labour laws) are not illegal immigrants (or non-nationals) just as legal immigrants may not necessarily be legally employed. In France, for example, a study recently published by the Employment Ministry revealed that, contrary to common belief, the large majority – more precisely, seven out of 10 – of clandestine or illegally employed workers are nationals of the country, and not foreigners.[3] In the Hessen state of Germany, a recent report by the labour office revealed that most illegal or unregulated jobs in the underground economy were filled by German citizens, not foreigners.[4]

---

[3] *Liberation*, 22 October 1992; *Migration News Sheet*, November, 1992.

[4] Cited in *Migration News*, Vol. 3, No. 7, July, 1996.

Indeed, in the past the holding of a job in the receiving country has sometimes been a main criterion for regularising the status of an irregular immigrant. Experience shows that in times of labour shortage in the destination country, irregular entry and residence of non-nationals may be tolerated or even positively viewed not only by the prospective employers, but also by the authorities concerned. Between the 1950s and early 1970s, when their economies were expanding fast and labour demand was high, most Western European countries used to take a benign attitude towards irregular entry of non-nationals. In France, often irregular immigrants could easily regularise their status on the strength of their finding employment. In the United States, until the provisions were modified in November 1986, it was not illegal to engage non-nationals whose status as immigrants was irregular. In other words, the entry and stay of the immigrant might have been illegal, but offering or holding the employment was not! In the late 1940s many Mexicans arrived in the United States, found jobs and then had their status regularised.[5] In the Netherlands, as recently as 1994 the government was examining the situation of those foreigners who resided illegally but who worked legally and paid taxes.[6]

The practical implications of such a situation are clear. When there are positive prospects or specific offers of employment for immigrants who are in an irregular situation, it is likely to encourage further irregular immigration to the country. Unauthorised (or irregular) employment and irregular immigration are then likely to go hand in hand. As will be further discussed in Chapter 2, this is exactly what is currently happening in many industrial countries where the expansion of the informal sectors and the continued existence of inefficient and non-competitive industries have created a demand for cheap and illegal immigrant labour, thus encouraging further irregular immigration.

Trafficking in migration (discussed separately below) has reinforced the links between clandestine immigration and irregular employment, as the traffickers often act in collusion with employers of irregular immigrants in the destination country or they themselves control, directly or indirectly, the syndicates which run the business activities concerned. A new dimension to the problem lies in the fact that many of these business operations – such as trafficking in drugs and arms – are unlawful. The engagement of the non-nationals in these operations thus implies a two-fold illegality; not only is their employment unauthorised but the activity itself is unlawful.

The above discussion has shown that irregular employment often encourages, or is combined with, irregular immigration, although in itself it does not

---

[5] In 1949, for example, 87,000 Mexicans arrived illegally in the United States and subsequently had their status regularised; by contrast, only about 20,000 Mexicans received contracts at recruitment centres in Mexico and legally entered the United States as contract workers. Presidents' Commission, 1951, p. 53. Philip Martin 'Guest Workers' Policies: An International Survey' (mimeo), 1995, pp. 11–12.

[6] *Migration News Sheet*, November, 1992.

constitute illegal immigration.[7] However, when the entry and stay of a non-national is authorised specifically to enable him/her to pursue a particular activity (e.g. participation in a training or research project, provision of services, participation in a conference, or establishing a business) the situation could be different. Non-compliance with these conditions (e.g. taking up an unauthorised, longer-term job) may not be only an issue of irregular employment; it would in principle render immigration itself irregular. In the Gulf States, for example, the residence and work permits may be issued on the understanding that the immigrant would be working for a particular employer. In such a situation, accepting a job with some other employer may render both the employment and residence illegal.

Other familiar examples include legally authorised entry and stay of East European workers for training and/or fixed term employment in West European countries (notably Germany) under bilateral agreements, leading to unauthorised, longer-term employment, often with the support and connivance of the employers. The latter clearly has the effect of placing the immigrants in an irregular situation.[8]

Malicious defiance of established laws or institutional deficiency?

A closer analysis of these three elements brings into focus a host of complex issues. As regards entry and residence, an irregular immigrant, who seeks admission in defiance of established regulations, may wilfully avoid having the necessary documents or may carry with him false documents. But a movement with inadequate documentation, be it in the sending or the receiving country, may also reflect an institutional deficiency rather than a deliberate intention of the migrant to circumvent the legal requirements. Such deficiency may relate to administrative and procedural constraints including the absence of competent official agencies in remote areas, unhelpful attitude of the officials responsible for processing the documents or simply lack of information and knowledge about the legal requirements and procedures. [Further discussed in Chapter 2, Section 2.6 Institutional and administrative deficiencies.]

The traditional cross-border movements of the nomads in the Sahel region of Africa, patterned after cycles of climatic change and pastoral needs, provides an extreme example. Distribution and processing of documents to authorise and monitor these movements may have been well beyond the administrative capacity of the governments concerned. And yet in so far as the migrants

---

[7] It is important to note that irregularity concerning the activity or employment of a non-national may arise in different circumstances such as: (i) when the activity itself is unlawful, or (ii) when the non-national does not possess the required authorisation (e.g. work permit), or (iii) when he/she fails to fulfill the conditions to which such authorisation is subject.

[8] The fact that under other bilateral agreements, nationals of many of these Eastern and Central European countries do not need visas to travel as tourists to the Western European countries is not relevant in this context.

remained undocumented, they would be considered to be in an irregular situation.

Incomplete documentation may also reflect or stem from unrealistic government policies. For example, under recent regulations of several countries of Western Europe, failure to produce travel documents such as passports would make an asylum-seeker non-eligible, with the result that he/she would have an irregular status. These measures are generally justified on the grounds that in a growing number of cases the asylum-seekers destroyed the travel documents to conceal information showing the country of origin and enhance the prospects of acceptance of their requests for asylum.[9] But there could also be many cases where a genuine asylum-seeker, haunted by the fear of persecution in a hostile political climate, would be unable to secure all the travel documents and complete the necessary formalities before fleeing the country. Non-compliance may also be due to lack of information about the regulatory requirements. In Russia, for example, a recent sample survey revealed that more than half of the migrants without a residence permit knew nothing about the government regulations on foreigners in the country.[10]

An important implication is that when incomplete documentation and the consequent irregularity in movements are due to institutional deficiencies, unrealistic policies or information gaps, the main challenge lies in removing these deficiencies. Also, both ethically and legally, it would be wrong to equate such irregular migrants with those who deliberately seek to circumvent established migration laws and regulations for purposes of illicit gains, for example, through drug trafficking.

Links between asylum-seeking and irregular migration

Complications in defining and measuring irregular migration also arise as it often gets intertwined with unsuccessful asylum-seeking. As the experience of Western Europe, especially during 1985–1993, revealed, a substantial proportion of non-bona fide asylum seekers (who are unlikely to qualify as refugees under the United Nations Convention of 1951 and the Protocol of 1967 relating to the status of refugees) tended to go underground as irregular immigrants when their applications were turned down or even when their applications

---

[9] For example, according to the UNHCR sources, the proportion of asylum seekers without documentation or with forged documents was about 90 per cent in the Netherlands and Switzerland; 80 per cent in Norway; and 70 per cent in Sweden in 1989. A rough estimate placed the overall average for Western European countries between 50 per cent and 80 per cent. See, Jonas Widgren, 'Movements of Refugees and Asylum-seekers: Recent trends In A Comparative Perspective', 1991. (OECD, Paris). Paper presented to the OECD Conference on Migration, Rome, 13–15 March 1991.

[10] IOM, Migration Information Programme, *Transit Migration in the Russian Federation.* July 1994, Geneva, p. 34.

were being considered.[11] Some individuals who escape to a foreign country and are eligible for refugee status may prefer for various reasons not to apply. Unless otherwise granted legal status, they are considered irregular immigrants by the receiving states. There are others who may have held refugee status but may subsequently lose it because of withdrawal of the status by the receiving state following political changes in the home country. Many of them may decide however not to return home, and thus swell the ranks of irregular immigrants either in the host country or in a third country where they might move.[12]

Problems of common definition and measurement of irregular migration also arise because of divergent legal systems and practices governing refugee flows. Some developing countries, which have not signed the 1951 UN Convention (and the 1967 Protocol) may consider as irregular immigrants all foreigners not admitted as legal immigrants. Also worthy of note is the fact that the Organisation of African Unity (OAU) Convention on refugees and the Cartagena Declaration on refugees of Latin American States are both of wider scope (though not in an identical manner) than the UN Convention.[13] Individuals recognised as refugees under these regional instruments may be considered illegal immigrants if they move to countries which are not a party to these arrangements.

In Western Europe a similar problem arises in connection with rejected asylum seekers. In some states, those appealing against a negative decision on asylum application are given the right to reside legally for the duration of the process, but in others, the appellant is considered to have an irregular status and can be repatriated. In the Netherlands, under a broad (and controversial) definition proposed by the government in 1995, 'illegal aliens' should include both clandestine immigrants and foreigners awaiting a decision on their asylum applications.[14]

---

[11] According to an estimate made in 1992, some 75 per cent of the asylum applicants in industrial countries in the late 1980s actually stayed on, half of them legally (after having obtained the refugee status), but the other half stayed illegally or semi-legally. See, Jonas Widgren 'Movements of Refugees and Asylum-seekers: Recent Trends In A Comparative Perspective', 1991, op. cit.

[12] Reinhard Lohrmann, 'Irregular Migration: An Emerging Issue in Developing Countries' in Reginald Appleyard, *The Impact of International Migration On Developing Countries*, 1989 (OECD, Paris), p. 131.

[13] In 1969, the Organization of African Unity (OAU) adopted a Convention Governing the Specific Aspects of Refugee Problems in Africa, which expanded the UN definition of a refugee. It included those persons who are outside their countries 'owing to external aggression, occupation, foreign domination or events seriously disturbing public order'. The Declaration of Cartagena, adopted by Latin American governments in 1984 as a non-binding statement of policy, went even beyond the OAU definition. It included not only those individuals who met the UN criteria, but also those 'who have fled their country because their lives, safety, or freedom have been threatened by generalized violence, foreign aggression, internal conflicts, massive violation of human rights or other circumstances which have seriously disturbed public order'.

[14] *De Volkstat*, 5 October, 1995 and *Migration News Sheet*, November 1995.

Two general points emerge from the discussion so far. First, the forms and characteristics of the irregular movements and the part played by the various actors involved in the process, vary widely. At one extreme, irregular movements may be directly linked to the pursuit of illegal gains by unscrupulous migrants and traffickers; at the other extreme, migrants can be seen as unfortunate victims of deficiencies in institutions, policies and information systems and/or their own ignorance of the relevant rules and regulations. This diversity also lends special justification to the use of a somewhat neutral and flexible term like 'irregular migration' to describe generically all inter-country movements that take place outside the regulatory norms of the sending, transit and receiving countries. Second, there is a need for a more harmonised definition and clearer classification of irregular migration in order to better identify the problems involved and formulate appropriate policy measures to deal with them.

1.2. Increasing volume and changing features

No one can be sure of the total number of irregular migrants around the world. The difficulties of estimation arise both from the nature of the movements themselves and the absence of a uniform definition of irregular migration. Linked to these is the problem of methodology: different states use different methods to assess the extent of the problem.[15] And the wide divergence in the methodology used reduces the comparability of the available statistics for individual countries. Not surprisingly, even within the countries, widely different figures are used by different groups and institutions, often reflecting their respective political, economic or ideological biases. Official agencies may consider a non-national to be in an irregular situation, but this may be challenged in a court of law if the immigration legislation is ambiguous.

Magnitude of the problem

United States of America In the United States, the country with the largest number of irregular immigrants, the magnitude of the problem has been a subject of speculation for many years, with the past estimates varying between 1.9 million and 4.5 million. Recently, however, the US Immigration and Naturalization Service (INS) has developed a relatively more reliable method of estimating the number of irregular immigrants through the combined use of several sets of statistics. The estimate for 1992 showed that the United States probably had 3.3 million irregular migrants living in the country.[16] The US

---

[15] For an indication of the different methodologies used, see IGC, *Illegal Aliens: A Preliminary Study*, IGC Secretariat, Geneva, June 1995, p. 14–15.

[16] Based on Census Bureau data, including information from the Bureau's Current Population Surveys and INS statistics from the IRCA legalisation programme. See Robert Warren, *Estimates of the Undocumented Immigrant Population Residing in the United States, by Country of Origin, and State of Residence: October 1992*. INS Statistics Division.

Census estimate indicated a similar figure of about 3.5 million irregular aliens in the United States in 1992. Revised estimates suggested that the irregular immigrant population was 3.8 million in October 1992. The country may now have some 15 million of them (during the 1996 US Presidential election campaign the National Committee of the Republican Party claimed that there were five million irregular immigrants – a figure confirmed in the OECD *SOPEMI* report for October 1996[17]), and the number is estimated to be increasing by 250,000 to 300,000 a year. According to one estimate, Mexico alone accounted for at least 200,000 irregular immigrants each year – 160,000 entered without inspection and 40,000 overstayed visas.[18] These figures are, in general, confirmed in the estimate released by the INS in February 1997 (see Table 1.2). Separately, projections based on earlier INS data suggest that by the year 2000 the United States would have 5.8 million irregular immigrants.

Irregular immigrant population is mainly concentrated in six states – California, New York, Texas, Florida, Illinois, and New Jersey – which account for 85 per cent of all irregular immigrants in the USA.

Since 1989, the number of illegal aliens apprehended while attempting to enter without inspection has increased by nearly one-third, to about 1.2 million in 1992, and to 1.3 million in 1993.[19] It is estimated that for every illegal alien apprehended, two or three manage to cross the border (although the ratio depends also on the effectiveness of border control which has recently been considerably tightened. See Chapter 4, including Box 4.1: US Illegal Immigration Reform and Immigrant Responsibility Act of 1996). Persons entering without inspection constitute the vast majority of irregular immigrants, and a second group consists of non-immigrant visa overstayers, who numbered 318,000 in 1991. In 1996, the number of overstayers may have reached the level of 370,000.

Western Europe Reliable figures for Western Europe are even more difficult to come by. But rough estimates would seem to suggest a figure of around three million, mostly concentrated in countries of southern Europe, particularly Italy, Spain, Greece and Portugal, although Germany, too, now has a large share of irregular immigrants. Earlier, in 1991, the European Commission had estimated that of the approximately three million foreigners living in these countries about one half were in an irregular situation. A recent report by the inter-agency working group set up by the US government estimated that 500,000 irregular aliens enter Western Europe each year, many transiting through Moscow.[20] Western Europe's irregular population is of mixed origins, drawn from North Africa, sub-Saharan Africa, Asia and the Middle East.

[17] *Trends in International Migration (SOPEMI)* 1996, OECD, Paris, 1997.
[18] See *Migration News*, Vol. 3, No. 7, July 1996.
[19] *SOPEMI* 1993, op. cit, p. 105.
[20] *Migration News*, Vol. 3, No. 1, January 1996.

Table 1.2. United States: Estimated resident irregular population by continent and top 25 countries of origin

October 1992 and October 1996

	Estimated resident undocumented population				Average Annual Change:
	October 1996	Range (+/−)	Pct of Total	October 1992	1992–1996
U.S. TOTAL	5,000,000	400,000	100.0%	3,900,000	275,000
North America	3,920,000	325,000	78.3%	3,015,000	224,000
Asia	365,000	25,000	7.3%	305,000	16,000
Europe	235,000	20,000	4.7%	205,000	6,000
South America	200,000	15,000	4.0%	155,000	12,000
Africa	115,000	10,000	2.3%	95,000	6,000
Oceania	14,000	–	0.3%	13,000	–
Stateless and unknown	151,000	5,000	3.1%	112,000	11,000
Mexico	2,700,000	250,000	54.1%	2,090,000	154,000
El Salvador	335,000	20,000	6.7%	290,000	11,000
Guatemala	165,000	10,000	3.3%	115,000	12,000
Canada	120,000	8,000	2.4%	85,000	8,000
Haiti	105,000	8,000	2.1%	80,000	6,000
Philippines	95,000	8,000	1.9%	95,000	1,000
Honduras	90,000	6,000	1.7%	55,000	8,000
Bahamas	70,000	5,000	1.3%	40,000	7,000
Poland	70,000	5,000	1.4%	75,000	−2,000
Nicaragua	70,000	4,000	1.4%	60,000	2,000
Colombia	65,000	4,000	1.3%	55,000	4,000
Ecuador	55,000	3,000	1.1%	40,000	3,000
Dom. Rep	50,000	3,000	1.0%	37,000	4,000
Trinidad	50,000	3,000	1.0%	35,000	4,000
Jamaica	50,000	3,000	0.9%	37,000	2,000
Pakistan	41,000	3,000	0.8%	28,000	3,000
India	33,000	3,000	0.7%	26,000	2,000
Dominica	32,000	3,000	0.6%	21,000	3,000
Peru	30,000	2,000	0.6%	20,000	3,000
Korea	30,000	2,000	0.6%	18,000	3,000
Ireland	30,000	3,000	0.6%	30,000	–
Portugal	27,000	2,000	0.5%	26,000	–
Iran	25,000	2,000	0.5%	27,000	−1,000
China	25,000	2,000	0.5%	23,000	–
Italy	25,000	2,000	0.5%	17,000	2,000
All other	612,000	36,000	12.3%	475,000	36,000

– Less than 500.
Source: INS Office of Policy and Planning.

The difficulty in coming up with an accurate estimate is illustrated by the fact that in 1991, the number of irregular immigrants in Spain was estimated at between 300,000 and 350,000 by associations working for the immigrants. At a trade union conference held by the International Confederation of Free Trade Unions (ICFTU) in the same year the number was mentioned to be even higher – 450,000. But a report prepared by an expert for the European Commission put the number between 72,000 and 124,000.[21] Prior to the initiation of its 1992 regularisation programme, it was estimated that Portugal could have as many as 200,000 irregular immigrants.[22]

Italy probably hosts the largest proportion of illegal immigrants in Western Europe, but there is no accurate estimate of the total number. In 1991, it was variously estimated at between 400,000 and 800,000.[23] More recently, it was claimed by a deputy in Italian Congress that the number might well be one million. Charity organisations which are closer to the ground thought that the figure was nearer 300,000. According to the Ministry of Foreign Affairs, there were between 300,000 and 600,000 illegal residents in the country in 1994, which included both undocumented arrivals and overstayers.[24]

In France, official organisations believed that there were between 200,000 and 350,000 irregular immigrants in 1996, and according to an adviser to the former Minister of Interior, Mr. Charles Pasqua, 30,000 new ones entered the country each year.[25] In the United Kingdom, the Immigration Service Union recently claimed that for every legal immigrant another two get into the country illegally. The Home Office makes no attempt to estimate the number of illegal immigrants but it is believed that the flow of irregular immigrants as estimated by the Immigration Service Union may have been an exaggeration.[26] Unofficial estimates placed the number of irregular immigrants at around 250,000 in 1993.[27]

It was recently estimated that in Switzerland there were between 100,000 and 200,000 immigrants with an irregular status.[28] There is similar uncertainty

---

[21] *El Pais*, 23 April 1991 and *Migration News Sheet*, May 1991, p. 4.

[22] *Expresso*, 15 August 1992.

[23] *Financial Times*, 27 March 1995. In 1991, at a conference held in Tunis by the International Confederation of Free Trade Unions it was reported that there were, prior to legalisation, between 700,000 and one million irregular immigrants in Italy. *El Pais*, 23 April 1991.

[24] United Nations Economic Commission for Europe, *International Migration Bulletin*, No. 7, November, 1995, United Nations, Geneva, 1995, p. 8.

[25] *Financial Times*, 20/21 April 1996.

[26] *The Economist*, London, 1–7 April, 1995. An important reason lies in the fact that without a social security number it is almost impossible for an irregular immigrant to get a job except as a low-paid manual worker. Another relevant point is that EU citizens who can have free entry are not entitled to income support as unemployed if they were not seeking work (High Court decision of 20 March 1995).

[27] Patricia Golay, 'United Kingdom', in Solon Ardittis (ed.), *The Politics of East-West Migration*, The Macmillan Press, London, 1994, p. 187.

[28] *Migration News Sheet*, January 1995; *Journal de Geneve and Liberation*, 5 December 1995.

about the exact numbers of irregular immigrants in Belgium and the Netherlands. The official sources estimate the number with a wide margin of flexibility – at between 40,000 and 80,000 for Belgium and between 50,000 and 100,000 for the Netherlands.[29] According to some estimates Germany probably has 500,000 irregular immigrants,[30] but no official figures are available. In a 1993 communication to the Council of Europe, the German Ministry of Labour and Social Affairs reported a figure of 23,587 as 'registered illegals', but this did not include arrivals by air nor the very large numbers of irregulars who remain unregistered. The total number of persons arrested for illegal entry into Germany during the first five months of 1993 was 37,000 – about two times more than during the same period in 1992 and five times more than between January and May in 1991.

Japan, Australia and New Zealand In Japan, estimates by the Ministry of Justice suggested that the number of foreigners illegally overstaying in the country was 280,000 in May 1992; the number was estimated at 300,000 by the end of 1994.[31] Unofficial estimates place the number between 300,000 and 400,000. Between 1986 and 1990, the number of refusals at the border increased five-fold to 13,934, and between 1986 and 1991, the number of expulsions of foreigners tripled to 35,903, of whom more than 90 per cent were irregular immigrant workers.[32] In 1993, the number of expulsions rose to 70,404, mainly involving Thais, Malaysians, South Koreans and Iranians.[33]

Irregular immigration into Australia and New Zealand – which are both relatively secluded by the sea – takes mainly the form of overstaying beyond the authorised period. In Australia, the number of such overstayers increased from 70,000 in 1988 to 90,000 in 1991. Since then, the number has substantially decreased, the figure being 48,000 in December 1995.[34] The increase in irregular immigration during 1988–89 may have been caused largely by the considerable number of overstayers who visited the country during the Bicentennial and Expo events. In New Zealand, there were some 20,000 overstayers in 1991.[35]

Central and Eastern Europe Central and Eastern European countries, too, are now hosting large numbers of irregular immigrants not only from within the

---

[29] These figures were provided to the Council of Europe in 1993 by the official agencies concerned.

[30] R. Böhning, 'Integration and immigration pressures in Western Europe' in *International Labour Review*, Vol. 30, No. 4, 1991. According to a *Der Spiegel* article (1995) about 100,000 foreigners illegally enter Germany each year and stay in the country. 'Illegale-der heimliche Trek nach Deutschland', *Der Spiegel*, no. 49, 1995.

[31] P. Wickramsekara, 'Recent trends in temporary labour migration in Asia'. Paper presented to the seminar on Migration and the Labour Market in Asia in the year 2000, Tokyo, January, 1995.

[32] *SOPEMI* 1993, op. cit.

[33] '93 Deportations hit high of over 70,000' Jiji Press Ticker Service, 16 May 1994. 'Deported foreigners top 70,000 for first time in '93', *Japan Economic Newswire*, 15 May 1994.

[34] *SOPEMI* 1996, op. cit.

[35] *SOPEMI* 1993, op. cit.

region but also from countries further afield. The earlier southern European route for irregular entry into Western Europe is now shifting to the East, as many irregular migrants, including those from developing countries, increasingly use the bordering states as the bridgehead or transit points for entry into Western Europe. [See also Chapter 2, Section 2.8.] In 1992, Poland was estimated to have between 50,000 and 70,000 irregular workers from the former Soviet Union alone. Unconfirmed press reports suggest that the total number of foreign workers illegally employed in Poland may be close to 200,000.[36] Romanians and Bulgarians visiting Poland for 'fly-by-night' commercial activities sometimes take up irregular employment, while some others try to use it as a base to cross over to Germany.[37] During the first eight months of 1992, more than 25,000 foreigners were prevented from illegally crossing the Polish–German border. The Polish Government estimated that in 1995 there were 100,000 migrants in the country who were waiting to cross illegally into Germany.[38]

Similarly, Hungary, whose eastern, northern and southern borders are not heavily protected, has been exposed to a significant level of illegal crossings mainly by Romanians and Chinese; in addition, it has had irregular immigrants from countries like Vietnam, Pakistan, Somalia and Iraq. In 1991, some 20,000 persons were arrested at the Western border for attempts at illegal entry and 4,500 at the former Czechoslovak border. During the last quarter of 1991, about a half million irregular immigrants were expelled from Hungary; another half million were expelled in the final ten months of 1992.[39] According to the OECD, there was an estimated 50,000 irregular workers in 1992.[40] Some more recent estimates placed the number of foreigners working illegally in the country, (mostly from Romania) at between 70,000 and 100,000.[41] In 1995, a total of 87,000 persons were arrested on suspicion of being traffickers or having used their services to enter Hungary.[42]

The Czech and Slovak republics have witnessed a similar pattern of irregular immigration. In 1994, 43,302 persons from 74 states were intercepted trying to cross the Czech–German border illegally.[43] Among the 10,291 persons who attempted to cross the former Czechoslovak Republic (CSFR) borders illegally during the first half of 1992, only 15 per cent were planning to stay in the

---

[36] IOM, Migration Information Programme, *Transit Migration in Poland*, Geneva, April, 1994.
[37] Marek Okolski, 'Poland', in Solon Ardittis (ed.), *The Politics of East–West Migration*, op. cit, p. 55–56.
[38] *The Economist*, London, 5–11 August 1995, p. 25.
[39] *Süddeutsche Zeitung*, 16 May 1995; *SOPEMI* 1993, op. cit, p. 128 and p. 130.
[40] OECD, *SOPEMI* 1992, Paris, 1993, p. 103.
[41] OECD, *SOPEMI* 1996, Paris, 1997.
[42] *Migration News Sheet*, March, 1996. Based on information provided by the Hungarian Association for Migrants.
[43] *The Economist*, op. cit. 5–11 August 1995, p. 25.

former CSFR and the remaining 85 per cent were heading for Germany.[44] Some 35,000 citizens of the former Soviet Union, 20,000 Romanians and up to 10,000 from Bulgaria and the former Yugoslavia were reported to be illegally present in the Czech Republic and Slovakia in 1992.[45] In Bulgaria, the Ministry of Interior records showed a total of 12,789 irregular immigrants at the end of 1992. Transit travel was a main source of irregular immigration.

It is difficult to make even a rough estimate of the total number of irregular immigrants in the Commonwealth of Independent States (CIS). But on the basis of the information recently provided by the governments, it was estimated in 1996 that there were some 580,000 irregular immigrants from within the CIS region alone.[46] The number is considerably increased when irregular migrants from Africa, Asia and the Middle East are taken into account. According to the government sources, Russia, for example, hosted more than 500,000 irregular immigrants, with 180,000 of them living in Moscow. A recent sample survey revealed that 33 per cent of immigrants who came from the non-Russian republics of the former Soviet Union thought that they were staying in Russia illegally. About 40 per cent of the migrants from the Middle East (mainly from Iraq) and 25 per cent of the Afghan immigrants felt the same way.[47]

Belarus and Ukraine, too, are faced with an increasing flow of irregular immigration from Africa, South-West Asia and the Middle East. The Belarussian government, for example, reports the presence in 1995 of about 200,000 irregular aliens from the CIS, the Baltic states and Asian, African and the Middle Eastern countries. In Ukraine, the number of irregular migrants is estimated at between 20,000 and 30,000.[48] Some of the irregular immigrants in the two countries are transit migrants heading West, and some are overstayers who were previously living in these countries as students or contract workers. Moldova has also been hosting irregular transit migrants, mostly from Asian countries. In 1993, about 6,000 such persons were arrested at the border, although there was a significant decrease in the flow in 1994.[49]

---

[44] *SOPEMI* 1993, op. cit, p. 126. Zednek Pavlik and Jarmila Maresova, 'Former Czechoslovakia' in Solon Ardittis (ed.), *The Politics of East–West Migration*, 1994, op. cit, p. 123.

[45] Economic Commission for Europe, 'International migration in the ECE region: Contemporary critical aspects', paper presented at the Expert Group Meeting on Population Distribution and Migration, New York, United Nations, (mimeo) 1994.

[46] Information provided by the government to the secretariat of the CIS conference on refugees and migrants, Geneva, May 1996. See IOM/UNHCR/OSCE, *CIS Conference on Refugees and Migrants*, Geneva 1996; also, UNHCR, *The CIS Conference on Refugees and Migrants*, European series, Vol. 2, No. 1 January, 1996, pp. 19–21.

[47] IOM, Migration Information Programme, *Transit Migration in the Russian Federation*, Geneva, July 1994.

[48] *Migration News*, Vol. 4, No. 2, Feb. 1997.

[49] Statistical information in this paragraph is based on the reports transmitted by the governments to the secretariat of the CIS conference on refugees and migrants, May 1996. See UNHCR, *The CIS Conference on Refugees and Migrants*, op. cit, pp. 19–21.

Developing countries Many developing countries are also hosting large numbers of irregular immigrants. Taiwan, China, probably has some 200,000 irregular immigrants[50] and the Republic of Korea, where a regularisation drive carried out in 1992 elicited 61,000 applications, was estimated in December 1995 to have over 81,000 irregular workers, representing some 62.6 per cent of all foreign workers.[51] In Malaysia, irregular immigration reached crisis proportions in the mid-1980s when the government stepped up measures to control it. More than 800,000 irregular immigrants still worked on plantations, construction sites and elsewhere; 320,000 applied for regularisation under an amnesty programme in 1992.[52] About 3,000 Filipinos are currently in Malaysian jails for illegally entering the country and up to 100 Filipinos are said to be entering Malaysia's eastern provinces each day.[53] Although an important labour-exporting country, the Philippines nonetheless has its share of irregular immigrants. In 1994, the government ordered a crackdown on an estimated 100,000 foreigners who had lived in the country illegally for more than three years. In the same year the *Manila Chronicle* suggested that about 500,000 irregular immigrants resided in the country.[54]

In Thailand, the Interior Ministry estimates that there are between 600,000 and 700,000 irregular workers, mainly from Mynamar (Burma), Laos and Cambodia.[55] The numbers of those coming from China and South Asia are also increasing. Before the 1989 law to discourage irregular immigration came into force, there was an amnesty for irregular workers in Singapore, and more than 10,000 workers took up the offer.[56] In Jordan, 70,000 irregular foreign workers – out of a total of between 200,00 and 250,000 foreign workers – were ordered to leave the country by 26 October 1995. Most of these irregular foreign workers had agricultural work permits, but were engaged in non-farm jobs.[57]

Africa, too, has its share of irregular immigrants. In a continent where political borders often cut across territories of culturally and ethnically homo-

---

[50] Reginald Appleyard, 'International Migration in East Asia', *International Migration*, Vol. XXXI, No. 2/3, 1993, p. 269.

[51] Kang, S.D., 'Globalization of labour market also in South Korea?', February, 1996. Paper presented to the international conference on the dynamics of labour migration, Nihon University, Tokyo, 6–7 March 1996.

[52] United Nations, *Review of Population Trends, Policies and Programmes*, Economic and Social Council, E/CN.9/1995/2 17 January 1995, p. 35. See also P. Stalker, *The Work of Strangers: A Survey of International Labour Migration*, ILO, Geneva, 1994. Unofficial estimates of the number of irregular immigrants in Malaysia varied between 200,00 and two million, and centred on 1.2 million. *Migration News* Vol. 1, No. 3, April 1994.

[53] 'Some 3000 Filipinos are in Malaysian jails', UPI, 18 June, 1996.

[54] *Migration News*, Vol. 1, No. 3, April 1994. *The Straits Times*, 14 March, 1994.

[55] *Financial Times* (London) 14 February, 1996.

[56] OECD, 'Migration Trends in Some Asian Countries', (mimeo) Paris, 1993, p. 21.

[57] 'Foreign workers in Jordan reduced by 70,000', Xinhua News Agency, 3 December, 1995. *Migration News*, Vol. 3, No. 1, January, 1996.

geneous population groups, hundreds of thousands of people belonging to the same ethnic group continue to cross borders without formalities and often with no records. Given these circumstances, it is difficult to assess exactly the scale of total irregular migration, but from all accounts it is quite significant. In the past, this was reflected in the large numbers of irregular immigrants who were affected by the expulsion orders of Ghana in 1969 and Nigeria in 1983 and 1985. The expulsion from Ghana was estimated to involve half a million irregular immigrants, mostly nationals of Nigeria, Burkina Faso and Niger. Prior to the 1983 expulsion, the number of irregular immigrants in Nigeria was estimated at one million by the Ministry of the Interior and three million by the Ministry of External Affairs.[58] Some other estimates suggested that the number in 1982 might have been 2.5 million.[59] Recently, Nigerian immigration officials estimated that about 300,000 irregular immigrants, mostly from Chad, Niger, Benin, and Cameroon lived in Lagos. They were required to obtain residence permits by June 1994 or leave the country.[60]

Latin America is not an exception. Like other developing regions, it sends irregular migrants outside but there are also irregular migratory movements within the region. Except during the economic recession of the 1980s, Venezuela, for example, has long been a magnet for irregular immigrants from several neighbouring countries, particularly Colombia. The results of the amnesty granted in 1980 provide an indication of the scale of such immigration – some 246,192 Colombians responded. By 1985, the number of irregular immigrants had again risen to reach the level of half a million.[61] Venezuela also attracted irregular immigrants as prospectors from Brazil who slipped across the border in search of gold, diamonds and other precious minerals. Many Brazilians, including the Brazilian Indians, smuggle themselves into Guinea. In the past, with its relative prosperity, Argentina, too, attracted irregular immigrants from neighbouring countries. According to recent press reports, 800,000 to one million foreigners, mainly Bolivians are working illegally in the country.[62]

In Central America since the late 1970s there have been massive, volatile population movements, mainly caused by political conflicts. But since only a small proportion of them were officially registered as refugees – only 146,000 out of two million – many were in an irregular situation.[63] With peace slowly

---

[58] A. Adepoju, 'Undocumented migration in Africa: Trends and policies', *International Migration*, Vol. X, No. 2, 1983, p. 206.

[59] Sharon Russell, K. Jackobsen and W.D. Stanley, *International Migration and Development in Sub-Saharan Africa*, World Bank Discussion Papers, Africa Technical Department Series, Washington DC, 1990.

[60] 'Nigeria to flush out illegal immigrants', *The Xinhua General Overseas News Service*, 17 March 1994. *Migration News*, Vol. 1, No. 2, April, 1994.

[61] A. Pelligrino, 'Colombian migration in Venezuela' in R. Appleyard (ed.) *The Impact of International Migration on Developing Countries*, OECD, Paris, 1989.

[62] Agence France Presse, 14 February 1996.

[63] United Nations, 'Update on the CIREFCA Process', United Nations General Assembly, Executive Committee of the High Commissioner's Programme, Forty-third session, A/AC.96/INF.176, 21 September 1991.

returning to Nicaragua and El Salvador the situation has changed, but as of 1989, Central American governments estimated that 893,000 undocumented persons were externally displaced within the region.[64] Of the 475,000 Nicaraguans who live in Costa Rica, more than half are probably in an irregular situation.[65] As of 1991, over one million Haitians were estimated to be present in the Dominican Republic, many as irregular (undocumented) workers on sugar plantations.[66]

The above discussion reveals the difficulty of making accurate numerical estimates of irregular immigrants. Even in the case of the United States and Western Europe, the estimated figures of 5 million and around three million, respectively, should be used cautiously – more as an indication of the order of magnitude of irregular immigration in the two regions. At the world level, some rough estimates suggest a figure of between 15 and 30 million. On the debatable assumption that this is a close approximation to realities, between one-eighth and one-fourth of the world's stock of migrant population is in an irregular situation.

Significantly, yearly arrivals of irregular migrants are estimated at between 250,000 and 300,000 (one quarter or more of the total flow) in the USA and between 300,000 and 500,00 (about one-third of the total flow) in Europe.[67] In 1997, the INS suggested that up to one million foreigners might be considering migrating illegally to the United States or Europe.[68] Even more than the quantitative increase of irregular migrants, it is the qualitative change affecting the nature and characteristics of the movements that causes concern. Not only is irregular migration becoming a highly organised international activity, but it is also becoming increasingly intertwined with crime and violence both within and across countries. This applies particularly to trafficking in migrants, which, if unchecked, could emerge as a most dominant and abusive form of irregular migration in the years to come.

Occupational and social characteristics of irregular migrants

The increasing scale of irregular migration and its changing forms make it more difficult than in the past to discern the profile of a typical irregular migrant. They are not a homogeneous group, and with changing forms of irregular migration, including the rise in trafficking, the occupational, social and personal characteristics of irregular migrants are also changing. It is, however, possible to have insights into the characteristics of the different types

---

[64] Conferencia Internacional sobre Refugiados Centroamericanos (CIREFCA), First International Meeting, May 1989.

[65] *Migration News*, Vol. 3, No. 7, July, 1996.

[66] United Nations, 'Update on the CIREFCA Process', op. cit.

[67] Inter-Governmental Consultation, IGC Work Plan for 1995, Annex 1: *Illegal Aliens*, 14 October 1994, Geneva.

[68] *Migration News*, Vol. 4, No. 7, July 1997.

of irregular migrants through special surveys; also, data based on regularisation programmes in specific countries shed some light on the situation.

A comparative analysis of the regularisation experiences in four countries – France, Spain, Italy and the United States – undertaken by the OECD in 1989, for example, revealed that irregular migrants are generally young and that they tend to cluster in the sectors and areas where legal immigrants or foreigners are already working.[69] This would seem to suggest a preference of employers in certain sectors for foreign workers, whether or not they are legal. The situation also reflects the tendency of irregular immigrants to draw upon ethnic network links to enter the destination country and find a living place and a job there.

In the United States, as in Western Europe, most irregular immigrants have been traditionally in low-wage, low-skill jobs in small and family-run enterprises; the employment is generally temporary or seasonal; and the economic activities are often in the informal sector or form part of the underground economy. Notwithstanding some changes in recent years (see discussion on irregular flows of skilled workers in Chapter 3), these occupational characteristics remain largely valid.

This is not surprising, given that firm characteristics and geographical location are known to have considerable influence on the use of irregular workers. In general, activities that are less competitive, less visible and less amenable to immigration control and labour inspection are more likely to use irregular labour. Thus, small and family enterprises as well as firms in the underground economy and in declining industries normally have a large share of irregular workers (further discussed in Chapter 2). In the United States, several analysts have argued that because of their low visibility and the presence of large numbers of competitors, small firms are more likely to employ casual or irregular labour and disregard labour laws.[70] In Italy, the concentrations of irregular workers are largely explained by the regional and firm or industry characteristics – in Lombardy they are mostly in industry and handicrafts; in Latium in the construction industry, hotels and catering and domestic services and in Sicily in agriculture.

In Central European countries, notably in Poland, most irregular immigrants are in the construction industry, agriculture and small manufacturing enterprises. An interesting occupational feature of irregular immigration in Central and Eastern European (including the CIS) countries is the predominance of small traders and intermediaries, especially among those temporary visitors or

---

[69] OECD, *Trends in International Migration (SOPEMI)* Annual Report 1989, Paris, 1990.

[70] See, for example, A. Portes and S. Sassen-Koob, 'Making it underground: Comparative material on the informal sector in Western market economies', *American Journal of Sociology*, 1987 93(1); M. Grantover, 'Small is beautiful: Labour markets and establishment', *American Sociological Review*, 1984, 49(3). pp. 323–334; and 'The relationship between the Immigration Reform and Control Act of 1986 and Labour Standards: An exploratory essay', 1990. Paper prepared for the Division of Immigration Policy Research, US Department of Labor, Washington DC, 1984.

Fig. 1.1. Occupational distribution of irregular workers (confirmed cases) in Japan, 1989.

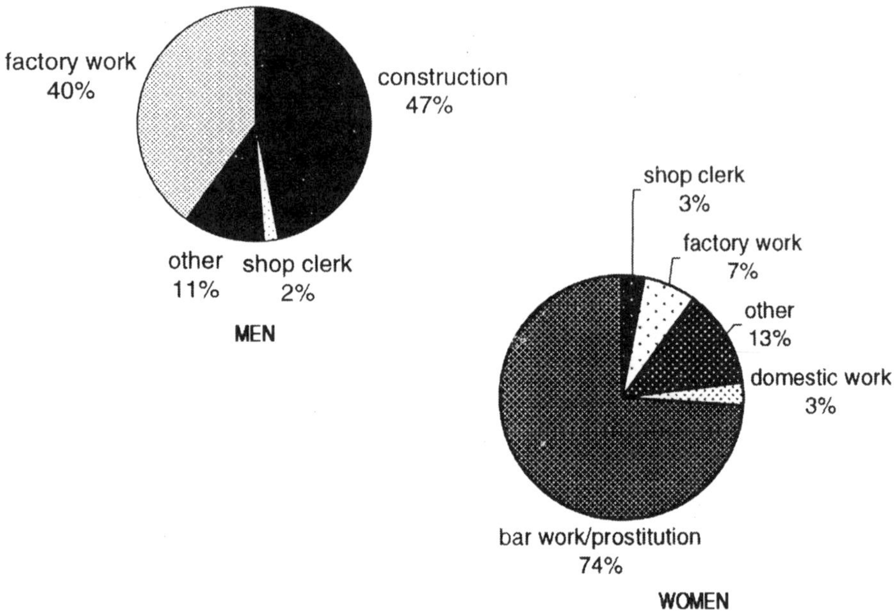

tourists who are illegally involved in commercial tourism, popularly known as 'fly-by-night' or 'suitcase' trade.

In Japan, a study made in 1992 suggested that 47 per cent of the irregular foreign workers (only confirmed cases) were engaged in the construction industry, 40 per cent in factory jobs, and two per cent as shop assistants in 1989 (Figure 1.1). In Malaysia, aside from plantation and construction industries which engage large numbers of irregular foreign workers, many irregular immigrants are now conducting business as night market traders in Gombak, Jajang and Bangi.

As with migration in general, women, from all indications, are becoming an increasingly important part of irregular flows. In the United States, for example, of about 1.8 million persons who applied for legalisation under the general regularisation programme of the 1986 Immigration Reform and Control Act, 43 per cent were women. In the case of the special agricultural workers programme, however, the share of women was much lower, only 18 per cent; this was mainly because the majority of farm workers were men. In many cases the proportion of irregular women immigrants even in the same country seems to vary according to nationalities or countries of origin. For example, a study made in 1991 for Spain (intra-EC freedom of movement was not applicable to Spain before 1 January 1993) showed that for every 100 irregular immigrants from the Dominican Republic, 89 were women; the percentages were 79 for

Cape Verdeans, 71 for Filipinos, 62 for French, 61 for Brazilians, 59 for Guineans and 58 for Germans.[71] The share of women is also becoming important in trafficking of migrants. Many such trafficked women are engaged in prostitution and domestic work. As discussed below, acceptance of such employment may be voluntary but more often, especially in the case of prostitution, the victims are deceived or forced into accepting these activities.

1.3. Trafficking in migration

Definition and characteristics

How does migrant trafficking differ from other forms of irregular migration? The wide and increasing concern over trafficking in migrants does not imply that a clear, simple and commonly accepted definition of such activities is readily available. To meet this lacuna, a working definition of migrant trafficking was proposed at a recent international seminar organized by the International Organization for Migration (IOM).[72] Under this definition trafficking in migrants contains four main elements. First, it requires a trafficker or intermediary who undertakes to facilitate the cross-border movement. Second, it involves a payment to the trafficker by the migrant or on his/her behalf. Third, the intended movement itself is illegal and needs to be supported by various illegal acts. Fourth, in as much as the migrant is a willing party to the transaction, the choice is a voluntary one.

These elements are useful starting points to discern the nature of migrant trafficking as distinct from other modes of irregular migration. If further refined and elaborated to take full account of the varying circumstances under which the trafficking activities actually take place, they could, as the discussion in the IOM seminar revealed, help in formulating an adequate definition of migrant trafficking, and provide at the same time a sound framework for designing effective policy and operational measures to combat it. Three specific points deserve attention in this connection; they relate to (a) the method of payment, (b) illegality of movements, and (c) voluntary nature of the transactions involved.

Payment is an essential element in all transactions implicit in migrant trafficking. It is however important to note that the payment may not in all cases be in the form of cash and that the claim of the trafficker is not necessarily settled in full by the end of the journey. The process of payment may – and in some of the worst forms of trafficking it often does – extend well beyond that point. The form and method of payment assume importance in the whole transaction since in a growing number of cases they largely explain the continu-

---

[71] *El Pais*, 18 March 1991; *Migration News Sheet*, April 1991.

[72] International Organization for Migration, 'International Response to Trafficking in Migrants and the Safeguarding of Migrant Rights', Geneva, 1994 (Eleventh IOM Seminar on Migration, Geneva, 26–28 October 1994).

ing hold of the traffickers on the migrants even after their arrival in the destination country, making them easy victims to exploitation and abuses, ranging from extortion to drug peddling and prostitution. In many cases the potential migrants, who are unable to pay the fees in advance or at the end of the journey, are in fact encouraged by the traffickers to opt for deferred payment. Not only does the business flourish through easier recruitment of candidates for irregular migration, but the situation also enables the traffickers to tighten their grip on the migrants and use their virtually indentured services for unlawful and even criminal activities.

Findings of a study of trafficked women (further discussed below) in Belgium, for example, revealed that although most women did not have to pay a fee to a trafficker in advance, on arrival a high proportion of women found themselves in debt to the recruiting network.[73] In some cases, as in the Netherlands, the debt was to be repaid to the 'new owners' (e.g. night clubs) who bought them from the trafficking network. The continuing hold of the traffickers over the migrants also explains how in some cases even families left behind in the home country become victims of extortion. Much of the social abuse and criminality associated with trafficking is thus ingrained in the form and methods of payment used in migrant trafficking. Thus, as noted above, the payments for trafficking are not a simple and straightforward transaction in cash at the beginning or even at the end of the journey; often it is a long, complex and tortuous process intertwined with the various ramifications of trafficking as an organized and lucrative activity involving several parties.

The illegality of the movements, another essential feature of migrant trafficking, also calls for elucidation. As already noted, the general tendency is to view the illegality of the movements from the standpoint of the immigration laws and regulations of the receiving country. But, as in other cases of irregular migration, migrant trafficking may, and often does, contravene the established laws of the sending and the transit countries as well. In such cases the illegality of the movement affects all the three categories (sending, transit and destination) of countries: this constitutes an additional reason for them to cooperate in evolving a joint approach to the problem.

The forms and sequence of illegality could also vary. The trafficked persons may be brought to the destination country through a legal channel, for example on a tourist visa or a visa linked to temporary work permit, but they soon become illegal when they overstay in the country, are engaged in work without a labour permit and/or are employed in illicit activities. These can be preplanned by the traffickers as part of a package deal – in some cases with the connivance of the trafficked persons, in others they are forced to accept jobs, whether lawful or not, as dictated by the traffickers, upon arrival.

---

[73] IOM, Migration Information Programme, *Trafficking and Prostitution: The Growing Exploitation of Migrant Women from Central and Eastern Europe*, Geneva, 1995.

As regards the voluntary nature of the transaction, here too, there is more than what meets the eye. On the surface and from a formal point of view, the migrant's choice may well be considered voluntary since the individual is a willing party to the transaction. In reality, however, the situation can be markedly different. In some cases migrants do turn to traffickers as a deliberate attempt to circumvent existing migration laws and regulations and make economic gains following entry in the target country. But there are also many situations where the migrant's recourse to the traffickers may be less a matter of free choice than of compulsion. In the absence of other channels of escape, such compulsion may be caused by such factors as extreme economic despair, political oppression, large-scale violence or environmental disaster or perhaps a combination of them. In probably many more instances the potential migrants are lured by false promise and propaganda about the opportunities in the target country or are misled by disinformation concerning migration laws and regulations.

Clearly, in all such cases the migrant's freedom of choice is seriously impaired so that the transaction ceases to be truly voluntary, although seemingly the migrant may be a willing party to it. Even in instances where the original contract may have been of a voluntary nature, the subsequent process may not be so. When, for example, the precariousness of their situation in the destination country places them under the full control of the trafficking network, and makes the trafficked persons totally vulnerable to manipulation, they can hardly be considered to have had a free choice.

Unravelling the web of trafficking activities Human trafficking is not a new phenomenon (see Box 1.1). But its configuration, including the types of traffickers and the activities undertaken by them, has significantly changed in recent years, marked by growing complexity and increasing abusiveness. Trafficking may take the form, for example, of illegal entry through informal modes supported and facilitated by social networks of migrants' relatives and countrymen in the sending, receiving and transit countries. The activities may be carried out by small operators to provide a specific service needed by a migrant such as transport for crossing the border or locating an employer willing to engage him/her despite the illegal entry. Some of them, especially in border areas, are occasional or casual traffickers. They usually are owners or operators of taxis, trucks or small boats which help them carry individuals or groups into the target country in a clandestine manner against payment. The occasional activity may not be their main source of income but a supplementary one. Some other small operators, by contrast, specialise in trafficking as their main economic activity and conduct their business in an organised manner and as frequently as possible.

Finally, trafficking may be part of a well-organised commercial activity run by large-scale operators with international networks, providing a whole range of services such as securing travel documents (which may often be forged or false), transportation and assistance in border crossing, arranging safe places

Box 1.1. 75 YEARS AGO
1922: SMUGGLING BY THE SEA

New York – A new industry has developed since the new US immigration restriction law has become effective. This industry has been responsible for the smuggling into the US of thousands of immigrants across the narrow strip of seas from Cuba. A large number of Chinese, Germans, Spaniards, Austrians, Italians, and Polish and Russian Jews are paying from $100 to $500 each to be landed from the West Indies on the Florida coast. This smuggling is known as 'dummy running' to distinguish it from another profitable source of West Indian smuggling called 'rum running'.

Source: *International Herald Tribune* 13 February 1997

in transit, and finding residence and (illegal or unlawful) employment in the destination country. The operational elements of trafficking, prior to the arrival of trafficked persons in the country of destination, include planning and conspiracy for smuggling, collection of information on travel documents for purposes of producing forged documents or falsification of travel documents, intelligence gathering concerning processing of asylum applications to justify false claims, arranging hideouts for migrants before the arrival of transport and during transit, and camouflaging vehicles and other means of transport to avoid apprehension.

It is these large-scale operations in migrant trafficking that are in many cases intertwined with the international networks of organised crime and often pose a serious threat to law and order in the target country and to the migrants themselves. As the organised networks control, often through fraudulent means, the whole process of migration – from the departure of the migrant from the sending country to providing accommodation and means of living in the destination country – they can have a complete hold over the migrant. Vulnerable to legal prosecution under the immigration laws of the destination country and devoid of financial means, the migrants, once outside their country of origin, may find their freedom of movement severely curtailed and their basic human rights virtually non-existent. The migrants can thus be used as a source of cheap labour for establishments directly or indirectly controlled by the networks or for illegal activities such as drug trafficking. Migrant trafficking is often one activity in a series of criminal, but highly lucrative and inter-locked operations. With sophisticated telecommunications and other means, traffickers can keep in touch with their networks spreading world-wide and command enormous financial resources and operational capability.

A recent document issued by the German Directorate of Border Controls provides a succinct description of the characteristics and operations of the large international human trafficking organisations engaged in smuggling foreigners from Asian countries to Western Europe and the USA.[74] According to this document, these organisations possess extraordinarily well-equipped workshops to falsify all necessary documents, visa and stamp marks. They react flexibly and are able to change their routes in case of intensified border controls. They also possess operations centres, hideouts and accommodation in all potential transit countries. Financially strong, the organisations are in a position to use large sums of money, for instance in the form of bribes, and are often active in various types of crime including organised crime. [For further discussion of trafficking, including trafficking of women, see Chapter 3.]

Trafficking in women and children

Trafficking in women for purposes of prostitution or similar forms of sexual exploitation (e.g. 'mail-order brides') is becoming an important and particularly disturbing part of migrant trafficking. It has the same negative features and consequences as other forms of migrant trafficking, but the human cost of trafficking in women is often much more devastating.

The problem is not altogether new. In Germany, for example, trafficking in women was extensively debated in the nineteenth century.[75] In one case a joiner found bills and receipts covering years of international traffic in women in the secret drawer of an inherited desk. This then led to the exposure of a ring of slave traders who were also involved in trafficking in women. However, it is particularly since the 1970s that the problem in Germany (as in many other countries) has rapidly gained in proportion, with trafficking activities supplying "bordellos and marriage markets of the major German cities with tens of thousands of young women from South-east Asia (especially, the Philippines and Thailand) and other parts of the Third World, as well as from Poland".[76] In a recent report, the Committee of Experts on Women Trade, set up by the regional parliament in Berlin, graphically describes how the cartels of drug traffickers active in the market of sexual exploitation have been experiencing an extraordinary business boom. It estimates that there are some 7,000 prostitutes in Berlin; about 3,000 of them are from Thailand. Many, though not all of them, are victims of traffickers. From Thailand these women are

---

[74] Directorate of Border Controls 1993, cited in IOM, *Chinese Migrants in Central and Eastern Europe: The Cases of the Czech Republic, Hungary and Romania*, Geneva, September 1995, p. 23.
[75] Jochen Blaschke, 'Gates of immigration into the Federal Republic of Germany', *International Migration*, Vol. XXX, No. 2/3, 1993, pp. 369–373.
[76] Ibid.

tricked into believing either that they would get a serious job in Germany or marry a well-to-do German. They have to pay up to DM 40,000 for the arrangements, and once in Germany they generally enter into a fraudulent marriage and are then obliged to work as prostitutes to pay off their debts.[77] Estimates by NGOs working in the field suggest that between one and two million women, including young girls, are being trafficked each year around the world.[78]

Young women are generally recruited in their home countries with offers of attractive jobs – as dancers in the entertainment business, lady companions or house maids. They are enticed to travel with the recruiting agents to Western Europe, and once there, they are often forced to sign promissory notes for their air fares, recruitment fees and other charges. Helpless and vulnerable, these young women, who generally do not know the local language, are soon obliged to work as prostitutes in brothels or for procurement agencies in order to redeem their debts. Like trafficking in illicit drugs, trafficking in women for sexual exploitation is now an organised cross-border criminal activity and raises a whole range of political and social issues, including care, assistance and rehabilitation of the victims. A recent European meeting of the INTERPOL warned how the activities of narco-traffickers are frequently combined with trade in women for prostitution and human smuggling. A most disturbing consequence is that the potential irregular immigrants are increasingly being used as drug carriers.[79]

Women trafficked to Western Europe come from different parts of the world, but the principal source countries are Ghana, Morocco and Nigeria in Africa; Brazil, Colombia and the Dominican Republic in Latin America; the Philippines and Thailand in South-East Asia; and more recently, Albania, the Czech Republic, Hungary, Poland, Romania, Russia and Ukraine in Central and Eastern Europe. Although the operations are becoming increasing global, existing networks and contacts and already established routes seem to play a part in influencing the geographical direction of the flow. For example, women from the Dominican Republic are trafficked mainly to Austria, Italy, the Netherlands and Spain and those from Thailand to Germany and the Netherlands. Also, within the countries of origin, women are trafficked more from some regions than others: for example, women trafficked from the Dominican Republic to Italy and Austria come mainly from Palmarito and La Vega and those trafficked to Spain from Vincente Noble and Barahona.[80] A similar but slightly different pattern is presented by another group of women who are recruited for the German marriage market. These women have to

[77] *Frankfurter Rundschau*, 12 April 1997; *Migration News Sheet*, May 1997, p. 7.

[78] United Nations, *World Population Monitoring 1997*, New York, 1996, (Draft), p. 213.

[79] *El Pais*, 25 April 1997; *Migration News Sheet*, May 1997, p. 6.

[80] IOM, 'Trafficking of Women To Countries of the Western European Union: Characteristics, Trends and Policy Issues', 1996. Paper submitted to the conference on trafficking in women for sexual exploitation. Vienna, June, 1996.

Box 1.2. Trafficking in Asian Women

Increasingly, prostitution in Asia is becoming interlocked with trafficking. The methods of trafficking include the normal lure of false job opportunities but even more disturbing, in many countries, village girls are abducted and smuggled across the border to work as prostitutes. Such incidents have been recorded in Bangladesh, Nepal, Burma, Vietnam and Thailand and they are undoubtedly more widespread than is known. In terms of numbers, it is estimated that 200,000 Bangladeshi women have been trafficked to Pakistan in the last 10 years, continuing at the rate of 200–400 women per month; other estimates demonstrate that 20,000–30,000 Burmese women are working as prostitutes in Thailand having arrived through trafficking devices such as deceptive job placements, abduction, and the sale of girls from hill tribes. At least 10 international crime syndicates are said to be trafficking 300 Thai women into Australia each year for prostitution; minors from Nepal and Bangladesh end up in the red light districts of India where it is estimated that 2.3 million women work as prostitutes. Between 5,000–7,000 women and girls from Nepal are trafficked to India each year; and finally, Japan has the largest sex market for Asian women, involving over 150,000 non-Japanese women who come primarily from Thailand and the Philippines.

Source: *Trafficking in Migrants* (Quarterly Bulletin), No. 15, IOM, Geneva, June 1997

marry the men for whom they are procured by the recruitment agencies: their doubtful resident status, and debts resulting from travel costs, combined with their lack of local contacts and insufficient knowledge of the local language, virtually leave them with no alternative.

Recent case studies of a limited number of trafficked women in countries of Western Europe reveal that, despite similarities in the methods of trafficking, the details could vary.[81] In the Netherlands, for example, most women from Central Europe entered the country legally as tourists; by contrast the majority of women from Eastern Europe including Russia entered the Netherlands illegally. Two-thirds of women from developing countries were illegal residents, at least one-third having entered the country illegally. In Switzerland, as in

[81] IOM, *Trafficking and Prostitution: The Growing Exploitation of Migrant Women from Central and Eastern Europe*, Geneva, 1995, p. 21.

Belgium, many trafficked young women entered the country legally with temporary work permits as dancers, entertainers or artists, but the precariousness of their situation made them vulnerable to manipulation by traffickers and night club owners who induced or forced them to take up prostitution and other activities of a dubious nature. Even when such activities are not prohibited by law, irregularity of their status may result from infringement of the conditions under which their visas were originally issued, adding to the vulnerability of their situation.

As with human trafficking in general, the methods used for trafficking women are often largely influenced by the type of organisation that handles the operation. Small and occasional traffickers may recruit only a few women at a time, as and when the owner of a night club or a brothel places an order through established contacts. The local contact recruits the women, accompanies them to the destination country or arranges for their transport and delivery to the club or the brothel.

By contrast, large-scale traffickers, with extensive networks and sophisticated infrastructure at their disposal, use a variety of legal and illegal ways to recruit and traffic the women from different countries. They are well equipped to use seemingly legal ways of recruiting, directly or through their networks, the women as artists, language students, dancers or tourists, and also have access to various fraudulent documents, if necessary. While using the same or similar methods, the medium-scale traffickers tend to specialise in trafficking from one or two specific countries and they are more likely to use the women in their own clubs and brothels, instead of selling them to a third party.

It would be misleading however to make a rigid distinction between these various methods or types of operations which can often be used in combination and with considerable flexibility, especially by the well-organised, large- and medium-scale traffickers. Also worth noting is the evidence from several sending countries, including the Dominican Republic and countries of Central and Eastern Europe, that informal contacts and social networking can also play an important part in the recruitment process.

Information on the personal and social profile of trafficked women is incomplete. But limited field studies recently carried out by the IOM shed some light on the characteristics of women trafficked to Western Europe for sexual exploitation. They reveal in particular important differences between the women recruited from Central and Eastern European countries and the developing regions. The former are generally young, between 15 and 25 years old, unmarried and, compared with the women from developing countries, have higher education. The latter are generally older, married and have children. They are mostly from the rural areas.

As with women, trafficking in children is increasing in scope and complexity as the international crime syndicates and traffickers recognise the potential profits they can derive from such activity. Commercial, including sexual, exploitation of children, in violation of various international instruments such as the

United Nations Convention on the Rights of the Child, is the main driving force behind the trafficking operations. The rising demand for children in the international market comes from different sources, making trafficking in them a highly lucrative business. Increasing threats of AIDS and other sexually-transmitted diseases are contributing to the ever-younger child prostitutes. Young children are trafficked across countries, and the complex operations managed through international networks renders it difficult to trace them. While the problem is global it has reached alarming proportions in Asia.[82]

How big and lucrative is the trafficking business?

Migrant trafficking, once a small part of irregular migration, has now become a dominant form of such movement, yielding vast amounts of money to the traffickers. Reliable data on migrant trafficking is however non-existent: gathering statistics on trafficking is often even more difficult than for other types of irregular migration. Estimates of migrant trafficking are thus generally made on the basis of indirect evidence, for example, as derivatives extrapolated from the numbers of other types of irregular migrants.

The Vienna-based International Centre for Migration Policy Development (ICMPD), for example, has calculated[83] that (a) 15 to 30 per cent of those who illegally crossed the borders of West European states for purposes of employment or residence (estimated at between 250,000 and 350,000 in 1993) and (b) 20 to 40 per cent of the non-bona fide asylum seekers (estimated at 300,000) during the same year used the services of traffickers.[84] This means that roughly between 40,000 and 100,000 of illegal migrants and between 60,000 and 120,000 of non bona fide asylum applicants relied on the services of traffickers at some point of the journey – for example to obtain forged documents, to cross the green border, or to have other forms of support. Thus, according to this calculation, migrant trafficking to Western Europe involved a total of 100,000 to 220,000 aliens in 1993.

There are several assumptions underlying these estimates. The number of illegal immigrants, for example, is calculated on the basis of two elements; (a) the known number of aliens – totalling 60,000 – apprehended in 1993 at the borders of Western European states; and (b) the assumption that four to

[82] *Migration News* 1996. IOM, *Trafficking in Migrants* (Quarterly Bulletin), No. 7, March 1996.

[83] Jonas Widgren, 'Multilateral Co-operation To Combat Trafficking In Migrants and The Role of International Organizations', 1994 (ICMPD, Vienna). Paper presented to the Eleventh IOM Seminar on Migration, Geneva, 26 28 October 1994), pp. 5–6.

[84] According to an estimate by the Slovak Republic the proportion of the irregular immigrants who arranged entry with the help of traffickers was as high as 31 per cent. In reply to a questionnaire, Turkey confirmed that all illegal entries to Turkey were organized by traffickers. Denmark, on the other hand, stated that irregular crossings were mostly facilitated by friends and relatives of foreign residents. See, 'Harmonization of Legislation to combat trafficking in Aliens', paper prepared for the Budapest Group (set up by the 1993 Budapest conference of ministers) Zurich, September 1995, pp. 17–18.

six times as many actually managed to freely pass through the borders. In a like manner, the number of bona-fide asylum-seekers is derived from (a) the recorded number of arrivals totalling 690,000 in 1993 and (b) the assumption that more than 43 per cent of these asylum seekers did not have well founded claims. Although the exact validity of such assumptions cannot be tested, circumstantial evidence seems to suggest that these may not be widely off the mark. Thus, the over-all estimate suggesting that traffickers smuggled 100,000 to 220,000 irregular migrants into Western Europe in 1993 – or nearly a half-million in 1993–1994 – could perhaps be a reasonable guess; at least it serves the purpose of revealing the order of magnitude of the problem.

An estimate can also be made on the basis of the assumption that between 20 and 30 per cent of the irregular immigrants into Western Europe used the services of traffickers in some part of the journey, and that the total annual flow of such irregular immigrants varied between 300,000 and 500,000 in recent years. This puts the total numbers of trafficked persons at 60,000–150,000. Using the average of each of these two sets of figures it is possible to conclude that in the past 2–3 years, there has been an annual flow of 100,000 trafficked immigrants into Western Europe.

The inter-agency working group on trafficking set up by the US government has estimated that a total of 100,000 trafficked migrants from 'outside the region' passed through one or more Central American countries on their way to the USA each year. As already noted, trafficking in women and children, too, is rising. For example, since 1990 the number of trafficked women from Central and Eastern European countries has more than doubled in Belgium and tripled in the Netherlands.[85] Indeed, if the estimates by NGOs of trafficked women are valid, the total volume of human trafficking around the world may be substantially larger than the figures cited above might imply.

A word of caution is however warranted. Depending on a number of variables, the levels of migrant trafficking could fluctuate widely and rather quickly. The number of asylum-seekers in Western Europe, for example, has fallen sharply since 1993. The potential high volatility of these flows makes it risky to make future projections simply on the basis of migrant trafficking figures for the previous years.

How lucrative is the business? Recent newspaper headlines suggest that trafficking in humans has become every bit as lucrative as drug smuggling and is already big business in Europe. How much money is involved? Again, hard figures are difficult to come by. Aside from, as noted above, the non-availability of reliable statistics concerning the volume of activity, complexity in calculations stems from the fact that the payments could vary widely depending on such factors as the types and range of activities covered in trafficking, the countries

[85] IOM, *Trafficking and Prostitution: The Growing Exploitation of Migrant Women from Central and Eastern Europe*, Geneva, 1995, op. cit, p. 8.

concerned and the distance and nature of risks involved. The fact that the payment, as discussed above, is not always a one-off cash transaction adds to the difficulty in calculating the fees.

Fragmentary evidence seems to suggest that the fees to traffickers per migrant could vary from US$ 500 (e.g. for an organized crossing over an East European or Middle Eastern border, or for an entry into South Africa from Zimbabwe through Botswana and Boputhatswana) to US$ 30,000 (e.g. for a full travel package from China to the USA or an entry visa to the Czech Republic and subsequent smuggling into Germany.[86] The Thai women seeking illegal entry into Japan are reported to pay high smuggling fees, typically US$ 40,000 in each case. Recent information suggests that traffickers charge migrants US$ 4,000 to be smuggled from South Asia to Germany via the former Soviet Union and Poland.[87] A fee of US$ 5,000 or even more for each migrant from a South Asian country to Germany is not uncommon. With an increasing demand for trafficking services, the fees seem to be going up. For instance, according to a recent report in *India Today*, some 280 people from India, Pakistan and Sri Lanka who were trying to enter Europe illegally but were drowned in the Ionin Sea on Christmas Day 1996 when the ferry carrying them capsized, had each paid US$ 8,000 to traffickers for the passage.[88] In November 1996, fees for migrant smuggling from South-East Asia to Toronto in Canada were reported to vary between $30,000 and $35,000 for each person.[89]

Depending on the element of risk taken by the traffickers, the fees could vary even for the same route. For example, according to a recent press report,[90] an important Maltese network transporting clandestine immigrants from Africa, the Middle East and Asia to the Sicilian coast of Italy via Malta charged two different prices depending on whether the client knew how to swim or not. In the former case the risk for the trafficker was less since the immigrant could leave the boat when it was at some distance from the coast thus reducing the possibility of the boat being intercepted by the Italian coast guard.

Enhancement of risk due to more strict surveillance can also push up the fees. Since the introduction of "Operation Gatekeeper", the US strategy to curb irregular immigration from Mexico, most people seeking illegal entry into the USA have been taking the help of traffickers and the fees have generally doubled.[91] Similarly, following adoption of measures by Morocco and Spain against clandestine immigration, the fee charged for the journey to Spain was reported to have doubled from 70,000 pesetas (about US$ 7,000) to 120,000 (or even 200,000) pesetas in 1992. At a cost of between 150,000 and 300,000

---

[86] *The Guardian*, 14 June 1995.

[87] British Broadcasting Summary of World Broadcasts (TV Polonia Satellite Service), 29 March 1995.

[88] IOM, *Trafficking in Migrants*, (Quarterly Bulletin), March 1997.

[89] *Migration News*, Vol. 4, No. 1, January 1997.

[90] *Corriere della Sera*, 20 August 1993.

[91] *Migration News*, Vol. 3, No. 2, February, 1996.

Belgian francs (between US$ 5,000 and US$ 10,000 at the prevailing rate of exchange), traffickers provided Moroccan migrants passports, visas, and even documents to enable their clients to claim certain social security benefits and in some cases arranged marriages of convenience.[92]

The gains from trafficking could be particularly attractive when compared with national levels of salaries and wages. The gangs in Morocco, for example, were reported in 1992 to be earning about 500,000 pesetas (about US$ 5,000) a month per member while the monthly average salary of a qualified person was 40,000 pesetas.[93]

At the average rates of US$ 5,000–10,000 per head and on the basis of a flow of 60,000–150,000 trafficked persons (as estimated at the lower and the upper end respectively), the traffickers smuggling migrants to Western Europe alone made an income of between US$ 300 million and US$ 1.5 billion in 1995. For the reasons already mentioned, such aggregate figures may not be a fully accurate estimate of the amounts of money that flow into migrant trafficking, but they are indicative of its considerable and growing importance as an illegal business activity.

As further indications of the importance of the business, it is estimated that in 1994, 100,000 Chinese were illegally smuggled into the USA against a payment of US$ 25,000 to US$ 35,000, generating for these operations alone some US$ 3 billion for the traffickers. A study completed by the University of Bangkok, on the basis of the number of Thai women smuggled into Japan, Germany and Taiwan for prostitution, estimates that the business yields US$ 3.5 billion a year.[94] The Vienna-based ICMPD speculated that at the global level, the total income derived from migrant trafficking might have been somewhere between US$ 5 and US$ 7 billion in 1995.

One further point needs to be noted in assessing the financial importance of the trafficking business. The amounts mentioned above are calculated on the basis of the payments made to the traffickers themselves; these do not take into account the value of the various activities that go with, or are 'generated' by trafficking. When these spread or multiplier effects are included, the value of trafficking is increased significantly. For example, a trafficking network that smuggled thousands of Turkish workers into France via the former Yugoslavia and Italy earned more than 400 million French francs between 1989 and 1990. While some 30 persons were full members of the gang, it was estimated that in the Italian frontier town of Veintimille alone almost 3,000 persons were benefiting directly or indirectly from clandestine activities in hotels, restaurants, transport and other businesses.[95]

---

[92] *Migration News Sheet*, February, 1991.
[93] *Ibid*, July, 1992.
[94] *Migration News*, Vol. 3, No. 2, February, 1996.
[95] *Migration News Sheet*, September, 1991.

As organized human trafficking becomes more closely intertwined with drugs and arms trafficking and other lucrative criminal activities through the networks of international syndicates, its financial attractions will be increasingly powerful. Trafficking in women, a high-profit (and so far low-risk) business, is an additional feature that helps swell the ill-gotten earnings of the syndicates.

CHAPTER TWO

Why irregular migration? Causes and conditions

Broadly speaking, any inter-country movement that takes place outside the regulatory framework of the sending or the receiving country, or both, is part of irregular migration. The discussion in the previous Chapter has revealed that the nature and degree of such irregularity vary widely as do the causes underlying them. This makes it difficult to enlist all the factors that cause irregular migration or delineate the varying circumstances that may surround it. It is none the less important, especially for policy formulation purposes, to identify at least the principal factors that cause or encourage irregular migration and unravel the complex interplay of forces that often characterise these movements. This is attempted in the present Chapter.

2.1. Emigration pressures and opportunities for legal entries: The mismatch

When there are no legal restrictions on movements of people either in the sending or the destination country, the question of illegal or irregular migration can hardly arise. This was largely the case in Western Europe before the First World War. Until 1875, anyone from anywhere could freely move into the United States and settle there. Today, however, national migration laws and practices limit the opportunities of such movements. People may be allowed to travel freely between countries under specific bilateral and regional agreements, but such freedom does not apply to nationals of countries outside the agreements.

In conditions of regulatory regimes, irregular migration basically results from a mismatch between the numbers or categories of persons seeking to migrate from a country and the legal opportunities available for this purpose. The restrictions on opportunities for movements may be found in the country of origin or destination, or both. As noted in Chapter 1, countries may for economic or political reasons place restrictions on emigration, especially of certain categories of persons such as skilled migrants or members of a political party in opposition. But more often, the legal restrictions on such movements come from the destination country which may be unwilling or unable to accommodate all the potential immigrants.

The mismatch between the numbers of people anxious or forced to emigrate and opportunities for legal migration could be due to conditions prevailing in the sending country. But the demand-pull of the destination country also often plays an important part in reinforcing the push for emigration, contributing to a mismatch between the actual flows and the legally available opportunities for immigration. Thus, when there is an excessive emigration pressure in the sending country or powerful pull factors in the destination country, and especially when the two converge, legal restrictions alone can hardly stop the movements: they tend to divert the flows to irregular channels. The conditions in both sending and receiving countries that contribute to the mismatch are analysed in the following sections.

2.2. *Emigration push in sending countries*

Economic factors – push of poverty and search for opportunities

The economic factors that cause or contribute to migratory pressure are well known – the urge to escape from economic distress and the search for better opportunities are two main elements in economically motivated migration. Poverty, unemployment and economic hardship serve as the main push factors in the first case (*survival migration*), and lack of opportunities to enhance economic welfare in the second (*opportunity-seeking migration*).[1] The urge to survive and the search for better opportunities often interact with two other conditions, namely, *relative deprivation* and *perception about the future* of the home country economy.

The distinction between survival and opportunity-seeking migration is useful as an analytical tool as it brings out the different circumstances and motivations which underlie the two types of movements. Those who move for better opportunities are more circumspect about the potential risks and rewards of irregular migration. When the risks of apprehension and punishment are high, they are less likely to opt for a move through irregular channels. Survival migrants who move more under compulsion than as a matter of choice are more likely to be candidates for irregular migration; the risks of apprehension and punishment may not be a very effective deterrent for them. Less skilled, less equipped and often desperate, they would be inclined to accept almost any job in the destination country. Not surprisingly, most (though not all) irregular immigrants are found in low-skilled, low-wage jobs.

Lack of employment and poverty are a particularly powerful source of pressure for irregular migration. And the present trends strongly suggest that such pressure will be rising in the years to come. About one-third of the

---

[1] For a detailed discussion, see R. Utuza, *Population Redistribution Mechanisms as Related to Various Forms of Development in Population Distribution Policies in Development Planning*, New York, United Nations, 1981. Bimal Ghosh, 'Migration, Trade and International Co-operation: Do the Interlinkages Work?' *International Migration*, Vol. XXX, No. 3/4, pp. 378–9, and 'Economic Migration and the Sending Countries' in Julien van den Broek (ed), *The Economics of Labour Migration*, Edward Elgar, Cheltenham, UK, Brookfield, USA, 1996, pp. 81–82.

Fig. 2.1. Informal sectors shrink with development.
Source: Barerji 1995, Summers and Heston 1991.

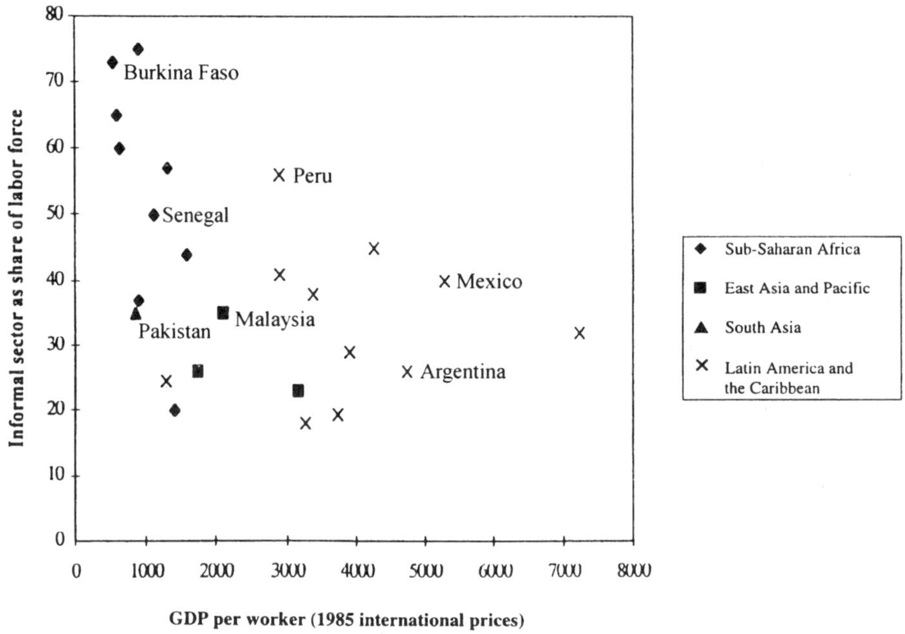

working age population in the low-income economies (with an annual income of US$ 695 or less per person in 1993) is not employed. Although the majority are employed, their earnings in most cases are appallingly low which explains the prevalence of widespread poverty. A high proportion of those under-employed in the developing regions (over 80 per cent of workers in low income countries and almost 40 per cent of those in middle-income countries) is in the informal sector, marked by its extremely low productivity and earnings. In Latin America, some 30 million people are working in the informal sector with a meagre and precarious income. In sub-Saharan Africa, the informal sector accounted in 1991 for about 60 per cent of all jobs.[2] Over all, probably 300 million people are employed in the informal sector of the developing countries of the world.[3] Informality and labour productivity are often negatively related. (Fig. 2.1).

In the past decade, growth in labour productivity in several regions – Africa, Latin America, the Middle East and countries in transition in Eastern Europe and Central Asia – was negative, and the recent trends, except in a handful of countries, have been less than promising. True, in the past few years the

[2] UNDP, *Human Development Report 1994*, Oxford University Press, New York, 1995, p. 25.
[3] ILO, *The Dilemma of the Informal Sector*, Geneva, 1991, p. 11.

proportion of people living below the poverty line in developing and transition economies has fallen slightly, with 29.4 per cent living on under $1 a day in 1993, down from 30.1 per cent in 1987.[4] But, the absolute number of those living below the poverty line in all developing countries has gone up; it was 1.3 billion in 1993, compared to 1.23 billion in 1987 (Table 2.1).[5] The proportion of the poor was 39 per cent in sub-Saharan Africa and 43 per cent in South Asia in 1993. Latin America and the Caribbean is not the poorest developing region in the world, but even there about a quarter of the population lives on less than one dollar a day. In migrant-sending Mexico, the number of people living below the poverty line has grown to 22 million, an increase of five million since the Peso devaluation in December 1994. In Central America, where poverty is widespread, 60 per cent of the population is considered poor. The absolute number of Latin America's poor today is twice what it was 40 years ago.[6] Poverty levels, though still relatively low, are rising in Eastern Europe and Central Asia, following the collapse of the command economy. The United Nations Seventh Annual Human Development Report estimates that, in all, there are 89 countries in which the average person has a lower per-capita income today than in the 1960s.[7]

High growth rates help in reducing poverty, although the exact impact of a given growth rate on poverty reduction could vary between countries depending on how the fruits of economic growth are distributed (further discussed below). As things stand now, growth rates of 6.5 per cent would be necessary in most countries of sub-Saharan Africa to achieve any substantial reduction in poverty.[8] It is doubtful that this can be attained without bold, new efforts. On the other hand, given the demographic expansion, it will be hard for developing regions to reduce the absolute numbers of the poor at the current rates of economic growth. To illustrate, projections for Latin America, (on the basis of growth at 1.9 per cent per capita in the first part of the 1990s) show that the number of the region's poor will continue to grow at a rate of one million people a year, reaching 176 million in 2025. This means two additional poor persons for every minute.[9]

Any major external or internal shocks to the economy imperil the very survival of these extremely vulnerable groups of population, contributing to the build-up of migratory pressure, or, as it often happens, actually pushing them to move. For many of those who already migrated from the rural areas

[4] World Bank, *Poverty Reduction and the World Bank: Progress and challenges in the 1990s*, Washington DC, 1996.

[5] UNDP, *Human Development Report 1994*, Table 3, op. cit, p. 135.

[6] Juan Luis Londono, *Poverty, Inequality, and Human Capital Development in Latin America, 1950–2025*, World Bank, Washington DC, 1996.

[7] UNDP, *Human Development Report 1996*, Oxford University Press, New York, 1997.

[8] World Bank. *Taking Action to Reduce Poverty in Sub-Saharan Africa*, Washington, DC, 1996.

[9] Juan Luis Londono, *Poverty, Inequality, and Human Capital Development in Latin America, 1950–2025*, op. cit.

TABLE 2.1. Population living below US$ 1 a day in developing and transitional economies, 1987–1993

Regions	Population covered by at least one survey (per cent)	Number of poor (millions)			Headcount index (per cent)			Poverty gap (per cent)		
		1987	1990	1993	1987	1990	1993	1987	1990	1993
East Asia and the Pacific	88.0	464.0	468.2	445.8	28.2	28.5	26.0	8.3	8.0	7.8
(excluding China)	(61.5)	(109.2)	(89.3)	(73.5)	(23.2)	(23.2)	(13.7)	(3.8)	(3.1)	(3.1)
Eastern Europe and Central Asia	85.9	2.2	n.a.	14.5	0.6	n.a.	3.5	0.2	n.a.	1.1
Latin America and the Caribbean	83.9	91.2	101.0	109.6	22.0	23.0	23.5	8.2	9.0	9.1
Middle East and North Africa	46.7	10.3	10.4	10.7	4.7	4.3	4.1	0.9	0.7	0.6
South Asia	98.4	479.9	480.4	514.7	45.4	43.0	43.1	14.1	12.3	12.6
Sub-Saharan Africa	65.9	179.6	201.2	218.6	38.5	39.3	39.1	14.4	14.5	15.3
Total	85.0	1,277.1	n.a.	1,313.9	30.1	n.a.	29.4	9.5	n.a.	9.2
Total (excluding ECA)	85.0	1,224.9	1,261.2	1,299.3	33.3	32.9	31.8	10.8	10.3	10.5

Source: World Bank, Poverty Reduction and the World Bank (1996).

to swell the ranks of the urban poor a further move – this time outside the country – is a natural step. Rural-urban disparity often contributes to the process (further discussed below). Urban prosperity, both real and perceived, serves as a powerful magnet for many of the rural poor, although the cities often fail to provide suitable jobs and housing for them. The urban informal sector has thus become a high pressure point for emigration.

In China, for example, the registration system to regulate internal migration has come under strain because of the uneven economic growth in the country – between 1985 and 1992, the economy witnessed a real growth rate of six per cent annually, but much of the job growth has been in the urban areas of the southeastern part of China. The very large numbers of internal migrants (both rural-urban and across regions), estimated in 1994 at 100 million, and widespread rural underemployment covering another 100 million are now causing concern in China's neighbouring countries/areas such as Russia, Taiwan, China, Japan and Indonesia that any deterioration in the internal conditions of the country could lead to a mass exodus.[10] Clearly, opportunities for legal entry will remain inadequate to match any such exodus, and the pressure for irregular migration will increase.

It would be wrong however to assume that survival or poverty-driven migration is always a two-stage process. Spectacular improvements in systems of transport and communications, spread of social networks and above all fast expanding operations of agents and traffickers are now making it possible for many to move abroad directly from rural areas.

Nor does lack of cash, even if an important constraint, necessarily prevent the poor from moving or at least trying to move abroad. When their survival is threatened, poor families would take almost any risks so that at least some members, usually the younger and the more enterprising ones, could have a chance abroad. If sufficient cash cannot be raised, for example, by selling the modest family possessions or by borrowing, there is now often a possibility of making a deal with a trafficker or an agent for deferred payment, for which both the migrant and the family at home may assume the responsibility. In the latter circumstances, the irregular migrant, as noted in Chapter 1, may end up being a victim of abuse and exploitation, and even the family at home could be subject to all forms of extortion.

Poverty and unemployment are generally more important causes of irregular migration than lack of upgrading opportunities at home or the pursuit of higher wages abroad (the pull effect of higher wages abroad is separately discussed in this Chapter). While, as noted above, it is thus useful to make a distinction between survival and opportunity-seeking migration, in certain circumstances the distinction becomes blurred. When, for example, skilled and professional people, though not poverty-stricken, feel that they have reached an economic blind alley, with little or no opportunities for using their skills or expertise in the

[10] BBC summary of World Broadcasts, 25 April 1994. *Migration News* Vol. 1, No. 5, June 1994.

home country, they may suffer from a feeling of despair not much different from the one that drives the survival migrants to look for escape through irregular migration. While the economic hardship in the first case could be severe in the absence of adequate social safety nets, the feeling of frustration resulting from 'de-skilling' and occupational downgrading may prove to be overwhelming, in the second. This is probably an important reason why in recent years skilled workers are also joining the irregular flows or are swelling the ranks of asylum-seekers even when the claim may be unjustified. The situation also explains why increasing numbers of skilled and professional people are becoming involved in trafficking and related illegal activities at a global level.

It is also important to be mindful of the close inter-relationship that exists at the macro-level between poverty and unemployment, on the one hand, and stagnant growth and lack of upgrading opportunities, on the other. Programmes of job creation and poverty alleviation can hardly be sustained over time without upgrading the economy, including the levels of skills and technology, and enhancing growth through improved efficiency and competitiveness. This is particularly so because of the growing interdependence of national economies and increasing globalisation of markets. When the economy continues to be upgraded and higher value added goods and services are produced, not only does it open up new opportunities for higher level jobs and improved earnings, but it also avoids economic stagnation leading, in the medium to long term, to problems of unemployment and under-employment. While economic growth and expansion of employment opportunities are thus correlated, this relationship is neither automatic nor precise. In the absence of certain employment-oriented, supportive policies, even a high-growth country can experience a contraction in job opportunities. This is shown in Figure 2.2. A recent study of a sample of 69 developing countries indicated that only about one-third (27) achieved both income growth and expansion of employment. In another 19 countries job opportunities declined despite growing per capita income. The other 23 countries all had declines in per capita income, but in some of them employment opportunities expanded. This was possible through the addition of a significant number of low-productivity jobs.[11]

These findings were based on official employment and labour force data which did not take full account of the informal sector. If this were done, the picture of low-growth or growthless jobs would be more complete. As already indicated, in recent years much of the expansion of job opportunities in a number of developing countries has taken place in the informal sector: productivity has often stagnated, and there has been little or no improvement in levels of poverty.

For many developing countries, an important source of unemployment-induced emigration pressure lies in lack of export opportunities of labour-intensive products in which they have a comparative advantage due to tariff

[11] UNDP, *Human Development Report 1996*, Oxford University Press, New York, 1997, p. 89.

Fig. 2.2. 'Jobless growth, growthless jobs'.
Source: UNDP. Based on ILO *Yearbook of Labour Statistics*, various editions, and World Bank, 1994.

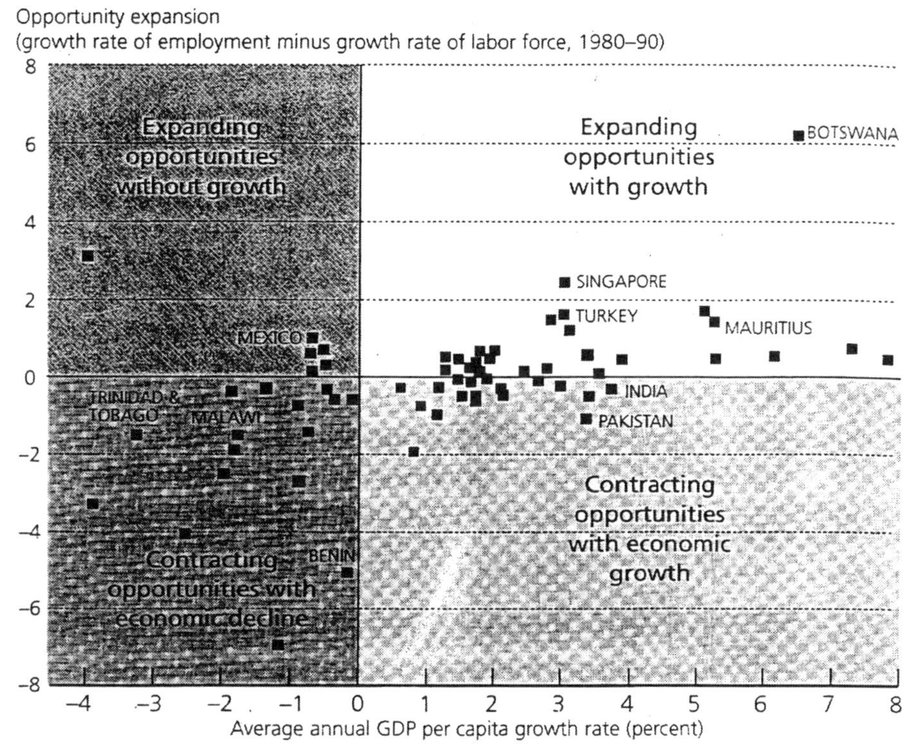

and other barriers against their access to industrial country markets (further discussed below). These include not only the traditional labour-intensive products such as farm produce, textiles and leather goods but also skill and knowledge-intensive services such as computer software and various business and professional services which create high value-added jobs and contribute to overall economic growth.[12]

Although the situation is set to improve as a result of the successful conclusion of the Uruguay Round of multilateral trade negotiations covering both goods and services, there are still a number of non-tariff restrictions that prevent many developing and transition economies from fully reaping the benefits of exports of a range of goods and services in which they have an actual or potential comparative advantage, and which have high employment potential. Industrial countries'

[12] A recent study shows that adequate market access (including freer movement of personnel) should over time, enable developing economies to create 6–30 million additional jobs and generate an income of $350 billion (an increase of $210 billion) from the export of knowledge-based, long-distance services alone. See, Bimal Ghosh, *Gains from Global Linkages: Trade in Services and Movement of Persons*, Macmillan Press, Houndmills and London, 1996.

trade protectionism thus contributes to pressures for both unemployment-induced and opportunity-seeking migration. At the same time, as further discussed later in this Chapter, many of the inefficient and protected industries create a demand for cheap and often irregular immigrant labour.

Relative deprivation, economic despair and skewed income distribution Knowingly or unknowingly, people tend to compare their economic situation with that of their neighbours. When they feel that others are making much faster progress due to their privileged position or inequities embedded in the social and economic system, the sense of relative deprivation[13] can be an additional inducement to move. This applies particularly to opportunity-seeking migration, both within and outside the country.

The outlook for the future also plays an important part. Even survival migrants, who generally are under greater pressure to move, may show more tolerance of hardship if they feel that tomorrow will be a better day. For those who move in search of better opportunities abroad and who can afford to take a decision on a more rational basis, prospects of a better economic future for themselves and their children weigh heavily in their decision against leaving the country. Conversely, an increasing pessimism about the future of the economy is likely to accelerate the outward movement.

Skewed income distribution can influence irregular migration by strengthening the push factor. Extreme inequality of income, in the form of both personal earnings and access to public services, would normally imply more poverty especially when a country's national income itself is low. But inequitable distribution also tends to heighten the sense of relative deprivation. As explained above, even in the absence of extreme economic hardship, the feeling of relative deprivation (often linked to a perception of injustice and discrimination) has been found to contribute to the propensity to migrate among the less privileged people.

Skewed income distribution can also contribute to the emigration pressure in yet another way – by injecting pessimism and eroding hopes about the future. As already noted, in many developing countries, income inequality, relative deprivation and pessimism about the future often go hand in hand, exacerbating emigration pressure. A more equitable distribution system may not be sufficient to reverse such a trend. But when the expectation of sustainable economic growth for several years is reinforced by a better distribution system, it can generate a new optimism and feeling of economic security even in a low-income country, leading to a decline in the migratory push.

In a large number of developing countries trends in income distribution are no more assuring than those concerning job creation and poverty alleviation.

---

[13] For a discussion on relative deprivation and perception of the future prospects as factors in migration see Bimal Ghosh, 'Foreign Direct Investment, Trade and International Migration', 1994 (mimeo).

In the period 1980–91, the ratio between the income share of the bottom 20 per cent of the population and that of the top 20 per cent was 1 : 32 in Brazil; 1 : 47 in Botswana; 1 : 30 in Guatemala; 1 : 29.9 in Panama; and 1 : 26 in Tanzania.[14] It was higher than 1 : 13 for countries like Colombia, Mexico and the Dominican Republic. In the developing world as a whole, the average share of the poorest 20 per cent of the population in total income is no more than 7 per cent. In Latin America, it is as low as 3 per cent.[15] In quite a few of these countries income distribution has become more skewed in recent years. In Mexico, for example, the richest 10 per cent received 34 per cent of national income in 1984; it rose to 41 per cent in 1994, according to a World Bank estimate.[16] The pattern of income distribution can be gauged by the Gini coefficient – a measure of inequality that ranges from 0 (perfect equality) to 1 (perfect inequality). For the developing countries as a whole the Gini coefficient was estimated at 0.50; for Latin America it was 0.56.[17] Economic inequality is pervasive in the rural areas of many developing countries as reflected, for example, in the pattern of land ownership. In Kenya, the Gini coefficient for land was 0.77 and in Brazil 0.86.[18]

Skewed income distribution makes poverty reduction more difficult. As already noted, growth is essential for poverty reduction, but the exact impact of growth on poverty varies across countries. An important determinant of such impact is the pattern of income distribution. Evidence shows that when income inequality is reduced, a given rate of growth is likely to have a more positive effect on poverty reduction. In most developing countries low growth rates and skewed income distribution correlate with high levels of poverty.

In a number of countries, economic discrimination against minorities or particular ethnic groups and skewed income distribution have become intertwined, one reinforcing the other. When this happens, it serves to heighten these groups' feelings of both deprivation and resentment. As further discussed below, the situation can easily lead to political tension, ethnic strife and often large-scale violence, building up pressures for migration, regular or irregular.

---

[14] UNDP, *Human Development Report 1994*, Oxford University Press, New York, 1995.

[15] J.E. Taylor, Micro Economywide Models for Migration and Policy Analysis. An Application to Rural Mexico, OECD, Paris, 1995.

[16] World Bank, *World Bank Development Report 1996*, Washington DC, 1997.

[17] See Pan Yotopoulos, 'The World Distribution of Income: Some Estimates', *Pakistan Journal of Economics*, 1976. Albert Berry, Francois Bourguinon and Christan Morrison, 'The Level of World Inequality: How Much Can One Say?' *The Review of Income and Wealth* 1983. Both cited in Juan Luis Londono, *Poverty, Inequality and Human Capital Development in Latin America, 1950–2025*, 1996, op. cit.

[18] UNDP, *Human Development Report 1994*, Oxford University Press, New York, 1995, p. 25. The importance of land ownership as a measure of income inequality has somewhat diminished in some developing regions (e.g. Latin America) as a result of the declining importance of agriculture, relative to, for example, education and human capital, in the rural economy. But factors such as the pattern of (uneven) expansion of education also reveal the extent of inequality in regions like Latin America. See in this connection Juan Luis Londono. 1996, op. cit.

Political and ethnic oppression and internal violence

When people's lives are at risk or their fundamental rights are suppressed, they flee or try to flee. Civil strife, ethnic conflicts and violation of human rights, including minority rights, are thus among the root causes of actual and potential mass movements.

As events in the 1960s in several developing countries, notably in Africa, demonstrated, protracted struggles for independence and bitter domestic strife over the political and social system in both old and emerging nation states can convert comparatively stable regions into areas of extreme social and political volatility, involving massive displacement of people within and across countries. Since the 1970s, alongside such conflicts, an increasing trend towards suppression of democratic freedom and flagrant abuses of human rights in a number of developing countries have forced people to flee. In many cases, the wider political environment dominated by the Cold War made it more difficult to resolve these conflicts.

More recently, the crises in the former Yugoslavia, the Horn of Africa, Liberia, the Caucasus and the central African states of Rwanda and Burundi have followed a broadly similar pattern of evolution. In each case tension arising from unresolved political, ethnic, religious or nationality disputes led to severe discrimination and flagrant human rights abuses which became increasingly violent. As the disputes then turned into armed conflicts, people were forced to flee in search of safety. Elsewhere, as witnessed in Haiti and El Salvador, political tension and civil strife, often combined with a deteriorating economic situation, led to large-scale migration or pressure for it. Analysts predict that political conflict or a collapse of the economy could force as many as two million North Koreans to seek refuge in other countries.[19]

When ethnic or other minority groupings cut across territorial boundaries of autonomous units within a nation state or have links across neighbouring countries, ethnic and nationality tensions, if unresolved, can be highly destabilising. The ethno-political conflicts in the former Yugoslavia should serve as a pointer to the delicate situation prevailing in the whole of the Balkans and the former Soviet Union. Macedonian Greeks and Turks in Bulgaria, Greeks in Albania, Albanians in Serbia and Romanians in Moldova are some of the well known examples. In such a setting, ethnic and nationality conflicts and potential irredentism can, if rekindled by aspirations long embedded in history, lead to violent challenges to existing frontiers and unleash instability and disorderly movements of people.[20]

The disintegration of the former Soviet Union has given rise to large-scale migratory movements within and between the successor Commonwealth of

---

[19] *Migration News*, Vol. 1, No. 5, June 1994, p. 9.

[20] Bimal Ghosh, 'Trends in International Migration: the European Perspective', *The Courier*. no. 129, September-October 1991, p. 51.

Table 2.2. Migratory movements following dissolution of the former Soviet Union

Refugees, IDPs and involuntary relocating persons	3,632,000*
Repatriants to country of ethnic origin	3,296,000*
Return movement of formerly deported peoples	1,184,000
Ecological migrants	689,000
Illegal migrants	580,000
Asylum-seekers/refugees from non-CIS countries	68,000
Total	8,845,000

*Overlap of 604,000 repatriants/involuntarily relocating persons is not included in overall total

Source: Secretariat of the CIS Conference on Refugees and Migrants, 1996.

Independent States (CIS). Some nine million people may have left their homes, but many of them are in legal and political limbo, with their status as migrants remaining irregular or unclear (Table 2.2). Even more disturbing, there are still a considerable number of flashpoints of potential movements across the whole area (Fig. 2.3). A study commissioned by the International Boundaries Research Unit, which was completed in December 1991, spotted no fewer than 164 ethno-territorial disputes and claims within the former Soviet Union. Many of them are still unresolved.

Past history and politics, especially of the Stalinist regime, have combined to make the ethnic composition of the CIS states most complex and highly sensitive. Central Asia has witnessed one destructive civil war in Tajikistan and two intra-ethnic conflicts in Kyrgyzstan and Uzbekistan, alongside large-scale migratory movements (one out of 12 inhabitants moved out since 1989). The potential for migration remains huge due to fears of on-going and future conflicts, widespread economic distress and environmental degradation. In the Caucasus, aside from the war between Armenia and Azerbeijan, which has so far caused 1.4 million people to leave their homes, there have been four more conflicts – two in Georgia (South Ossetia and Abkazia), and two in the Russian Federation (North Ossetia and Chechnya). Although these conflict spots have been relatively quiet in recent months, none of them seems close to finding a durable solution. Meanwhile, many of the uprooted are living in temporary sheds and the migration potential is still building up.

Of the 3.1 million people, belonging to 20 major national or ethnic groups who were deported from the Western borders of the Soviet Union about 50 years ago, some have returned to their ancestral homelands; some have become involved in new ethnic conflicts on their return; and some others (e.g. the Crimean Tatars and Meshetians) are still trying to return, but their situation remains precarious. Also, there is the frightening problem of nearly 65 million people who had been living outside their own republics or autonomous regions in the former Soviet Union. With its dissolution they became aliens in the newly independent republics, facing a most uncertain future. By 1996, of the 34 million Russians, Ukrainians and Belorussians, more than 3 million had

Fig. 2.3. Ethno-political minorities in the CIS as a potential source of migratory pressure.

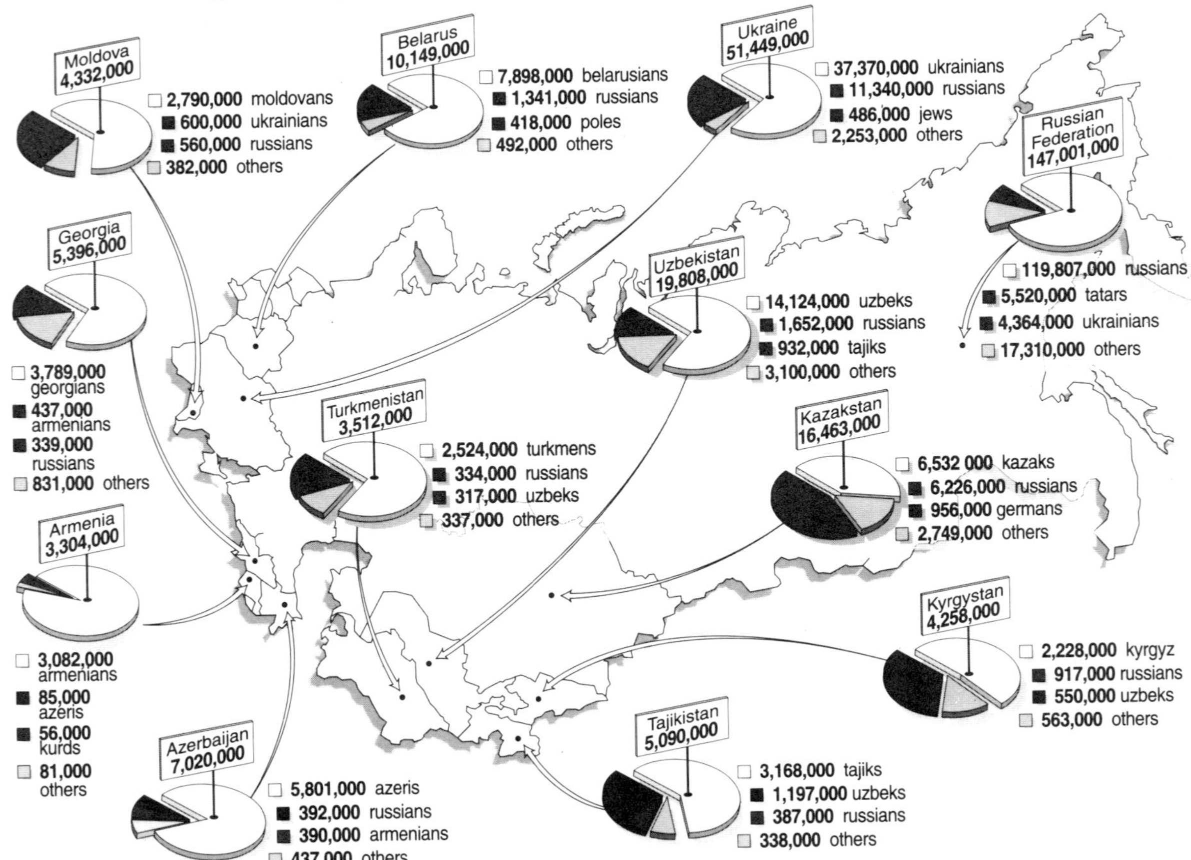

returned to their ethnic homelands, many more are likely to follow. But whether they move or not, their situation causes concern as a source of political tension and instability, exacerbated by the absence in most cases of well-defined migration and nationality laws to protect their rights and ensure them a secure future either in their countries of residence or in their ethnic homelands.

The end of the Cold War has brought into the open many of the unresolved nationality and ethnic disputes deeply rooted in history. Many strife-torn states have collapsed or are politically unstable. If these disputes and open conflicts cannot be resolved through a democratic process, with due respect for human and minority rights, the numbers of refugees and those in a refugee-like situation can only be expected to rise further in the years to come. Recent sample surveys[21] of immigrants in Poland and Russia have revealed that war, political hostilities and discrimination are among the important causes – accounting for 55 per cent of migrants in Russia and 27 per cent of those in Poland interviewed as part of a recent IOM survey – that pushed them to move from home countries. These political factors ranked high especially for those who migrated from the war-torn or politically unstable countries or areas like the former Yugoslavia, Azerbaijan, Armenia and Afghanistan.

Rarely do the political and ethnic factors act alone to propel people to move, except in extreme cases of large-scale conflicts and generalised violence. Political upheavals and conflicts often thwart economic development and accelerate environmental degradation. As resource scarcity increases, economic rivalry becomes increasingly fierce and discrimination more rampant. This in turn sharpens political conflicts, creating a vicious circle that induces or forces more people to migrate.

Having no compelling ideological or political reasons to welcome the victims in the post Cold War era, and given their domestic political and economic constraints, Western states are likely to continue with their restrictive refugee admission policies. There will not be many doors legally open for them. The numbers of those seeking refuge can be expected to far exceed the places that the potential receiving countries will be willing or able to provide. Unless the root causes can be effectively tackled, many of them will seek escape through irregular channels.

Growing menace of environmental degradation

In many instances in the past, particular migratory movements have been influenced by environmental factors. Movements of nomads and herdsmen in Africa, for example, have often followed a transhumance pattern in which environmental considerations, especially the search for pastures and water, have been a dominant element. Although it is difficult to establish a direct

[21] IOM, *Transit Migration in the Russian Federation*, Geneva, July 1994, p. 23; *Transit Migration in Poland*, Geneva, April 1994, p. 22.

causal relationship between the environment and irregular migration, there is little doubt that environmental factors, by themselves or, more often, in interaction with political and economic causes, can significantly contribute to migration pressures far exceeding the admission opportunities in the receiving countries. (See Table 2.3 for a list of environmental factors contributing to migration or migratory pressure.)

Environmental disruptions may take various forms with varying degrees of impact on migration. Some of them are chronic and long-lasting; others are more sudden and violent. These may be caused by natural disasters such as cyclones, earthquakes, volcanic eruptions and floods. It is believed that the number of people affected by natural disasters has increased in each decade since the 1960s. In the 1980s as many as 64 million people were affected by such disasters, compared with 28 million in the 1960s.[22] During 1967–91 disasters hit three billion people, mostly in Asia.[23] Natural disasters are not a major cause of external migration, but, in the absence of well established systems of relief and assistance they often worsen the conditions of poor people in developing countries. This in turn forces them to look for an escape elsewhere, both within or outside the country.

Environmental degradation, which (unlike environmental disruptions) is often accelerated by human activities over long periods, is generally a slower process but it can also be a serious source of migration pressure. Climatic change, desertification, deforestation, soil erosion, salinity and waterlogging are among the processes of such degradation. They often contribute to drought and famine. Climatic changes cause serious concern because they are likely to be continuous, largely irreversible and open-ended. There is now strong evidence that global warming may lead to a rise in the levels of the oceans of between 15 cm and 30 cm over the next four or five decades. Should this happen, some 200 million people may be overtaken by coastal flooding, disruptions in rainfall and droughts of unprecedented severity and duration. Internal displacements of such large numbers of people can only add to current pressures for external migration.

Desertification, a manifestation of the deterioration of the eco-system under the combined pressure of adverse climatic conditions and excessive exploitation of natural resources, is another cause of migration pressure; it may be even more so in the years to come. It is estimated that some 135 million people are threatened by desertification, mostly in the African Sahel, the Horn of Africa, Brazil, Mexico, China and parts of West and South Asia. As in most other cases of environmental degradation, desertification often goes hand in hand with poverty, inequitable land distribution and increasing population pressure

---

[22] UNDP, Central Evaluation Office, 'UNDP/UNRO Cooperation: An Evaluation', December 1989, p. 19.

[23] UNDP, *Human Development Report 1994*, Oxford University Press, New York, op. cit., p. 29.

Table 2.3. Environmental change as a cause of migration

		Time frame	Scale and intensity	Predictability	Reversibility
Natural causes					
Earthquakes, volcanic eruptions, flooding, etc. necessitating disaster relief		Short-term	Local and severe	Limited or none	Yes, in some cases
Man-made causes					
Global warming, acid rain Pollution of rivers, etc.		Long-term and gradual	Global, regional and incremental	To some degree	Partial and difficult
Industrial accidents		Short-term	Local and severe	Limited or none	Sometimes
Predictable environmental causes of displacement (reservoir construction, nuclear testing, hazardous waste site construction, megaprojects, etc.)		Medium- to long-term	Local and sometimes severe	Yes	No
Depletion of resources and/or environmental degradation	Localized problems (degradation of agriculture base; soil, water, wildlife resources)	Medium- to long-term	Basically local and could be serious	To some degree	Sometimes partial
	Irreversible problems (severe soil erosion and desertification)	Long-term	Local to regional and serious to severe	To some degree	No

Source: UNHCR/IOM/RPG International Symposium on 'Environmentally-induced Population Displacements and Environmental Impacts Resulting from Mass Migrations', Geneva. 21–24 April 1996.

on declining resources. Their combined effect often serves as a powerful push factor in internal and external movements.

Deforestation is still another example of slow but serious environmental deterioration which, combined with population pressure and resource constraints, may encourage migration. Forests are being lost at the rate of more than 11 million hectares a year. The Sahelian belt from Sudan to Mauritania has been almost entirely stripped of trees by the combined forces of drought, overgrazing and indiscriminate cutting of trees for domestic fuel. Haiti has lost most of its forests, while in Central America and parts of South America loss of forests have made sustainable development doubtful.[24] Deforestation, in turn, has led to soil erosion, affecting both farm productivity and income.

Biological disasters caused by pathogens, insects and pests, have in the past led to major population movements, especially when, as in Africa, they destroyed vital food production. Although the threat of such disasters is somewhat diminished today by modern pesticides, insecticides and other chemicals, locusts continue to be a serious threat in many areas already in the throes of ecological deterioration – for example the region extending from Western Sahel to east-central Africa. The onset of any large disaster in these areas can drive many of the affected people to move into neighbouring countries.

Industrial accidents, toxic waste dumps and the release of radioactive substances from nuclear stations can also make heavy onslaughts on the environment. Their immediate impact is generally limited to internal displacement, but, as the Chernobyl disaster has demonstrated, over a long period they may serve as an additional push factor encouraging external migration.

Ecological deterioration and armed conflicts often go together, one interacting with the other. Freshwater scarcity is now known to be an important factor in ethnic strife and political tension both within and between countries. For more than two decades, differences over the sharing of the waters of the Ganges had strained relations between Bangladesh and India. Water scarcity, alongside intrusion of sea water that destroys forests and farms, has led to massive irregular migration from Khulna, one of the worst affected districts in Bangladesh. Afghanistan, Chad, El Salvador, Ethiopia, Haiti, Honduras, Somalia and Sudan are among the countries which in recent years have experienced both ecological disasters and prolonged armed conflicts. Indeed, of around 50 such conflicts in 1994, about 20 were thought to have an environmental dimension. El Salvador is a good example of how ecological deterioration, poverty, inequitable land distribution and armed conflict can combine to create a vicious spiral propelling people to migrate.

In sum, environmental degradation and disasters hold powerful potential for inducing or forcing vast numbers of people to migrate. But, as opportunities for legal entry into destination countries will, even in the best of circumstances,

---

[24] IOM/The Refugee Policy Group (RPG), *Migration and the Environment*, Geneva and Washington DC, 1992, p. 12.

continue to be limited, many migrants are likely to try the irregular channels. A comprehensive policy response to irregular migration must therefore take due account of the environmental factor that contributes to migratory pressures.

2.3. Demand pull in destination countries

As already noted, irregular immigration may also result from a mismatch between the level of demand for immigrant labour and the opportunities offered by the receiving country for legal entry. When there is a significant amount of unmet labour demand, it is difficult to restrain immigration flows through legal restrictions imposed by the receiving country, unless the penalty for illegal entry is excessively high and can be rigorously applied.

Despite a shortage in labour supply, a receiving country may impose restrictions on labour immigration for various reasons, both economic and non-economic. Concern about the loss of cultural homogeneity and national cohesiveness may restrain a country from encouraging large-scale immigration even in the case of acute labour shortages in the economy. While most countries attach a certain importance to the preservation of national identity and cohesion, it weighs more heavily in the formulation of immigration policies in particular cases. In Japan, for example, large inflows of foreigners are widely regarded as a potential source of social disharmony, and the government is particularly concerned about the immigration of low-skilled foreign workers. It is fearful that this would lead to the formation of a racially different social underclass which could turn out to be socially and politically disruptive.

Even a country wedded to a multi-cultural model may be afraid of potential social tension that may result from a sudden and large influx of foreigners and of the problems of integration that it may entail. Also, excessive dependence on foreign workers is often perceived as a source of economic and political vulnerability which most countries try to avoid. To illustrate, Switzerland, a capital-rich country with high labour productivity and a structural shortage of labour, had followed a liberal immigration policy since the end of the 19th century. But by 1963, when the number of foreigners reached the level of one million and constituted more than one eighth of the total population, an increasing 'belief in a political danger that national traits would be debased' gained ground.[25] As it overtook economic and labour market concerns, the Government introduced a ceiling system based on a firm's total work force to control the inflows of foreign workers. This was refined and reinforced by an overall ceiling system in 1970, with entry quotas set for each canton.

Most analysts believe that Germany's post-war economic miracle was closely linked to the inflow of guest workers. Even in the face of today's high unemployment, many continue to see the need for Germany to import foreign workers

---

[25] A. Macheret, *L'immigration etranger en Suisse al'heure de l'integration europeenne*, Georg, Geneva, 1969, p. 37.

to meet its labour needs in specific industries and occupations.[26] Nonetheless, history, tradition and political concerns combined with real and perceived social costs have prevented Germany from considering itself an 'immigration' country.

Shortages of housing, transport and other infrastructural facilities, along with the rising cost of social welfare, are also often an immediate constraining factor, although these need to be balanced against the costs of immigration restrictions (e.g. loss of national output and cost of controlling irregular immigration). In the recent debate on admission of foreign workers in Japan, for example, the Ministry of Labour argued that an inflow of 500,000 foreign workers would cost the country an annual minimum of 1,413,400 million Yen to look after their social welfare.[27] As discussed in Chapter 3, in the USA as in Western Europe, rising social welfare cost has become a dominant theme in the current discussion on immigration restriction policies.

Pursuit of increased productivity through technological restructuring is an important economic reason why a country may not encourage the import of unskilled or semi-skilled foreign workers even when there is clear shortage at the lower end of the labour market. In recent years the concern has increasingly surfaced in most newly industrialising East Asian economies in the face of shortage of low-skilled workers. For example, in the Republic of Korea, where the country's increasing dependence has become the subject of wide debate, the Ministry of Labour has expressed concern that such dependence would retard restructuring and slow down increase in productivity and wages. Although there is less organized opposition to low-skilled foreign workers in Singapore, the government seeks to regulate the inflow of such workers by setting a ceiling on the percentage of foreign workers in a firm's work force and by placing a levy on permits for hiring foreign workers, while pressuring employers to upgrade and relocate. Taiwan, China, now follows a similar policy of imposing a levy on labour imports, and Malaysia does the same.

The general experience of these countries seems to suggest, however, that limited import of foreign workers, alongside measures to upgrade skills and technology, relocation of firms abroad and increasing domestic labour force participation, may not completely alleviate labour shortages at least in the short run. Should this be the case, the pressure for irregular immigration is likely to persist. As will be discussed in the next section, the capacity of national migration regimes in resisting through their unilateral action the process of labour market adjustment (e.g. by stopping labour outflows despite surplus in the potential sending country's labour market or labour inflows in the face of

---

[26] Some analysts put the 'immigration need' of Germany at 300,00 to 400,000 newcomers per year. *Migration News*, Vol. 3, No. 8, August 1996.

[27] Based on a simulation model of foreign workers living in Japan for 5–10 years, each with his/her spouse and 2 children. *Present Situation of Foreign Workers and their Social Cost*, Ministry of Labour, Tokyo, Japan, 1993.

unmet labour demand in the potential receiving country) is now increasingly circumscribed.

Labour shortages alongside immigration restrictions in the receiving country are not the only factors that contribute to irregular immigration. There are several situations in which unmet labour demand may encourage irregular immigration even though there may be a general surplus in the labour market of the receiving country. This can happen when, for example, local workers may be unwilling and unavailable to take up certain types of work, as exemplified by the aversion of the workers in many industrial countries towards dirty, dangerous and difficult jobs. Unemployment among local workers can then co-exist with labour shortages in certain segments of the economy. When this happens, employers look for foreign workers to fill the vacant jobs, and in the absence of opportunities for legal immigration, the unmet labour demand for these jobs is likely to be satisfied by irregular immigrant workers. In Western Europe, the non-availability of local workers for certain jobs, and the consequent segmentation of the labour market are major contributing factors of immigration pressure. The problem is somewhat less serious in the USA due to the presence of black and Hispanic populations representing a large reservoir of local labour for less attractive jobs.

Demand for (irregular) foreign workers may also co-exist with an availability of local labour because of wage differentials. Since irregular foreign workers are often paid wages that are much lower than the market rates, employers may have a special interest in engaging irregular immigrants. The temptation is likely to be greater when wage differentials are high enough to compensate for the risk involved in recruiting irregular workers and when geographical proximity and the existence of networks give them easy access to such irregular immigrant labour. The fact that irregular immigrant workers can be shunned more easily than regular workers is often an additional inducement.

In Germany, for example, a combination of many of these factors accounts for the prevalence of large numbers of irregular foreign workers in the construction industry – at a time when its competitiveness is threatened by high domestic labour costs. Recent raids by Berlin police on a large construction site revealed that some of the irregular foreign workers were paid DM 5 (US$ 3.40) an hour, less than one-tenth of what is payable to a legally employed German worker. In the state of Hessen, the Labour Office estimated that an irregular worker cost only DM 34 per hour whereas the official rate was DM 54.[28] Another attraction for employing irregular workers is the possible evasion of payroll taxes that finance social security schemes and can add up to 50 per cent to the hourly wage the employer pays. Some foreign workers, too, prefer to work off the books which could mean savings of between 20 and 30 per cent of their wages that are typically deducted for pension, unemployment and health programmes. In the Czech Republic, an irregular (mostly unskilled)

[28] *Frankfurter Allgemeine Zeitung*, 31 October 1990.

Status.

Wages

lack rights

savings for migrant + employer

worker, for example, in construction and textile industries costs the employer approximately half as much as a worker who is legally employed, and the risk involved (a fine of $400–800) is small relative to the savings made in salaries, taxes and social benefits.[29]

Over the years, irregular migration from Mexico to the United States has been fuelled by the demand for cheap labour. The nature of the flows, including the choice of the transit city, seems to have been largely influenced by the actual or perceived demand for clandestine labour in specific sectors of the US economy. This is reflected, for example, in the decreasing trend in the movement of agricultural workers in recent years, alongside a diversification in the occupational composition of the irregular flows. Table 2.4 shows how during the period from 1987 to 1992 these flows adapted themselves to the fluctuations in the US labour market.[30]

The level of such irregular migration has also been influenced by the economic cycles in the USA, with the demand for Mexican labour generally declining in times of high unemployment, as during the economic downturns of 1907, 1921, 1929–34, 1974, 1981 and 1992. The demand for low-cost, irregular labour however existed even during periods of economic slowdown. In fact, as has been argued by an analyst, the economic difficulties may have encouraged some US employers, who in normal times would not hire irregular immigrant workers, to do so during periods of economic downturn in order to reduce the cost of production.[31]

Not surprisingly, the demand for such irregular immigrant labour – even in the absence of shortages in domestic labour market – stems particularly from declining and non-competitive industries and marginal firms in the underground economy, which may find it difficult to survive without access to cheap and flexible labour provided by irregular immigrants. Many of these declining industries also seek, with the support of powerful lobbies, high tariff protection. As already noted, to the extent that these industries are labour-intensive, in which developing countries have a comparative advantage, trade protectionism in industrial countries contributes to irregular migration in a two-fold manner: it encourages the protected and less efficient industries to rely on cheap, irregular, immigrant labour, just as the loss of export-related employment and income undermines the efforts of labour-surplus countries to reduce emigration pressure.

Marginal firms which operate in the underground economy with low productivity and margin of profits are particularly anxious to use irregular immigrant workers for similar reasons. An additional factor that encourages them to

---

[29] IOM, *Transit Migration in the Czech Republic*, Geneva, May 1994, p. 26.

[30] Jorge A. Bustamante, *Undocumented migration: A theoretical – methodological framework*, OECD, Paris, 1993. Paper presented to the conference on migration and international cooperation, Madrid, March 1993, pp. 7–8.

[31] Ibid, p. 8.

Table 2.4. Distribution by economic activity of irregular Mexican immigrants into the United States (based on sample surveys, 1987–92) (in percentages)

Sector	1987	1988	1989	1990	1991	1992
Tourism	34.8	19.1	15.2	19.6	16.5	14.1
Domestic services	0.2	15.3	9.1	9.7	19.7	10.2
Other services		10.0	7.3	8.2	8.1	6.6
Agriculture	30.5	24.1	30.2	29.3	26.1	21.6
Manufacturing industry	17.0	6.2	17.5	14.0	7.3	6.2
Construction industry	17.1	20.2	19.0	16.3	21.5	41.2
Self-employment	0.2	–	1.6	1.5	–	–
Others	0.2	5.0	–	1.5	0.8	–
Total	100.0	100.0	100.0	100.0	100.0	100.0

Source: Proyecto Canon Zapata, El Colegio de la Frontera Norte, Mexico.

engage irregular immigrants is that they often remain outside the scope of the labour inspection system; and even if they do come under its purview, they cannot be easily reached. Thus, in several Western European countries the number of (mostly irregular) foreign workers in the underground economy has increased substantially in recent years. In Italy, for example, the proportion of persons employed in the underground economy increased from 21 per cent of the total labour force in 1980 to 23 per cent in 1994. But the proportion of foreigners in the total number of persons doing undeclared work rose faster, increasing from 6 per cent to 13 per cent during the same period.[32]

Three important points emerge from the above discussion. First, unmet labour demand due to imbalances between the supply of, and demand for labour in a country can be an important source of irregular immigration. Second, such imbalances may co-exist alongside a general excess of labour supply in the receiving country as a result of the fragmentation of the labour market and/or segmentation of the economy. Third, measures against irregular migration cannot be isolated from reforms in labour market, trade and other policies to redress segmentation of the labour market and the national economy.

2.4. *Migration regimes and interpenetration of national labour markets*

The discussion above has revealed how supply–demand imbalances in the labour markets both within and between different countries can encourage irregular labour migration. The sending and receiving countries' migration

[32] Information based on a report issued by the National Institute of Statistics, 30 November 1995, quoted in *Corriere della Sera*, 30.November 1995. The situation however varies between different Western European countries and areas. In the German state of Hessen, for example, a recent labour office report suggests that most of the jobs in the underground economy are filled by German citizens and not foreigners. *Migration News*, Vol. 3, No. 8, August 1996.

policies can be adjusted to redress these imbalances, but they can also serve to impede the process of such adjustment. When the latter happens, the migration regime is challenged by the market forces and irregular migration tends to increase in defiance of the regulatory framework.

This explains why many developing countries which are faced with the problem of an excess supply of professional and scientific personnel relative to the effective demand in the economy, are generally unable to preserve their (potentially important) human resources through a restrictive emigration policy. The root causes of such imbalances may lie in lopsided educational policies, or faulty development strategies, or both. As long as these root causes persist, a restrictive emigration policy tends to thwart or adversely affect the normal process of supply–demand adjustment through labour market mechanisms, and thus leads to irregular migration.

Implicit in this process of adjustment is the growing interpenetration of the labour markets. The experience of several African and Arab countries that sought to pursue such restrictive policies illustrates this point. As noted in Chapter 1, in the mid-1970s, Syria, for example, introduced a restrictive policy to prevent the outflow of qualified personnel. Although the government was able to bring the emigration of civil servants under a degree of control after 1979, the (mostly irregular) outflows of skilled and unskilled workers could not be stopped. The situation led Syria to promulgate a decree in 1980 granting amnesty to all unauthorised migrants if they returned to the country within six months.[33] Survival migrants are more easily attracted to such irregular movements because of the extreme economic pressure, and the little or zero opportunity cost involved. To put it differently, they have little to lose as they move from the home country.

Conversely, the immigration policy of a receiving country can contribute to irregular immigration if it negatively affects the labour market mechanism by restricting labour inflows despite unmet labour demand. When there are real shortages in the labour market, a country, within certain limits, may try to meet them either by restricting the demand (through, for example, technological upgrading or relocating firms and investing abroad), or by increasing the labour supply (through, for example, increased female participation in the labour force and raising the retirement age). But as long as there is an imbalance in the labour market in the form of unmet labour demand, a restrictive labour immigration policy would normally encourage employers to take recourse to irregular immigrant labour. This is clearly borne out by the experience of

---

[33] I.J. Seccombe and R.I. Lawless, 'State Intervention and the International Labour Market' in R. Appleyard (ed.) *The Impact of International Migration on Developing Countries*, OECD, Paris, 1988, pp. 69–86. Bimal Ghosh 'Economic Migration and the Sending Countries' in Julien van den Broek (ed.), op. cit., p. 85. A situation roughly similar to that in Syria largely explains why several other countries (e.g. Turkey and Tunisia) which had tried to enforce selective control of emigration on the basis of skills and/or geographical regions in the 1960s and early 1970s had very little impact in the years that followed.

countries or areas like Japan, Republic of Korea, Malaysia and Taiwan, China. Once more, this basically reflects the growing internationalisation of the labour market. The employers would seek to circumvent the immigration restrictions unless the anticipated risks outweigh the expected 'rewards'; and for the reasons already mentioned, the survival migrants would probably be the ones to be most easily attracted to irregular entry and employment. The situation largely explains why employer sanctions (discussed in Chapter 4) as an isolated policy measure often fail to stop the use of irregular immigrant labour.

Half-hearted or distorted labour market measures to meet labour shortages may encourage irregular migration, instead of alleviating it. A typical example is provided by the so-called technical trainee scheme in the Republic of Korea. Although in principle designed to provide technical training to foreign workers, including those employed by Korean companies abroad, a substantial part of the scheme is now used to supply cheap foreign workers to small manufacturing firms which have been experiencing acute labour shortages and financial difficulties since the 1990s. Most of them are basically used for unskilled jobs, but as trainees they are paid at a much lower level than workers in comparable jobs. According to a recent report, while the trainees receive about $300 a month, the illegal workers are paid about $600. As a result, it is estimated that about 30 per cent of the trainees – in 1996 their total number was around 70,000 – leave their original work places and become irregular workers because of the attraction of higher earnings. The scheme is thus considered to be a source of irregular foreign workers in Korea.[34]

In short, migration policy can be prudently used to facilitate, or manage in an orderly manner, supply–demand adjustment in the labour market over time; but when used to counteract such adjustment it creates a perverse effect in the form of irregular migration. The greater the degree of internationalisation of the labour markets, the higher the risks. The situation becomes worse when irregular immigration is allowed to become a part of a government's response to a tight labour market. Not only is it a poor substitute for a sound labour market and economic policy, but it shakes public confidence in other government policies and weakens general credibility of the government, while also leading to a host of negative social and ethical consequences as discussed in Chapter 3.

An additional point to note is that non-economic immigration, notably the refugee and family reunification flows, may eventually serve to meet the labour market needs of the receiving country. Indeed, it can be argued that without the authorised refugee and family reunification flows there could have been a greater pressure for irregular immigration in response to industrial countries' unmet labour demand in specific sectors and occupations in recent years. It is

---

[34] S.D. Kang, 'Globalisation of Labour market also in South Korea?', paper presented to the international conference on the dynamics of labour migration in Asia, Nihon University, Tokyo, March 1996. (mimeo) pp. 19–20.

thus important to take careful account of the effects, over time, of authorised refugee and family reunification flows on the labour market. However, the policy considerations governing these flows are not the same as, and cannot be substituted for, those that are relevant to labour market management.

2.5. *Income differentials as a factor in irregular migration*

An important question that has not been specifically addressed so far is: To what extent does the pull of higher income in rich countries contribute to irregular migration? It is well known that disparities in levels of both income and employment encourage internal and external migration. For example, a study in the United States shows that a state with a per capita income 10 per cent below the national average experiences a net emigration of 0.25 per cent of its population per year, other things being equal.[35] Experience in Western Europe seems to suggest that emigration is high when income inequality between countries is at a ratio of 10 to 1 and that it tends to decline when the ratio drops to 3–4 to 1. As for the effect of employment disparity, it has been estimated by some that when the unemployment rate in one European Community (now European Union) country is 10 percentage points higher that the EC average, the country can be expected to have one per cent additional emigration.[36]

Limited studies made in several countries seem to indicate that, all other things remaining equal, employment differentials are generally a more powerful factor than income differentials in internal migration. For example, in Britain a 10 per cent lower wage in a region increases its annual net emigration by 0.6 per cent of its labour force. But a fall of 10 per cent in its employment rate increases annual net emigration by 0.8 per cent of its labour force.[37] This may also be true for inter-country movements, but, it is difficult to generalize. In reality, much depends on the type or main underlying motivation of the migratory movement. For example, for the survival migrants (who are driven mainly by unemployment, poverty and extreme economic insecurity), the prospects of finding a job may be the most powerful attraction. Opportunity-seeking migrants, on the other hand, are likely to be more sensitive to higher wages and incomes in a foreign country. What is important to underline in this connection is that irregular migration entails considerably higher risks

---

[35] R. Barrow and X, Sala-i-Martin, 'Convergence across States and Regions', Unpublished, Harvard University, 1991.

[36] Prognos, *The Development of the EC Labour Market*, Basel, 1989, p. 25.

[37] R. Layard, S. Nickell and R. Jackman, *Unemployment: Macro-economic Performance and the Labour Market*, Oxford University Press, 1991, Chapter 6. Comparable figures for Spain are 0.025 $/u$ per cent for the effect of a 10 per cent lower wage, and 0.09 $/u$ per cent for the effect of a 10 per cent lower employment rate, where u is the national unemployment rate. see, S. Bentolila and J. Doldado, 'Mismatch and Internal migration in Spain. 1962–86' in Padoa-Schioppa (ed.), *Mismatch and Labour Mobility*, Cambridge University Press, 1991, pp. 212–213.

than legal migration and that such risks have a differentiated effect on the attitude of these two groups of potential migrants.

As already discussed, given the high risks involved in irregular movements, it is easy to see why the majority of those propelled to take such risks belong to the category of survival migrants. For many of them, finding a remunerative job – almost any job – is the primary goal; levels of wages or incomes are of less immediate importance. There are, however, situations when prospects of very high earnings or quick gains in the destination country may be a powerful factor in irregular migration, and when even some of those who migrate mainly in search of better opportunities (opportunity-seeking migrants with a high income threshold to emigrate) may join the irregular flows. This happens especially when not only are the anticipated rewards from irregular migration quite high, but the risks of apprehension are low and the eventual punishments likely to be small. If the anticipated rewards or benefits outweigh the risks or costs involved in moving to a foreign country through unlawful channels, then individuals who are anxious to improve their conditions (but have no compulsion to move) may rationally decide in favour of irregular migration.

A sizable part of irregular, often pendular, migration from Eastern Europe, especially Poland, to Western Europe since the 1980s can be attributed to substantially high earnings that the migrants could secure, with little risk of apprehension or punishment, from the sale of highly subsidised, low-priced goods or from considerably better paid short-term employment in the countries of Western Europe. The income differentials were further accentuated by the rates at which the East Europeans could exchange their earnings into their national currencies. Their combined pull effects led to considerable short-term, irregular migration. After 1989, while such differences in incomes and prices between Western and a number of Eastern European countries narrowed, those between various countries of Eastern Europe widened, encouraging irregular migration within the eastern region.[38] In Africa, following the devaluation of the CFA franc, used in 14 west African states, in January 1994, the value of Nigeria's currency, the naira (pegged to the US dollar) rose by 54 per cent, and immigrants poured into northern Nigeria to profit from the higher exchange rate.[39] Mexico–US migration, as most migration flows, is determined by a complex set of factors. It is interesting to note, however, that according to one recent study, a 10 per cent peso devaluation increased Mexico–US migration, regular and irregular, by 17 per cent.[40]

At the global level income inequalities seem to be widening, rather than narrowing. In 1870, the average income per head of the richest countries was

[38] Marek Okolski, 'Poland' in Solon Ardittis (ed), *The Politics of East-West Migration*, op. cit., pp. 54–55.

[39] 'French currency move provokes unrest in Africa', *New York Times*, 23 February 1994, p.A.1.

[40] J.E. Taylor, *Micro Economywide Models for Migration and Policy Analysis. An Application to Rural Mexico*, OECD, Paris, 1995.

Italy!

11 times that of the poorest. In 1985, the ratio had risen to 52 times.[41] Between 1960 and 1991, the share of world income for the richest 20 per cent of the world population, mostly in industrial countries, increased from 70.2 per cent to 84.7 per cent. Over the same period the poorest 20 per cent of the population (mostly in developing countries) saw a decline in their share from 2.3 per cent to 1.4 per cent.[42] In other words, the ratio of the shares of the richest and the poorest rose from 30:1 to 60:1 in 31 years.

True, policy reorientation in the past two decades in a number of emerging economies, notably in East Asia, has enabled them to achieve remarkable success in catching up with the high-income countries. But conditions in a large number of poor countries exclude any such speedy economic growth. To illustrate, one estimate suggests that even at three times the rise in per capita GDP increase in the countries of Central America, the absolute income disparity between these countries and the USA would increase before it started to narrow. Indeed, it could take 150 years for the disparity to be erased.[43] According to another recent estimate, even with policy improvements all round, 'the ratio between the wages of the richest and the poorest groups in the international wage hierarchy – skilled industrial country workers and African farmers – could fall from an estimated sixty to one in 1992, to fifty to one by 2010'. If, however, things go bad, it may even rise to 70.[44] For other developing regions, the gap may be less striking but it is nonetheless quite important (Fig. 2.4). For example, the differences in average wages between Eastern and Western Europe or between Mexico and the United States are, roughly speaking, around one to eight or ten.

Such income disparities will continue to be an important factor in international migration. It is doubtful, however, whether they would be a very powerful driving force for *irregular migration* in the face of stricter border control and provision of stiff punitive measures against such movements. As discussed above, the situation may be somewhat different when risks involved in irregular movements are negligible and the anticipated gains are immediate and extremely attractive. It is worth noting that both by minimizing, at least seemingly, the risk factor and exaggerating the potential gains from moving abroad, organized traffickers seem to fuel irregular migration.

Some general conclusions can be drawn from the above discussion. More than the attraction of higher earnings, it is the push of poverty and unemployment, combined with the pull of unmet labour demand in the destination country, that will normally continue to be a dominant force in irregular

---

[41] World Bank, *World Development Report 1995*, Washington DC, 1996.

[42] UNDP, *Human Development Report 1992; 1995*. Oxford University Press, New York and Oxford, p. 34 (1992) and p. 63 (1995).

[43] ILO, S. Weintrraub and S. Diaz Briquet, 'The use of foreign aid for reducing incentives to emigrate from Central America', in W.R. Böhning and M.L. Schloeter-Parades, *Aid in Place of Migration*, Geneva, 1994, pp. 138–140.

[44] UNDP, *Human Development Report 1992*, 1995, op. cit., p. 18, 5.

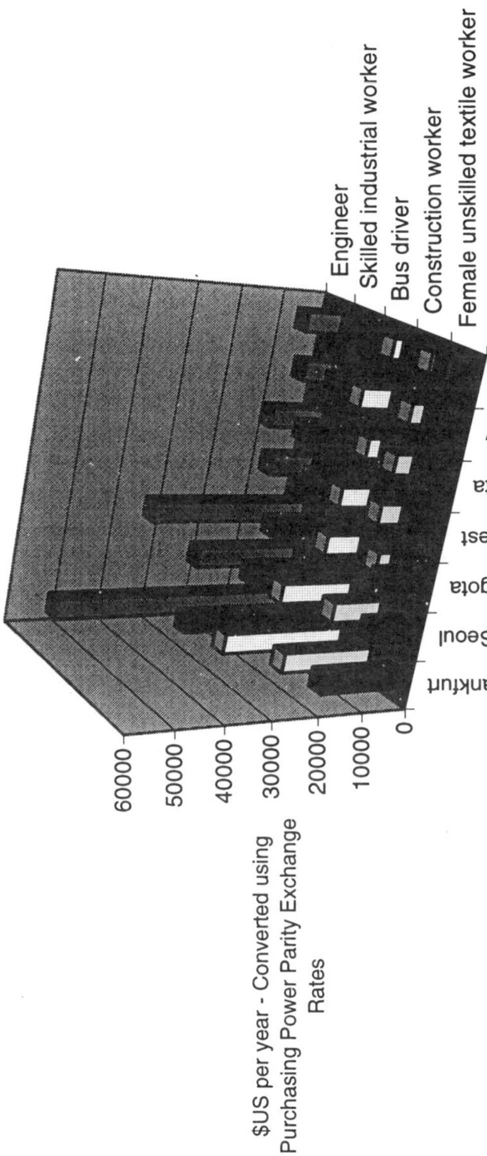

Fig. 2.4. Differences in earnings across the international wage hierarchy. *Note:* Earnings adjusted to reflect purchasing power parity. *Source:* Union Bank of Switzerland, 1994.

movements. This, however, does not mean that the irregular migrants will be confined exclusively to unskilled and low-skilled workers; in situations of extreme economic despair and insecurity, skilled and professional workers could also swell the ranks of irregular migrants. Nor does it mean that income inequalities between countries do not play a role in irregular migration. In particular, when the destination country offers prospects of quick and substantial income gains, with low risks for irregular entry and work, it may be an important source of attraction for irregular migrants.

Pressures for non-economic migration and restrictive migration regimes

The preceding discussion has focused on irregular flows in the context of labour migration. But, as already noted, even in the case of other types of migration, if the pressure for outward movement, be it due to political, environmental or other reasons, is high, a restrictive emigration policy is more likely to lead to irregular migration – or movements in defiance of the established rules – rather than stop it. This is particularly so to the extent that there is an actual or perceived assurance of admission opportunities in the destination country. During the whole Cold War period and until the fall of the Berlin Wall, people from Eastern Europe continuously migrated to the West despite the emigration restrictions imposed by the communist governments. While the escape from political oppression and the quest for freedom were basic motivating factors, the assurance of admission and asylum in Western countries which ratified the 1951 UN Convention relating to the Status of Refugees played its part in encouraging the people to move. The fact that the movement was unauthorised by the regime of the home country (and entailed considerable risks for those who tried to escape) did not stop the flow.

The same may be true of family reunification flows. Most migrants who are separated from their families feel strongly about family reunification. Should the migration policies and laws in the sending or the receiving country impede such reunification, and unless the punishment to contravene the legal restrictions is excessively heavy, there will be a natural tendency for the migrants and their families to look for reunification possibilities through irregular channels. The rush for smuggling children into Hong Kong before the transfer of power to China on 1 July 1997 is a case in point (See Box 2.1).

As already noted, should there be an unmet labour demand in the destination country offering possibilities of employment, either immediately or in the near future, this is likely to serve as an additional inducement for the political refugees and candidates for family reunification to seek entry into the country in defiance of emigration or immigration restrictions.

2.6. Institutional and administrative deficiencies

As noted in Chapter 1, irregularity in movements may sometimes be a direct consequence of institutional and administrative deficiencies in the sending or

Box 2.1. Urge for family reunification: Smuggling of children

Hundreds of children were reportedly being smuggled from mainland china into Hong Kong to join their parents. More than 1,500 children crossed the border illegally between January and June 1997, making up already twice the number that crossed during all of 1996. Almost all the migrant children were from Guangdong Privince, born to Hong Kong residents who went to China to marry and start families. In most cases the residents returned to Hong Kong, but the children were put on a long waiting list for the right to enter. Before the transfer of power, 66 children were allowed into Hong Kong from China each day, and about 130,000 children were still waiting to cross.[1] There was fear, however, that the borders would be tightened after China resumed power on 1 July 1997. Under the Basic Law, the children who managed to cross would be allowed to reside in Hong Kong after it would revert to Chinese control.

[1] This was the figure in June 1997.

Source: *Trafficking in Migrants – Quarterly Bulletin* No. 15, IOM Geneva, June 1997.

receiving country, or both. The deficiencies, which in some cases are closely linked to historical and political circumstances affecting the countries concerned, reflect an administrative weakness in the migration management system. In most of Africa, for example, the arbitrariness in drawing up country boundaries in the colonial era, which often split the same ethnic group into two or more different but adjacent countries, created artificial barriers to traditional intra-ethnic movements. The adherence in the post-independence period to such boundaries, and the absence of an adequate administrative structure to prevent or control the flows, meant that much of the traditional movements have continued, but not necessarily in keeping with the new regulatory requirements.

At times the colonial governments also deliberately encouraged and actively helped migratory labour movements from within and across countries for the development of mines and plantations and production of cash crops for export. Movements of workers from Mali, Togo and Burkina Faso (Haute Volta) to Senegal and Cote d'Ivoire and from Tanzania (Tanganyika) and Rwanda to the plantations in Uganda and Kenya, for example, used to take place in keeping with such policies, but few migration formalities were involved. In a like manner, workers used to move to South Africa and Rhodesia (now

Zimbabwe) from countries like Botswana, Lesotho, Malawi, Swaziland and Zambia.[45] Following independence, the development of migration regulations, including the introduction of systems of work and residence permits, created a distinction between regular and irregular migration. But the administrative structures were not sufficiently well developed to control or regulate the continuing movements; nor were the workers who followed the long established patterns of movement always aware of the new regulatory requirements.

Clearly, in all such cases the surplus in the labour markets of the sending countries was matching the labour demand in the receiving countries. But the irregularity of the movements was not just a matter of the supply push outstripping the opportunities for legal entry. Rather it was the absence of well developed migration structures and control mechanisms that largely explained why much of these movements were taking place outside, or at the margin of, the newly established regulatory framework.

Political changes leading to a realignment of national borders or the emergence of new nation-states and sudden changes in nationality and migration laws can make the status of a country's erstwhile citizens and legal immigrants uncertain, ambiguous or irregular. For example, as discussed in Chapter 1, with the break-up of the former Soviet Union in 1991, millions of people living outside their ethnic republics or autonomous regions suddenly became aliens in their own 'homelands'. Given that the successor states of the USSR use divergent and to some extent conflicting criteria for determining citizenship and in the absence of clearly defined migration laws, many of these people are at present either stateless or are technically in an irregular situation. Similarly, since few of the CIS states have clear legislation on refugees, thousands of asylum-seekers from non-CIS countries are now in legal limbo: their current status is at best uncertain, and at worst, irregular.[46]

Discussion in Chapter 1 has also revealed that ambiguity in migration legislation and differences in admission criteria between countries may cause, or contribute to, irregularity in international movements. Non-compliance with legal requirements governing entry, residence and employment of foreigners may also be the consequence of cumbersome legislation. In the Czech Republic, for example, much of the current problem of irregular stay and employment of foreigners is attributed to cumbersome and time-consuming procedures and formalities involved in obtaining a work permit and a residence permit. In Malaysia, many employers argue that some foreign workers arrested by the

---

[45] W. Elkan, 'Labour migration from Botswana, Lesotho and Swaziland', in W.M.J. Van Binsbergen and H.A. Melnik (eds.), *Migration and the Transformation of the Modern African Society*, Leiden, 1978.

[46] As of mid-April 1996, only four CIS countries had acceded to the 1951 UN Convention on refugees and its 1967 Protocol, with a fifth, Krgyzstan on the point of doing so. Only four had adopted sound national legislation to deal with refugees; and even these were yet to develop their institutional capacity to deal fully and effectively with their national and international obligations. Cf. *CIS Conference on Refugees and Migrants*, 1996, op. cit.

police because of their alleged irregular status are in fact legally recruited workers and that it is only the delay in processing the employers' applications by a slow-moving government bureaucracy that makes the workers technically illegal.[47]

Sometimes sudden changes in national migration laws can also create a legal vacuum or ambiguity, making the status of foreigners already in the country uncertain or even irregular. In France, at least some political leaders believed that many among the 300 undocumented Africans who went on hunger strike in June 1996 to protest against expulsion and press their demand for the right to stay in France were "victims of ambiguous or contradictory measures of the new laws on immigration".[48] Changes in migration legislation can place erstwhile legal immigrants into an irregular situation, as it happened in Hungary when stricter rules under the new Aliens Act became effective on 1 May 1994.

In a migrant-receiving country the regulations may permit the recruitment of foreign workers, but if the procedures are cumbersome or involve payment of excessive fees, then the employer may be tempted to opt for irregular methods of recruitment rather than the legal procedures. Likewise, a worker in a sending country may be in touch with a potential employer abroad through informal contacts, and may even have a firm offer of employment. In the absence, however, of well established official or private recruitment agencies the worker, especially if he or she is from a remote area, may face real difficulties in formalising the arrangements; or the costs involved – official fees and bribes – may be too high. In such situations the migrant may be tempted to take up the employment abroad without adhering to all the legal requirements. In Taiwan, China, for example, in order to evade paying excessive brokerage fees – which are often deducted from the wages on the basis of promissory notes signed by them – many foreign workers leave their designated jobs and thus become irregular foreign workers.[49] The problem can be compounded when full and updated information regarding the regulatory requirements is not available or at least not easily accessible to the migrants.

2.7. Gaps and weaknesses in migration-related information system

Lack of credible and objective information on migration laws and regulations and on employment, housing and living conditions in the potential destination countries can be an important factor in irregular migration. Discussion above and in Chapter 1 has indicated that non-compliance with migration laws and regulations – be it in the country of origin or destination or both – does not

---

[47] *Migration News*, Vol. 1, No. 3, April 1994, p. 7.

[48] See, for example, an open letter dated 16 August 1996 to the hunger-strikers from Mr. Bernard Statsi, Vice President of the centrist party, Force démocrate, a member of the Union pour la démocratic française (UDF), one of the two main governing parties. Cited in *Migration News Sheet*, September 1996, p. 4.

[49] *Migration News*, Vol. 1, No. 8, September 1994, p. 5.

necessarily imply a deliberate defiance of the regulatory system. At least in some cases, the non-compliance may well be due to information gaps: when the migrant does not have complete, unambiguous and up-to-date information on the regulatory requirements, he or she may quite unknowingly fail to meet the requirements. For example, although regulations in countries such as Pakistan and Sri Lanka require all labour migrants to register themselves with a designated official agency, some fail to do so simply because they are not aware of this requirement. In Russia, as already noted, more than half of the irregular immigrants (who were without residence permits) knew nothing of the regulatory requirements.

An interesting example of how lack of accurate information on immigration regulations in the destination country can be conducive to irregular migration is provided by the transit migrants in Ukraine. A recent sample survey[50] of those who entered Ukraine legally or illegally in order to a move to a Western country revealed that few of them had realistic ideas about visa regulations in Western countries before leaving their country of origin, and that about 20 per cent of them had chosen Ukraine as a transit point in the belief that they could easily obtain a visa to a Western country from there. When the migrants finally came to know of the real situation, more than 60 per cent of them were willing to move illegally to a Western country; and at least 26 per cent of those interviewed were likely to attempt illegal movements. Another survey made in Albania in the early 1990s found that about half of the country's population believed that it was possible to claim asylum in Western Europe if the economic conditions in one's own country became unbearable.

When new and complex migration regulations are issued, it may not be enough that the potential migrants are aware of them. Unless the other parties directly involved in the migration process, including in particular, the employers of migrant workers, are properly informed and sensitised about their obligations, irregular migration may result due to non-compliance – which may well be inadvertent rather than deliberate – with the regulatory requirements. In the USA, an important impediment to effective employer compliance with the requirements of the 1986 Immigration Reform and Control Act related to the fact that many employers were not fully aware of the provisions of IRCA and their obligations under it. In 1990, the General Accounting Office, the investigative agency of Congress, noted that although within two years after the law came into effect employers' awareness of IRCA increased to 83 per cent, there was a significant decrease in the percentage of employers who understood IRCA's major provisions, for example, those concerning employment eligibility verification requirements and hiring restrictions.[51] Such a situation clearly

---

[50] IOM, *Transit Migration in Ukraine*, Geneva, August 1994, p. 34–37.

[51] John R. Fraser, 'Illegal Immigration in the United States and the Limits of Sanctions Against Employers' in *Migration and Development: New Partnerships for Cooperation*, OECD, Paris, 1994, p. 77.

militates against the application of the legal standards (further discussed in Chapter 4).

Often irregular migration is also encouraged by wrong information and consequent unrealistic expectations of job opportunities and housing and living conditions in the destination country. Although the newly found freedom to travel was a main propelling force in the massive East–West movements (both irregular and regular) that took place in 1989–91, they were was also fuelled by exaggerated expectations, even fantasies about job opportunities, housing facilities and living conditions in the countries of destination.[52] This was not surprising as few of the migrants who had lived and worked for decades under a regimented political and economic system had access to reliable and up-to-date information of the conditions in the destination countries. Despite expansion of mass media and spectacular progress in communications across countries, lack of objective information or, more importantly, false and misleading publicity about the legal provisions and regulatory measures on entry, residence and employment as well as the housing and living conditions in the destination country continues to be a major contributory factor in irregular migration.

A recent investigation in Poland revealed that those who live abroad or returnees to the home country are a main source of information about the migration possibilities abroad. But, as a rule migrants pretend to be better off than they actually are. Failure abroad is not readily admitted. Thus, the information disseminated gives an exaggerated picture of their success and the opportunities abroad. The information is often transmitted through informal channels, and at each new link in the transmission process the success story tends to be further magnified, with the result that the distorted information serves as a strong incentive for outmigration. Information disseminated through mass media, which had long been controlled by the government to propagate the official points of view under the communist regime, is widely suspected, unless the information is in line with that received by the potential migrant through the informal channel.[53]

The use of misleading publicity concerning employment and living conditions in the destination country by agents and traffickers to recruit potential candidates for clandestine migration presents an even more disquieting aspect of the problem. The practice is not entirely new. For example, following the virtual ban introduced in most Western European countries in 1973 on regular recruitment of foreign workers, many unscrupulous agents, often in collusion with employers and/or their agents in the receiving country, relied on misleading information to recruit irregular migrant workers and arrange for their clandestine movement. By the mid-1970s, the problem had assumed such importance

---

[52] Bimal Ghosh, 'Migratory Movements from Central and Eastern European Countries to Western Europe' in *People on the Move: New Migration Flows in Europe*, Council of Europe, Strasbourg, 1992, pp. 148–150.

[53] IOM, *Transit Migration in Poland*, April 1994, Geneva, p. 42.

that in 1978, the Council of Europe felt it necessary to urge sending and receiving countries to cooperate in eliminating misleading publicity material that fueled irregular migration.[54]

In the past few years, with a rapid increase in the number of unauthorised agents and expansion of the network of traffickers the problem has become more disturbing than ever before. In Bangladesh, examples of false publicity to recruit potential migrants include the use of video tapes to present a rosy, often fictitious, picture of the working and living conditions in the target countries. The credibility of such publicity is sometimes sought to be enhanced by arranging the presence of a person, usually from the destination country, during meetings and interviews with the potential migrants. The foreigner is falsely presented as an employer in the destination country or his/her agent; in effect, however, the person is more likely to be hired specifically for the purpose of convincing the prospective migrants.[55] In Malaysia, many irregular immigrants in the country are foreigners who pay bogus job agencies in their home countries, such as Indonesia and the Philippines, for what they believe to be a valid work permit. They are then brought into the country illegally and issued false work permits.[56] Discussion in Chapter 1 has indicated how the traffickers and their agents use wrong information, misleading publicity and false promises to entice potential migrants who often do not have the possibility of verifying or counter-checking them and, in many cases are unaware of all the risks that the process of trafficking involves. Wrong information often goes hand-in-hand with false promises and duplicity by unscrupulous agents.

Traffickers in particular rely widely on the use of misleading publicity for recruiting women who are looking for other jobs but are tricked or forced into prostitution (further discussed in Chapter 3). The process may involve irregular entry or irregular employment even if prostitution itself may not be illegal in the destination country. Many of these women are offered what they thought would be jobs outside the sex industry. But even in cases where the women knew they would work as prostitutes, the actual working and living conditions would have little to do with what had been offered or promised; and once they started working as prostitutes they were unable to extricate themselves from the situation. The use of misleading information and recourse to dubious promises are no less frequent in cases where the recruitment takes place through an agent or a so-called 'impresario', as is often the situation in, for example, Belgium.

---

[54] Resolution (78) 44 on clandestine migration and illegal employment of foreign workers, adopted by the Council of Ministers on 26 October 1978.

[55] Raisul Awal Mahmood, 'Clandestine Foreign Workers and the Domestic Labour Market: Process of Integration and Implications'. Paper presented to the IOM/UNFPA Policy Workshop on Emigration Dynamics in South Asia, Geneva, September 1996. (mimeo).

[56] *Migration News*, Vol. 1, No. 3, April 1994, p. 7.

2.8. *Dynamics of irregular migration*

Irregular migration, like migration itself, has now emerged as a global process. Geographical contiguity and regional affinity, political and cultural ties and other historical links, including those established during the colonial administration, still continue to influence the pattern and direction of migratory flows, both regular and irregular. But other forces such as globalisation of the world economy, inter-penetration of markets, expansion of world trade and investment and spectacular improvement of transport and communication are opening new avenues and opportunities for movements of people, alongside those for movements of goods, services and capital.

It is normal for people to take advantage of these new conditions and avenues to move across countries especially when, as discussed above, there are rising pressures for emigration in countries of origin and unmet labour demand or better opportunities elsewhere. What is special about contemporary movements of people, be they regular or irregular, is that they are part of, and are often helped by, these new global linkages constituting the dynamics of global change. Organised trafficking which as will be further discussed below has become a multi-country operation increasingly managed by international networks of crime syndicates, is a striking example of the globalisation of irregular migration. An important policy implication of this new situation is that an effective response to the problem cannot be designed only at the national or bilateral level. It calls for a wider – regional and global – approach.

Trends in globalisation of irregular migration are considerably reinforced by the emergence of a market for trafficked migrants which is becoming increasingly global. This includes trafficked women and children who can be easily placed, as already noted, in a growing market in industrial countries, because they are exotic or docile, easier to exploit and keep as virtual slaves or, as in the case of young girls and children, they are more likely to be free from the AIDS virus. Market expansion is also helped by the rise of 'sex tourism' in several countries, which provides the opportunity for first contacts to be made between the women and the traffickers or their agents. At the same time this shows the women the huge imaginary gains they can make from prostitution abroad. Underlying the whole situation there are of course wider social issues such as the pressure of poverty and absence of social safety nets, lack of opportunities and marginalisation of women, often coinciding with an increasing burden of family responsibilities.

There is also considerable truth in the suggestion that irregular migration creates its own internal dynamics to encourage further irregular inflows in the receiving country. As will be discussed in Chapter 3, new irregular immigrants are more likely to compete directly with the irregular immigrants who have the same ethnic and labour market characteristics and are already in the country. From an economic point of view, it may not be in the general interest of resident irregular migrants to encourage new inflows of a similar type. In practice, however, things work out differently: resident irregular immigrants are often found to be a source of help and attraction for new irregular flows from the same ethnic and geographical community in the country of origin.

Social and family considerations and kinship factors play an important part in the networking that sustains a cumulative process of irregular movements. As mentioned in Chapter 1, irregular movements, including trafficking through informal modes, may be supported and facilitated by social networks of migrant's relatives and countrymen in the sending, receiving and transit countries. Local knowledge and contacts of the resident irregular (and regular) migrants could be of immense value to the newcomers because of their vulnerable situation. Assurances of support in the form, for example of food, shelter and initial business contacts would encourage new irregular inflows, especially if the receiving country has a long tradition of accommodating irregular immigrants. It has already been noted in Chapter 1 that social contacts and kinship sometimes play an important part in the recruitment of women for sex trade abroad.

Ethnic affinity sometimes serves as an important element in the dynamics of irregular migration including trafficking. Some of the Chinese and Vietnamese immigrants who have established themselves as traffickers in receiving countries provide typical examples of how the ethnic networking operates. The large number of restaurants set up by the Vietnamese and Chinese traffickers in Eastern Europe are often used as fronts to secure entry and work permits for many more people from the home countries. In Prague, for example, police raided a Chinese restaurant which had only eight tables but over 800 registered employees. Many of these so-called employees were reported to have been smuggled into Germany.[57] A recent police investigation in Belgium revealed a huge human trafficking network linked to Chinese restaurants in the country, with the Czech Republic as a key transit point for the network's operations.[58] When the resident immigrants establish themselves as part of an international network that uses strategic routes and transit points across countries and regions, irregular migration tends to flourish and combatting it becomes a formidable task. This is further discussed below.

2.9. Organized trafficking and the role of transit countries

Irregular migration in general and trafficking in particular are now increasingly channelled through third countries. True, since the mid-1980s, southern European countries, notably Italy, Spain and Greece, have served as transit points for many irregular migrants who ultimately moved to Western and northern European countries. But today's situation is different in many ways.

---

[57] *The Economist*, London, 5–11 August 1995, p. 26.

[58] IOM, *Chinese Migrants in Central and Eastern Europe: The Cases of the Czech Republic, Hungary and Romania*, 1995, Geneva, p. 22.

Progress in transport and communications, multi-country networks of organized traffickers, and inter-locking of human smuggling with trafficking in drugs and arms have all contributed to the globalisation of human trafficking in which the transit countries play an increasingly important role. Recruitment may start in distant impoverished lands, and the journey may run though several countries to evade government vigilance and take advantage of countries that have liberal visa laws or less stringent border control. The strength of the local organization of the trafficking syndicates and the possibility of bribing the border police in case of apprehension are also among the considerations that influence the selection of the transit countries.

In short, since for organized, large-scale traffickers human smuggling is a global operation, they tend to choose the routes and transit countries as part of an overall strategy. There are several established networks to reach countries in Western Europe, while some others extend beyond Europe and are linked to the United States. The route from Central Asia, for example, runs through the former Soviet Union to the Baltic states where boats are hired to traffic the human cargo to Scandinavian countries. According to press reports,[59] Swedish immigration officials had long suspected that the *Estonia*, the ferry which sank in 1994 drowning more than 900 persons, regularly carried migrants hidden in cargo containers. The Balkan route, preferred by traffickers for smuggling people from Africa and East Asia, runs from Turkey through Hungary to Germany and other Western European countries.

As noted in Chapter 1, Central European countries, notably, Poland, Hungary and the Czech Republic, are frequently used as transit points not only because of their geographical contiguity or proximity to countries in Western Europe, but also because border controls are chaotic and visa requirements at least until recently have been lax. Gangs from Vietnam and China, who are among the best established traffickers in these countries with the most sophisticated methods and with local links that go back to the days of the communist regime, are ingenious and well equipped to smuggle people to Germany and beyond.[60] Lately, as control in other countries of east and west Europe have become more strict, some foresee that if peace returns to Bosnia, the Balkan region could become a preferred route of transit for irregular migrants wanting to move to the USA.

Poland, which according to one estimate,[61] receives over 100,000 transit migrants annually, has two transit routes that run through the country: (i) the south-west route, mainly used by migrants from Africa, Asia and the Middle East, that goes through Russia or by air from Hong Kong and Bangkok to

---

[59] *Economist*, op. cit. p 25.

[60] Ibid, p. 26.

[61] IOM, *Transit Migration in Poland* op. cit, p. 10. The figure which includes all transit migrants represents the lower estimated limit. A transit migrant is defined as a migrant who moves to one or more countries with the intention of moving to yet another country as the final destination.

Poland, and from there to the West; and (ii) the east-west route, mainly used by the nationals of the former Yugoslavia, and other Balkan states, that runs through Ukraine, Belarus or the Baltic states to Poland and beyond – to the West.

Lately, as control in countries of Western Europe, and even those in Eastern Europe, have become more strict, Russia has become a preferred country for many Asians who are seeking to move to the USA via Moscow with the help of traffickers.[62] Preliminary research in Russia by Investigative Network, a Washington-based research organization, indicates increases in trafficking by the Russian Mafia and other traffickers to locations throughout Europe, Israel, the USA, and more recently, into Asia through northern China to Hong Kong and Macau. Prostitution rings are increasingly active in Moscow, St. Petersburg, Khabarovsk, Chita, Tver, Barnaul and Vladivostok. The Russian Mafia has established bases in several major cities in the USA, including Miami, New York, Seattle and Los Angeles. Together with their Ukrainian counterparts, the Russian gangs now have the exclusive control of the prostitution trade throughout formerly communist Europe and the eastern fringes of Western Europe.[63]

The remarkable ingenuity and alertness of the traffickers help them to change their strategy, including the route and the transit points, at short notice and with surprising flexibility. When, for example, a few years ago, with financial assistance from Germany, the Polish authorities tightened control along the long borders running through forests and marshes, the traffickers changed the route – Mediterranean ports such as Marseilles and rocky inlets in the heel of Italy became the favoured landing places.

The growing importance of transit countries in irregular migration, especially in the form of trafficking in migrants, raises a number of policy issues. Among such issues is the question of securing the cooperation of transit countries in dealing with these irregular movements through exchange of information, coordinated surveillance and other forms of joint action. A specific aspect of such concerted action concerns the widening of the geographical scope of anti-trafficking legislation so that the operation carried out in transit countries can be brought within the purview of punitive action. These issues are further discussed in Chapter 4.

---

[62] *Der Stand*, 2 January 1996; *Migration News Sheet*, February 1996. According to a Russian diplomat in Prague quoted in these papers, some 250,000 Asians were living in Moscow waiting to arrange their travel with the help of traffickers.

[63] Gilian B.Caldwell, *The Sex Trade: From Russia With Love: A Project of the Investigative Network*, Washington DC, 1995, (mimeo) p. 4.

CHAPTER THREE

Social and economic consequences of irregular migration

The social and economic consequences of irregular migration have been an issue of considerable discussion in Western Europe since the late 1970s; and in the USA since the 1980s. Indeed, the US Immigration and Naturalization Act of 1986 was largely motivated by an increasing concern in the early 1980s over irregular immigration. During the past few years it has once more become a focus of wide attention in both North America and Western Europe. The rise in the level of irregular migration, its changing ethnic and cultural composition, its impact on the public welfare system and, even more importantly, the increasing social tension and political sensitivity that now surround migration in general, have contributed to this trend. In the past, problems of irregular migration received relatively little attention in, or from the perspective of, the sending countries. This also is changing at least for two important reasons: the emergence of irregular migration as an important issue affecting relations between sending and receiving countries; and the growing concern over the involvement of international crime syndicates in human trafficking, its interlocking with smuggling of arms and drugs and the abuse of human rights that it often entails.

3.1. Effects on workers, employers and consumers

Economically motivated irregular migration often takes place between countries with contrasting labour market situations (shortages of labour in one country and surplus in the other) and sharply different levels of income. As already noted, if the richer country is passing through a phase of economic expansion and there are labour shortages which cannot be met through regular channels, it will attract unemployed or under-employed workers from the labour-surplus country, even if the entry is illegal. Unless the perceived benefits are outweighed by the financial and non-financial costs, including anticipated risks and penalties, that the move might entail, irregular migration at least from the point of view of the migrant may even be considered a 'rational process'.[1]

---

[1] United Nations, *International Migration Policies and Programmes*, Population Studies, No. 80, New York, 1982.

It can be further argued that to the extent that such movement contributes to a better matching of labour supply and demand within and between sending and receiving countries, the process is also beneficial to the economies of both. Whether or not this will actually happen of course depends on several factors, including the size and relative importance of the flow, the structure of the labour markets and the skill composition of the migrants. If, for example, low-skill, low-wage irregular immigrants complement the receiving country's workers (who may be unavailable or unwilling to take on such jobs) the possibility is that the employers of low-wage labour and consumers of labour-intensive products in the receiving country will gain, and the upward mobility of its workers will be sustained by the inflow of irregular foreign workers. Assuming that there is a high degree of complementarity between unskilled irregular immigrants and skilled workers of the receiving country, the latter in theory should benefit from higher wages resulting from a higher demand for skilled labour. And, to the extent that the move will enable the migrants to have higher earnings than at home, they, too, will gain.

Countries in Western Europe, for example, derived some of these benefits from both regular and irregular flows in the 1960s and early 1970s when their labour demand, especially for less skilled jobs, was high.[2] As already noted, this also partly explains why some of them (including Italy and Greece after the mid-1980s) continued to draw irregular migrants even long after a formal ban on recruitment of foreign labour had been introduced in 1973–74.

As mentioned above, when clandestine migrants are employed in occupations shunned by nationals, they alleviate labour shortage and do not compete with the local workers. It has been argued that irregular flows from Mexico to the USA satisfy a real demand for cheap labour that cannot be met domestically. As noted in Chapter 2, when the US demand for cheap labour shifted from agriculture to other sectors such as textiles, construction and services, there was a corresponding shift in the composition of the new irregular flows from Mexico. Irregular migration has thus been a factor of flexibility in the US labour market[3] (Table 2.1).

The situation may not be very different even in labour-surplus developing countries. For example, after the mass expulsion of undocumented Ghanian workers from Nigeria in 1983, many jobs held by them remained vacant and finally had to be filled by other irregular migrants[4]. A similar situation of acute

---

[2] Klaus Zimmermann, for example, recently estimated that Germany's annual growth rates which topped 10 per cent in the 1960s were up to 4 per cent higher than they would have been without foreign workers. Cited in *Migration News*, Vol. 4, No. 4, April 1997.

[3] Jorge Bustamante, 'Undocumented migration: A theoretical-methodological frame work', 1993, op. cit.

[4] A. Adepoju, 'Undocumented Migration in Africa: Trends and Policies', *International Migration*, Vol. XXI, No. 2, 1983.

labour shortage arose in Ghana's cocoa farms in the wake of the strict enforcement of the Aliens Compliance Order of 1969.[5]

The effects of irregular immigrants on employment and wages in the receiving country thus depend on whether or to what extent they complement or compete with the nationals and legal immigrants. The experience both in the United States[6] and Western Europe tends to confirm that there is usually little or limited direct competition between local workers and undocumented immigrants. But this can only be measured in the country-specific situation. In the United States, one study made in 1987–88 sought to measure these effects by using the 1980 census data from five southern states (Arizona, California, Colorado, New Mexico and Texas) and assuming that all Mexicans entering the United States after 1975 have done so illegally.[7] The econometric study showed that the presence of illegal Mexican immigrants had only a slight impact on the wages of other workers and that competition for nationals (including those of Mexican origin) came more from legal than from illegal immigrants. The reason for this is that irregular immigrants find jobs in an inferior, and therefore complementary, labour market. In such a situation there is little competition between the irregular immigrants and the national workers.

The complementarity of irregular Hispanic immigrants in the US labour market is borne out by other studies. For example, using micro-data from the 1980 Census, an investigation was made into the effects of Hispanic immigrants who arrived between 1975 and 1980, 'the majority of whom appeared to be illegal'. It indicated that the inflow had no significant negative impact on the wages of low-skilled domestic workers (the only exception was black women, but this negative effect was relatively small).[8] In fact, the irregular inflow had 'a significantly positive influence on the Anglo-male earnings'. Two experimental programmes which were carried out in California in the 1970s to fill jobs formerly occupied by irregular immigrants with unemployed US citizens or regular foreign workers seemed to confirm that many of the jobs that the irregulars held would not be filled by local workers in the absence of irregular immigrants. Significantly, the experiments also implied that if irregulars were not available, the jobs might simply disappear – some would be automated, and still others would not be filled if employers had to pay higher wages.[9] This,

---

[5] Akomako-Sarfoh J., 'The effects of the expulsion of migrant workers on Ghana's economy, with particular reference to the cocoa industry', in S. Amin (ed.), *Modern Migration in West Africa*, Oxford University Press, London, 1974.

[6] F.D. Bean, E.E. Telles and B.L. Lowell, 'Undocumented migration to the United States: Perception and evidence', *Population and Development Review*, Vol. 13, No. 4, December 1987. F.D. Taylor, 'Undocumented Mexican immigrants and the earnings of workers in the United States', *Demography*, Vol. 23, No. 1, February, 1988.

[7] F.D. Taylor, 'Undocumented Mexican immigrants and the earnings of workers in the United States' *Demography*, 1988, op. cit. See also *SOPEMI*, 1993, p. 164.

[8] Gregory DeFreitas, 'The Impact of Immigration on Low-Wage Workers', 1986 (mimeo), p. 23.

[9] See M. Villapondo et al, *A Study of the Socio-Economic Impact of Illegal Aliens, County of San Diego*, Human Resources Agency, San Diego, CA, 1977, p. 16, 23 and 61–2. Julian Simon, 1989, op. cit, pp. 298–300.

in turn, helps to understand the effects of irregular immigration on economic and technological restructuring and trade protectionism, as will be discussed later in this Chapter.

As for the sending countries, irregular migration may provide a temporary relief to their unemployment situation or serve as a safety valve in the face of social tension, but the flows generally remain too small and too uncertain to solve the problem of unemployment. Given the large pool of surplus labour and the conditions of supply, it is also unlikely that, except in special situations or specific sectors, irregular migration can have an appreciable effect on raising wage levels in the sending countries.

The situation is however quite different when the receiving country faces no labour shortage and irregular immigrants directly compete with the local workers in the same sectors and types of skill. This would depress wages and other benefits at the lower end of the receiving country's labour force or may lead to some job displacement, given that the irregular immigrants are likely to be paid at lower rates than the local workers. At a lower wage level there could however be an increase in the net employment of unskilled workers (especially if the trade union had set a higher than the equilibrium wage in the market for unskilled labour). Assuming that skilled and unskilled workers are complementary, in a flexible economy the situation could lead to an upward shift in the demand for skilled workers and an increase in their wages.

A recent study in Germany found that a one per cent increase in the share of foreign workers in general leads to a fall of 5.9 per cent in the wages of blue collar workers, but a rise of 3.5 per cent for white collar workers.[10] True, given the fragmentation of the labour market, direct competition between irregular immigrants and low-skilled local workers is not likely to take place very often. There are however exceptions. For example, in Germany, although a large proportion of foreign workers are engaged in jobs shunned by German nationals – according to one study two-thirds of all foreigners who found employment in 1988 were in jobs turned down by the latter[11] – the situation is far from uniform across industries and occupations. To illustrate, in 1994, the construction industry was estimated to employ some 500,000 irregular workers, many of them immigrants, at low wages and the trade union has been complaining that the situation was endangering job prospects for regular German workers, while causing losses in trade union income and social security contributions.[12] This is largely explained by the fact that many German workers who, due to their relatively low geographical mobility, do not move away from immigrant areas, wind up, especially in times of high unemployment, competing with

[10] Klaus Zimmermann, 'European Migration: Push and Pull'. Paper presented at the World Bank's Conference on Development Economics, April 1994.

[11] Cited in *Migration News*, Vol. 3, No. 8, August 1996.

[12] *Migration News Sheet*, February 1994 and July 1994, *Süddeutsche Zeitung*, 14 January 1994 and 8 June 1994.

immigrants, both regular and irregular.[13] Even in the United States some of the more recent studies seem to suggest that in the absence of labour market segmentation or lack of geographical mobility of local workers, inflows of unskilled immigrants, especially if they are unauthorised, may displace American workers and depress their wages. This applies particularly to black workers who are more likely to compete with low-skilled irregular immigrants in the same jobs and areas. Mexican immigrants, for example, are now doing the work that black janitors used to do in Los Angeles.[14]

As for the employers, in the absence of employer sanctions against illegal employment, and their strict enforcement, the effects of irregular immigration would be uneven: those using irregular migrants will have a differential advantage over the non-users. In the Netherlands, for example, the Ministry of Social Affairs reported that in 1991 the 373 convicted employers who had hired irregular immigrants, made a gain of DFL 800,000 even after paying the fines, including payments made as out-of-court settlements.[15] Over the long-term, however, this may also imply, as will be argued below, that they will be less anxious to improve productivity through technological change and development of the skills of the labour force.

Irregular flows of skilled workers

In general, economically motivated irregular migration has traditionally involved low-skilled workers. However, as already noted, in recent years the situation has somewhat changed, with several regions now witnessing outflows of skilled and professional personnel through (regular and) irregular channels. Further, empirical evidence seems to suggest that irregular migration of unskilled workers often fuels irregular migration of skilled workers.

The negative effects of large-scale skilled migration in some of the transition economies (e.g. 11 per cent decline in the number of scientists in Russia in a single year, 1989–90[16]) and in sub-Saharan African countries are now well documented.[17] When the skills are critical for the domestic economy and cannot be easily replaced, the outflows can negatively affect both output and future

---

[13] According to some estimates, a one per cent increase in the number of foreign workers reduces unskilled and semi-skilled workers' wages by six per cent. *Migration News*, Vol. 3, No. 1, January 1996, p. 7.

[14] Philip Martin and Elizabeth Midgley, 'Immigration to the United States: Journey to an Uncertain Destination', *Population Bulletin*, Vol. 49, No. 2, Washington DC, September 1994. However, as noted in a most recent report (17 May, 1997), issued by the US National Research Council, most blacks do not live in places with large concentrations of immigrants. The report does not specifically refer to irregular immigrants.

[15] Annual report, 1991, Department of Labour Inspection, Ministry of Social Affairs, cited in *Migration News Sheet*, June 1992.

[16] J.P. Dufour 'Le naufrage de la science russe', *Le Monde*, 24 April 1992, p. 11.

[17] See, for example, Bimal Ghosh, 'Economic Migration and the Sending Countries' in Julien van den Broek (ed.) *'The Economics of Labour Migration'*, Edward Elgar, Cheltenham, United Kingdom and Brookfield, USA, 1996, pp. 88–109.

economic growth of the sending country. Skilled migration through irregular channels makes the problem more serious. This is because the irregular and unpredictable nature of the outflows makes it particularly difficult for the government to monitor the skilled outflows and for the employers to plan anticipatory measures for skill replacement and timely adjustment in the production processes. Since human skills act as a complement to capital and technology, skilled migration tends to depress wages of unskilled workers, and thus aggravates poverty in a developing economy.[18] It is worth noting that in government replies to a survey on clandestine migration conducted by the Council of Europe in 1993, 'brain drain' was the most commonly cited negative effect of clandestine migration on the sending countries.[19]

The destination countries and their employers, on the other hand, are likely to gain from the entry and employment of the skilled personnel, even if the entry is irregular. In most industrial countries as in the newly industrialising economies, there is now a growing demand for skilled and highly-skilled workers, which remains unmet in specific sectors and occupations. Even with an increased emphasis on upgrading training of their labour force and human resources development, these countries are unlikely to be able to overcome these shortages in the coming years. To the extent that the incorporation of skilled irregular migrants into the local labour force does not present a problem, the access to additional skills is likely to help the employers of the destination countries to restrain rises in wage costs, increase exports and enhance their profits. Assuming a high degree of complementarity between skilled and unskilled labour, there could at the same time be a higher demand for unskilled workers. The economy gains through improved productivity, a higher level of employment and savings on human capital development expenditure.

The discussion made so far briefly indicates several situations in which movements of workers across countries could be beneficial to one or more of the parties involved. But it does not reveal the merits of irregular migration as such. The benefits may arise from the movements, *even when they are irregular but not necessarily because they are irregular or illegal.* In fact, as will be discussed below, when movements are irregular, they entail a wide range of risks and pitfalls, the direct and indirect cost of which could be high, outweighing the benefits. From an economic point of view, irregular migrants tend to differ from regular migrants in two important respects: participation in the social security or public welfare system; and fragmentation of the labour market.

---

[18] This will be the case for a two-fold reason: (i) shifts in distribution of the wages and salaries in favour of highly skilled workers and against relatively low skilled workers and (ii) a possible decline in the average incomes of those left behind. *Cf.*, Keith Griffin and A.R. Khan, 'Globalization and the Developing World: An Essay on the International Dimensions of Development in the Post-Cold War Era', Occasional papers, Human Development Report Office, UNDP, New York, 1992, p. 34.

[19] Council of Europe Parliamentary Assembly, *Traffickers and Employers of Clandestine Migrants*, January 1993. Restricted document AS/PR (44) 26.

Irregular immigration and the welfare system

The effects of irregular immigration on the welfare system of the receiving country can differ sharply from those of regular immigration. Even when the irregular immigrants neither receive nor pay into the social security and public welfare system, the inflows can have an important distributional effect. This could happen when, for example, irregular immigrants (rather exceptionally) compete with local workers and take away their jobs. As a result the financial burden of the legally employed increases, as they need to pay higher taxes to finance unemployment benefit schemes unless of course there is a reduction in the rate of unemployment benefits.

On the (debatable) assumption that most of the irregular immigrants are unskilled, the situation, in theory, may have several consequences. Given that the irregular immigrants are generally cheaper than the legally employed local workers, the employers can now employ more irregular immigrants for the same amount of money they used to pay for (unskilled) local workers. In a flexible economy, as factor prices decrease output is likely to rise. As already discussed above, if unskilled workers continue to be complementary, and assuming that the supply of qualified workers is fixed, irregular immigration would mean that the skilled workers would benefit from higher wages as a result of increased productivity and output. This can possibly compensate for the burden of higher taxes on the skilled workers to finance unemployment benefit schemes as discussed above.

Several of these neo-classical assumptions may not however be fully valid or applicable in the real world. For example, as already discussed above and in Chapter 1, irregular immigrants have been found to compete at least in the first instance more directly with those irregular immigrants who are already in the country and not necessarily with the legally employed workers. Even if they do compete with legally employed local workers, they are more likely to displace legal immigrants with the same or similar ethnic and labour market characteristics than the local workers in general. Thus, to the extent that the new irregular immigrants replace existing irregulars in the country there may not be an increase in the tax burden to finance increased unemployment benefits, given that in theory neither group is covered by unemployment benefit schemes. If on the other hand, new irregular immigrants replace legally employed (low-wage, low-skilled) local workers, leading to an increased tax burden to finance unemployment benefits, the question remains whether the rise in wages of skilled workers is adequate to compensate for the increase in their tax burden. Or, to put it differently, whether the loss in legal employment and wages is balanced by the rise in marginal productivity for the skilled sector.

In the real world, the situation is more complicated for at least two reasons. First, the assumption that irregular workers may neither pay to, nor receive benefits from, the unemployment insurance schemes does not necessarily hold. In the absence of strict vigilance there may be scope for the irregular immigrants to make fraudulent claims for benefits, adding to the tax burden to finance additional unemployment benefits. Second, the exclusion of irregular immigrants from a country's unemployment benefit system does not necessarily imply that they do not have access to other public welfare schemes such as education and health and medical care, especially in emergency situations.

Thus, to the extent that the irregular immigrants derive benefits from social services without contributing to them, they accentuate the tax burden of the local population – an argument that is now being widely used in Western Europe and especially in the USA in support of stronger and more stringent measures against irregular immigration, including the denial of social services to them.[20] In 1992, a study of San Diego by the auditor general of California estimated that the net cost of state and county services for 200,000 illegals was US$ 145.9 million. Another study by the Los Angeles County government concluded that the county services provided for 2.3 million immigrants, both legal and illegal, entailed a net cost (after deducting the taxes paid by them) of US$ 808 million. A statement made by Governor Pete Wilson of California in August 1993 suggested that illegal immigrants and their US born children (who are US citizens) were costing the state US$ 2.9 billion a year for only four services: welfare, education, health care and incarceration. The health costs alone for illegal aliens was estimated at US$ 369 million. In January 1994, the state requested a reimbursement of US$ 2.3 billion from the federal government for providing three federally-mandated services to irregular immigrants–education, incarceration and health care. The Governor of Florida has claimed that illegal immigration was costing his state US$ 884 million for the provision of education, health and incarceration. In April 1994, Florida sued the federal government for reimbursement of US$ 1.5 billion spent on irregular immigrants for the past two years (the amount included ' prescriptive relief' from future costs but excluded any revenues generated from irregular immigrants). In Texas, a study has placed the annual costs of government services to legal and illegal immigrants at US$ 4.6 billion.[21]

Several other studies try to assess the welfare costs of immigration in the USA. For example, a study made at Rice University concluded that the regular and irregular immigrants who arrived since 1970 cost the United States US$ 42.5 billion in 1992, and US$ 18.1 billion in the state of California, for the services provided to them.[22] It further estimated that the projected arrival

---

[20] Donald L. Huddle, 'Immigration: Stem the Flow, Savings Will Follow', *International Herald Tribune*, 7 September 1993.

[21] Ibid. See also Vernon M. Briggs Jr., 'International Migration and Labour Mobility: The Receiving countries' in Julien van den Broeck (ed.) *The Economics of Labour Migration*, 1996, op. cit, pp. 147–149; and *Migration News*, Vol. 1, No. 4, May 1994.

[22] Donald Huddle, *The Net Costs of Immigration to California*, Rice University, Houston, 1993; see also 'Immigration: Stem the Flow, Savings Will Follow', *International Herald Tribune*, op. cit. In a more recent study, Huddle estimated that immigration costs the US a net amount of $65 billion, including $15 billion for indirect worker displacement costs in the form, for example, of unemployment benefits. *The Net Costs of Immigration; the Facts, the Trends and Their Critics*, Carrying Capacity Network, Washington DC, 1996.

of 11.1 million immigrants, legal and illegal, in the next decade will cost the US tax payers a net amount of US$ 668.5 billion by 2002, including a net cost of some US$ 186 billion for illegal immigrants alone.

Several of these estimates, which covered both legal and illegal immigration, were based on a number of arguable assumptions, such as displacement of unskilled local workers by unskilled immigrants (legal and illegal) at an overall rate of 25 per cent. The assumption is open to question in view of several recent findings including those of the US National Research Council (NRC).[23] In its report, issued in May 1997, the Council observed, "All in all, the data suggest that the jobs of immigrant and native workers are different". In other words, the risk of displacement of local workers due to direct competition from immigrants is minimal.

More importantly, the extent to which irregular immigrants (a) use public social services and (b) contribute to their funding, and the nature of their economic impact remain highly debatable issues. Irregulars are typically young males and do not need to depend heavily on welfare services at least during the initial period. They are generally unaccompanied by wife and children who may be more frequent users of these services. Furthermore, they are often hesitant to request public assistance because of their fear of apprehension. Thus, in the Netherlands, a statement made by the Under-Secretary of Justice in 1991 suggested that not more than 5 per cent of foreigners claiming social security benefits were irregulars.[24]

This apart, by law irregular immigrants, in contrast with legal residents, may be excluded from certain social benefits. Under US legislation, for example, immigration status is a criterion for determining eligibility for several social welfare programmes. Thus, until the welfare reform of 1996, irregular immigrants were not eligible for federal benefits under a number of programmes. These included: aid to families with dependent children; medical aid, except for emergency conditions; supplemental security income; food stamps; public housing, legal services, unemployment compensation, post-secondary financial aid, and job training. Irregular immigrants' eligibility for social assistance was limited to a few narrowly defined types of benefits relating to emergencies and other compelling situations.[25] Public education, at about US$ 5000 for each child, accounted for two-thirds of the costs of these benefits. Elderly legal residents who entered under family reunification provisions and who did not work in the United States did not qualify for social security benefits, but they

---

[23] National Research Council, *The New Americans: Economic, Demographic and Fiscal Effects of Immigration*, Washington DC, 1997.

[24] *Migration News Sheet*, November 1991 (NRC 16 October 1991).

[25] These include children's access to public education and lunch programme, special supplemental food programme for women, infants and children; and community and health centre facilities. The disaster relief package that passed US Congress following the recent earthquake in Los Angeles permits emergency assistance to irregular immigrants but no long-term aid. See, in this connection, US Commission on Immigration Reform, *A Report to Congress*, 1994.

were none the less entitled to food stamps and supplemental security income benefits.[26] But this would not apply to irregular immigrants.

Nor is it certain that the irregular immigrants do not pay taxes. In the United States, for example, large numbers of them do pay social security and income taxes through the automatic withholding system. A sample study[27] made in 1976 showed that the proportions of irregular immigrants who paid social security and income taxes were 77 per cent and 73 per cent, respectively. Another study made in 1984 indicated that the average undocumented workers in the USA had more than US$ 1000 withheld each year for federal income and social security taxes alone (after allowing for the roughly one-third of workers who do not pay such taxes).[28]

It is worth noting that, according to a number of studies made in the USA in the 1980s, the taxes paid by the irregular immigrants far exceed the cost of services they use. One such study carried out in 1984 concludes, 'despite our biasing the costs upward and the revenues downward, tax revenues from undocumented aliens exceed the costs to provide public services to them.'[29] A more recent study at the Urban Institute in Washington which challenged the estimates made at Rice University showed that instead of a net cost of US$ 42 billion, there was a net benefit of US$ 29 billion for the USA on account of the immigrants since 1970.[30] For the state of California there was a net benefit of US$ 12 billion each year, instead of a net cost of 18.1 billion as estimated by the Rice University study. The substantial difference between the two estimates stems mainly from their calculations of the taxes paid by the immigrants. The study at the Rice University assumed that that the post-1970 immigrants paid US$ 20 billion in taxes to all levels of government, while the second study assumed the amount to be US$ 70 billion. The first study did not include the 15 per cent of each worker's earning paid as social security contributions on the grounds that these should be offset by the promise of benefit payments to immigrants on retirement. The Urban Institute study included them because the US federal government treats social security on a pay-as-you-go basis.

In assessing the net cost of welfare services provided for the irregular immigrants, it is of course important to take into account all contributions

---

[26] It is estimated that these benefits were annually costing the US federal government US$ 1.2 billion. *Migration News*, 1 April 1994, p. 2.

[27] David North and Marian F. Houston, *The Characteristics and Role of Illegal Aliens in the US Labour Market: An Explanatory Study*, Washington, DC Linton and Company, 1976.

[28] See Julian Simon, *The Economic Consequences of Immigration*, Basil Blackwell, Oxford, 1989, p. 293.

[29] Sidney Weintraub and Gilberto Cardenas, 'The Use of Public services by Undocumented Aliens in Texas', Policy Research Project Report, Lyndon Johnson School of Public Affairs, University of Texas, Austin, 1984.

[30] Donald Huddle, *The Net Costs of Immigration to California*, op. cit and Michael Fix and Jeff Passel, *Immigration and Immigrants: Setting the Record Straight*, The Urban Institute, Washington DC, May 1994.

made to (and benefits received from) different public authorities by the immigrants, and not to confine the assessment to the jurisdiction of a particular city or state in isolation (as has been done in some of the estimates made for specific areas or cities in the USA, referred to above). Under the federal system of a country like the USA, irregular immigrants may cost a city or a state more than they pay in taxes, but thc situation may be quite different for the country as a whole, given that the immigrants' may be paying more in the form of federal levies than under state and local levies. On such an over-all basis, the excess of government revenues over government cost incurred for the irregular immigrants in the USA has been estimated by some to be quite considerable.[31]

Indeed, it has been argued: 'every study that provides dollar estimates shows that when the sum of the tax contributions to city, state and federal government are allowed for, these tax payments vastly exceed the cost of services used by a factor of perhaps five, ten or more. On balance, then, the conclusion is quite the opposite of what is commonly supposed: natives exploit illegal immigrants through the public coffers by taking much more than is spent on them in public expenditures'.[32]

Whether or not irregular immigrants increase the fiscal burden of the local population (including legal immigrants) thus depends on the circumstances determining the extent of the use of the services by the irregular immigrants and their families, on the one hand, and the extent of their contributions to their funding, on the other. Also of relevance is the question of how or to what extent the integration of the immigrants, whether regular or irregular, into the economy of the receiving country affects the pattern of their use of welfare services over time. Will they remain poor and depend on public welfare as they become eligible; or will they have economic success and, as the earnings rise, avoid depending on public welfare even if they are eligible? The answers will depend on several factors such as access to economic opportunities, occupational mobility and the socio-cultural behaviour of the immigrant groups.

As for the attitude of immigrants to public welfare, it could vary widely for different immigrant groups depending on factors such as national origin, skill composition and the motivation underlying the movement. Studies in the USA, for example, suggest that recent immigrants are more likely to use welfare than the earlier ones. In 1970, only 5.5 per cent of the immigrant households that came to the USA during 1965–1969 used public welfare compared to 8.3 per cent of those arriving in 1985–89.[33] Part of the explanation probably lies in the differences in skill levels of the immigrant groups. Not surprisingly, according to the recent NRC study referred to above, newly arrived immigrants with

---

[31] Julian Simon, 1989, op. cit, p. 295.

[32] Ibid, p. 296. In a more recent study, Simon asserts that on average immigrant families contribute more than they draw in publicly-funded benefits. Julian Simon, *Immigration: The Demographic and Economic Facts*, Cato Institute, Washington DC, 1995.

[33] George J. Borjas, 'The Economics of Migration', *Journal of Economic Literature*, Vol. 23, December 1994, 1667–1717.

little education consume more state and local public services such as education than they pay in taxes. For example, taxpayers in California were found to pay about $1,178 each year for services used by immigrants but not covered by their state and local taxes.[34] Experience in countries like Australia and Canada, where skilled migrants have a lower than average propensity to depend on welfare, would tend to support such a view. In Canada, for example, 9.4 per cent of local households were receiving public assistance in 1991, while the rate for the immigrant households was 7.4 per cent.[35] There could also be considerable differences in welfare participation between regular and irregular immigrants just as there may be differences between various groups of legally admitted migrants such as refugees, labour immigrants and those admitted for family reunification. Thus, as already noted, irregular immigrants may be more hesitant to request public assistance because of fear of apprehension. On the other hand, to the extent that irregular immigrants may have less education and skills, have more limited occupational mobility and access to economic opportunities and are generally less integrated into the receiving society, they may be inclined or impelled to rely on public welfare more than the regular immigrants.

The welfare participation rate may also evolve over time. As indicated above, young, active and often single, migrants in the initial stage are less likely to depend on welfare. But as time elapses and family formation takes place, welfare transfers are likely to increase. Following a relative decline, these could rise again as the migrant population ages. Beyond all this there is the important question of the general attitude of the national population itself towards public welfare – a general aversion of the members of the receiving society towards public welfare dependency is likely to discourage the immigrant population, whether regular or irregular, from relying unduly on public welfare. The reverse could equally be true. Existing studies on the welfare costs of immigrants shed little light on these dynamic aspects.

There are several other elements that contribute to the difficulty in making an exact assessment of the welfare costs for irregular immigrants in a country like the USA. Aside from the assumed number of irregular immigrants which is a critical variable in determining how many immigrant children there are to benefit from public welfare, there is the complex question, for example, of how the welfare cost of citizen children of irregular immigrants can be imputed. To take another example, should the value of services provided for irregular immigrants be calculated on the basis of average costs or marginal costs? It can be argued, as some in the US have done, that only the marginal cost should be taken into account, since the receiving country will certainly need

---

[34] National Research Council, *The New Americans: Economic, Demographic and Fiscal Effects of Immigration*, 1997, op. cit.

[35] Michael Baker and Dwayne Benjamin, 'The receipt of transfer payments by immigrant in Canada', Working Paper, University of Toronto, 1993 (mimeo).

to maintain general infrastructures for such services as criminal justice and education even if there were no irregular immigrants. And the marginal costs can be higher than the average costs if new prisons or schools need to be built due to the arrival of irregular immigrants or lower if they use only the spare capacity of existing services. As far as the USA is concerned, with the signing of the 1996 welfare bill by President Clinton and the consequent reduction in welfare support (see Chapter 4 and Box 4.2), the net welfare cost for immigrants, regular or irregular, needs to be reassessed.

Finally, an important point to be noted in this context is that the issue of net welfare cost does not apply only to irregular immigrants but also to local workers who are illegally employed and may not pay welfare taxes.

3.2. Effects on structural adjustment, productivity growth and competitiveness

From a strictly economic point of view, a most serious negative effect of irregular migration is that it contributes to the segmentation and dysfunctioning of the labour market and inhibits restructuring and upgrading of the economy of the destination country. Given the technological change, high labour costs and global competition, a number of industrial countries' declining or less competitive industries – farm products, textiles and clothing, shoes and leather products–would normally have been upgraded or replaced by new and more productive ones, helping the general upswing of the economy. But with an easy access to low-cost irregular labour from outside the country and distortion in wages, there is less pressure for structural change in such industries.[36]

Many firms in these industries operate in the informal or underground economy, where the wages and overhead costs are low, working conditions are often unsatisfactory and labour inspection inadequate or non-existent. The possibility of avoiding a range of social charges applicable to employment of regular labour, which in some West European countries can increase wage costs by as much as 50 per cent, is a matter of special attraction. Once the segmentation of the labour market is firmly in place, the secondary labour market gathers its own momentum and tends to attract new irregular immigrants. Irregular workers, when legalized, tend to push the new irregular workers into jobs with still lower earnings in the service and light manufacturing

[36] The general argument is that a large supply of unskilled foreign workers allows firms to expand output and exports at stable wages with current technologies, but it also dampens the employers' urge to search for productivity increasing technologies. Since improved productivity is the basis of economic and wage growth, cheap foreign labour can be counter-productive in the long run. Some economists (e.g. Lutz, 1963) have further argued that as immigrants, initially confined to low wage sector, move into high wage sector which employs mostly national workers, the relative wage gains to nationals diminishes. This eventually depresses wage increases for all workers and reduces the short-term benefit of cheap goods for national workers. Whatever may be the general merits of this argument, it is certainly less valid for low-skilled irregular immigrants, most of whom, as discussed in this Chapter, continue to be employed in the low-wage sector because of the segmented labour market and their limited occupational mobility.

sectors or drive them to intermittent self employment in informal labour markets.

Declining competitiveness also propels some of the firms operating in the tradable sector to mount powerful lobbies to promote trade protection. As noted in Chapter 2, irregular immigration, trade protectionism and low productivity resulting from inefficient use of resources go hand-in-hand. Not only do the consumers suffer but the situation creates a vicious circle that impedes economic, technological and social progress. Although previously confined to the traditional labour-intensive industries such as those mentioned above, irregular immigrant labour is now also being relied upon as a means of fighting competition by employers of large firms and several skill-intensive sophisticated industries (e.g. software development) in which there is fierce competition in the world market. True, large firms find it difficult to engage irregular workers directly due to trade union pressures and labour inspection measures. But, as the experience in Italy shows, by decentralizing part of the production process to small firms using non-union labour, larger companies can keep their hands clean, and let smaller, shady firms do the dirty work of running sweatshops and homework operations.[37] If capital is mobile across sectors, then such a situation may indeed draw capital to the informal or underground economy, and in extreme cases it can deprive the rest of the economy of capital, causing it to stagnate.[38]

A most disquieting aspect of the situation is that the irregular migrants who are engaged in low wage, low productivity activities in the underground economy hardly have either the possibility or the urge to improve their performance or upgrade their skills. The past experience of industrial countries regarding the economic success and improvement of earnings of migrants is illuminating in this connection. Several studies in the USA, Canada and Australia have shown that in many cases an initial earnings gap between immigrants and local workers decreased over time.[39] Although the findings of these studies vary, they leave little doubt that the initial human capital characteristics and motivation of the immigrants play an important part in their subsequent advance-

---

[37] Linda Weiss, 'Explaining the Underground economy: State and Social Structure', *The British Journal of Sociology*, 1987, 38: 216–233; see also Bruno Contini, *The Second Economy in Italy* in Vito Tanzi (ed.) *The Underground Economy in the United States and Abroad*, D.C. Heathe and Co., Boston, 1982, pp. 199–208.

[38] Andrea Ichino, 'The Economic Impact of Immigration on the Host Country', Unpublished paper, Bocconoi University, Milan, Italy, 1992.

[39] See, for example, Barry Chiswick, *An Analysis of Economic Progress and Impacts of Immigrants*, Final Report to the US Department of Labour, Washington DC, 1980. On the basis of an analysis of the 1970 census, Chiswick came to the conclusion that the immigrants initially have lower incomes than the comparable groups of US nationals, but after 11–15 years their incomes equal those of the comparable groups, and become even higher after that period. There were however differences according to ethnic or national origins of immigrants.

ment.[40] When the immigrants are less endowed in these attributes, as exemplified by the immigrants who came to the USA after 1970, their advancement tends to be slower.[41] This is also reflected in the differentiated economic progress of different groups of immigrants who arrived in the United States between 1970 and 1990. Mexican immigrant men who entered the USA with education, language and skill disadvantages have continued to lose ground relative to US-born men during the past two decades. By contrast, immigrant men from China, Japan and Korea, who were better equipped, increased their earnings from 88 per cent of those of similar US-born men in 1970 to 110 per cent in 1990.[42]

Similar studies in Europe have shown that slow rate of economic success and advancement of immigrants may be due to a wide variety of factors such as the relative rigidity of the labour market, ethnic origin and under-valuation of the qualifications of foreign workers in the initial stage. A significant point that seems to emerge from these studies is that migrants who were less educated and low-skilled at the time of entry had more difficulty in making subsequent advancement[43]: not only do they enter as low wage workers, but they tend to remain at the lower end of the wage hierarchy. Irregular migrants who are employed in low-wage, low productivity activities in the informal or underground economy suffer from a two-fold disadvantage in this respect. First, their low qualifications or human capital endowments and lack of adequate motivation seriously limit the possibilities of occupational advancement through self improvement. Even when they are skilled and qualified, their qualifications are likely to be under-valued even more than in the case of regular immigrants. Second, rarely does the working environment of the non-competitive firms in the informal economy or declining industries provide the necessary scope and incentives to improve their skills and human capital. The convergence of these two sets of negative factors impedes any progress towards

---

[40] See George Borjas, 'Self-selection and the Earnings of Immigrants', *The American Economic Review*, September 1987, pp. 531 ff.

[41] An important reason why Borjas came to a more differentiated conclusion than Chiswick on the earnings growth of immigrants concerns the human capital characteristics and motivation of the immigrants. The immigrants examined by Chiswick, who came to the United States before 1970 were generally better endowed in terms of both qualifications and motivation.

[42] *The Mixed Economic Progress*, Rand Corporation, Santa Monica, July 1996.

[43] European studies on the subject do not suggest that immigrants are more successful than nationals, but rather confirm that much depends on the selection of immigrant workers, including the country of origin and their human capital characteristics. While duration of stay may influence immigrants' motivations and improvements in their qualifications and earnings, those who enter with relatively low skills tend to remain at the lower segment of the wage and occupational structure. For somewhat divergent findings on the earnings growth of immigrants in Germany see: Christian Dustmann, 'Earnings Adjustment of Temporary Migrants', *Journal of Population Economics*, 1993, pp. 153–186; Christoph Schmidt, 'The Earnings Dynamics of Immigrant Labour', Discussion Paper no. 92–28, Universität Munchen, 1992.

improved skills and productivity, and thus retards economic and technological progress.

When irregular flows of immigrant labour inhibit industrial restructuring and encourage trade protectionism in developed countries, the negative effects are generally not confined to the latter, but tend to spill over into sending developing countries and can serve as a drag on the world economy. As already noted, the receiving countries suffer due to lack of technological progress and productivity growth; at the same time, their reliance on trade barriers and irregular immigrant labour deny the developing countries the possibility of expanding exports through a dynamic use of the comparative advantage of their low-cost labour. The consequent depressive effect on both employment and earnings generates emigration pressure and thus creates a vicious circle. The world economy is denied the fruits of technological progress and increased efficiency through better allocation of resources.

True, irregular outflows can provide the sending country with some temporary economic and social relief, but in most cases this is likely to be marginal or insignificant. If, on the other hand, the relief is appreciable, it may induce the government of the sending country to avoid or postpone policy changes needed to address root causes of such movements, and important policy reform could be delayed.

Social costs and consequences

Even more disquieting are the social consequences of irregular migration: these can be particularly harmful for the destination country and the migrants themselves under certain circumstances. Irregular migrants' precarious legal status and often weak economic position in the destination country makes them vulnerable to employer pressure, mistreatment and exploitation. At the same time, by creating a low-paid and less protected social underclass, irregular immigration contributes to economic inequality in the receiving country.

In the USA, the *Economic Report of the President* presented by Mr. Clinton in 1994 declared that increasing the relative supply of less educated labour immigrants seemed to have contributed to the growing income inequality, although the effect has been small. Some have argued that rising inequality has meant stagnation or even fall in real wages in the bottom half of the US workforce. The recent report of the National Research Council (NRC) confirms that although US workers as a group may have gained from immigration, arrival of low-skilled workers depressed the wages of US workers without high-school education by about five per cent since 1980, accounting for about half of the total drop in unskilled workers' wages; newly arrived immigrants also depressed the wages of earlier arrivals.[44]

---

[44] National Research Council, *The New Americans: Economic, Demographic and Fiscal Effects of Immigration*, 1997, op. cit.

Most economists generally agree that excessive inequality in skills and earnings can slow economic growth because co-workers may lack the skill and motivation needed to enable those with higher skills and earnings to make full use of their productive capacity. Any such effect on inequality is most likely to be greater in the case of irregular immigration for several reasons: not only are most irregular immigrant workers low-skilled, but they also receive wages that are considerably lower than those paid to regular workers and are more likely to remain in low-grade jobs longer than the regular (especially non-immigrant) workers.

In Sweden, for example, irregular Polish workers in the southern municipality of Sjobo were reported to have received one-third of the official wages, without any social security benefits.[45] In Poland, the illegally employed migrant workers from Russia, Ukraine and Belarus, mostly in the construction industry, received salaries about less than half of the legal minimum.[46] In the Republic of Korea, a survey made of Filipino irregular workers in 1992 revealed that the monthly wages paid to them were 43.7 per cent of the wages earned by Korean workers in the manufacturing sector in 1991. Until 1994, when there was a sit-in strike to protest against their ill-treatment, irregular workers were not entitled to compensation for industrial accidents. Although in February 1994, industrial accident insurance coverage was extended to irregular foreign workers, many of those who suffered minor injuries avoided applying for compensation for fear of deportation. Many others were deported before receiving any compensation.[47] In Singapore, irregular immigrants from Bangladesh are recruited at almost half the market wage for many service sector activities such as cleaning, catering, and maintenance of public buildings. Studies in Japan revealed a similar trend.

In the USA, the sweatshops in, for example, the garment-making industry which employs large numbers of irregular immigrants, often operate in sub-human conditions. Reviewing these appalling conditions, a 1994 report of the General Accounting Office described the state of the US garment industry as being little different from that at the turn of the century. A recent survey by the Department of Labour of the garment-making industry in California, revealed that more than half of the firms were paying less than the minimum wage of US$ 4.25 per hour and 68 per cent were violating federal overtime requirements.[48] In Japan, a study made in 1988 by the Ministry of Labour found that the wages for irregular foreign workers were around 60 per cent lower than those paid to Japanese workers. Working conditions, including safety standards are often unsatisfactory, and, worse still, injured workers may

---

[45] *The Daily Telegraph*, 1 November 1990.

[46] *Migration News Sheet*, March 1995.

[47] S.D. Kang, 'Globalization of the labour market also in South Korea?', 1996. Paper submitted to the conference to the Dynamics of Labour Migration in Asia', Nihon University, Tokyo, 6–7 March 1996 (mimeo), pp. 32–35.

[48] *Migration News*, Vol. 1, No 9, October 1994.

be denied compensation either for fear of discovery, or because they were required to waive coverage as a condition of employment.[49] In Germany, irregular workers engaged in the construction industry (as discussed in Chapter 2) were in some cases encouraged or induced to claim 'self-employed status' so that their employers would not have to pay social security contributions, and they themselves would be in a position to avoid paying taxes. A study commissioned by the German Federal Labour Office calculated that the consequent losses in 1989 amounted to 5 per cent of the gross national product.[50]

In such situations exploitation of labour, loss in public receipts, erosion of respect for the law and weakening of ethical standards of business go hand-in-hand. Already in 1981, the US Select Commission on Immigration and Refugee Policy argued, 'illegal migration [if unchecked] will continue to undermine the most valued ideals of this nation – the integrity of the law and the fundamental dignity of the individual'.[51] The argument remains equally valid today.

Exploitation and abuses of human rights often assume alarming proportions when, as already noted, the irregular migrants are fully within the clutches of unscrupulous traffickers. Some of them die during the journey due to drowning as they travel, for example, by unsafe fishing boats, or because of suffocation as they hide themselves in the interior of trucks and containers of cargo ships. When detected, traffickers can react in exactly the same way as they do when trafficking in drugs – they throw the migrants overboard. In a recent case nearly one thousand Africans paid a ship's captain US$ 750 each to be illegally ferried to Italy. On reaching the shore they discovered that they were in the former Yugoslavia. Against an extra payment of US$ 600 each, they were promised to be taken to Austria by bus; in the event they were duped and abandoned in Hungary.[52]

As noted in Chapter 1, trafficked migrants are in many cases forced to work in legal or illegal enterprises controlled by the traffickers under sub-human conditions or to participate in various activities involving crime and violence. In Spain, for example, recent police reports revealed that trafficked immigrants from China were often forced to work mainly in restaurants and textile factories under conditions of semi-slavery simply for food and accommodation. Discussion in Chapter 1 has indicated how women and children can be exposed to special forms of exploitation such as prostitution and sexual harassment. To add to the examples already cited, recent press reports from Belgium revealed several cases of young Filipino women who were forced into prostitution; in one case, 17 of them arrived in Antwerp after having been trafficked through

---

[49] S. Spencer, 'Illegal migrant laborers in Japan', *International Migration Review*, Vol. 26, No. 3, 1992.
[50] *Süddeutsche Zeitung*, 8 June 1994 and 25 November 1994; *Migration News Sheet*, November 1994; *Frankfurter Rundschau*, 8 August 1991.
[51] Select Commission on Immigration and Refugee Policy, *US Immigration Policy and the National Interest* (Final Report), US Government Printing Office, Washington DC, 1981, p. 560.
[52] *The Economist*, London, 5–11 August 1995, p. 25.

Morocco, Turkey and the Netherlands.[53] In Spain, 2000 Dominican women, brought by a network operated by Spanish and Dominican nationals, were subsequently forced, and sometimes tortured, into prostitution.[54] A similar pattern of exploitation of women illegally employed in bars and as prostitutes is found in Japan. Their passports and return tickets are routinely taken away by traffickers, job brokers and club managers and they remain under the constant threat of being reported to the police if they try to run away. In some instances, women have been confined within a single building for months at a time and forced into prostitution; they did not even know where they were.[55] Irregular migration in these situations becomes closely associated with gross violation of basic human and workers' rights.

Irregular migration, as noted in Chapter 1, is now also closely intertwined with international crimes and acts of violence. In a growing number of cases in Western Europe it was found that trafficking in drugs, smuggling of migrants and money laundering often went hand in hand, the same criminal networks being involved in all these illicit operations. In Italy, for example, recent press reports suggest that the involvement of the Mafia is increasingly linking illegal immigration to the world of crime – drugs, arms trafficking and prostitution.[56] In several cases, Chinese and Bosnian rings were found to collude with the local Mafia, combining illegal immigration with arms trafficking.[57] According to the Italian police, in one case a young leader of an organized criminal gang, who controlled a clandestine organization in Milan, had specialised in, among other things, migrant smuggling, drug trafficking, and gambling and prostitution businesses. He was alleged to have practiced kidnapping, brutal beating and other tortures to his clients in order to extract money from them, in addition to a charge of US$ 10,000 per person from a trip from China to Milan.[58]

There are other links between irregular migration and criminal or illegal activities. In Canada, for example, it was recently found that one of the immigrant smuggling rings charged US$ 18,000 to US$ 20,000 for each person smuggled into the country, and subsequently collected half of the welfare payments received.[59]

Irregular migration, especially organized human trafficking, often encourages a whole range of illicit activities such as clandestine printing of false travel documents, forgery, bribery and corruption. The money earned from migrant

---

[53] *La Libre Belgique; Migration News Sheet*, September 1993.

[54] *El Pais*, 16 February 1993.

[55] M. Fukushima, 'Immigrant Asian Workers and Japan: The Reality I Discovered at "HELP"', 1991. Paper presented to the Conference on International Manpower flows and Foreign investment in the Asian Region, Tokyo (mimeo). Peter Stalker: *The Work of Strangers*, op. cit, p. 254.

[56] *Financial Times*, 27 March 1995.

[57] *Financial Times*, 13 April 1995.

[58] *Migration News Sheet*, May 1995.

[59] W. Bilal Syeed, 'Welcome to Ontario, welfare heaven', *Wall Street Journal*, 9 September 1994, A15.

smuggling often fuels official corruption. In Panama, Belize and Guatemala, for example, immigration officials were fired in 1995 for accepting bribes from foreign smugglers.[60] In Uruguay, two senior immigration officials were recently fired as they were implicated in smuggling Chinese immigrants into the country and then to Argentina.[61] Similar cases were reported in the United Kingdom· where an immigration officer was given a two-year prison sentence for having forged visas for irregular immigrants against payment of bribes[62], and in Spain where in 1993, eight Spanish consular officials, posted in Tanger, were accused of involvement in large-scale trafficking of Spanish visas.[63] It is not uncommon for staff members of Bangladeshi embassies in the neighbouring receiving countries to share with labour agents and intermediaries the payments made by the irregular migrants over and above the prescribed official fees for issuing, for example, duplicate passports.[64] Cases of alleged corruption involving government officials have been reported in a number of other countries, including Belgium and Morocco.[65] To illustrate further, in early 1997, the top US immigration officer in Hong Kong was relieved of his duties and his wife was arrested on visa-fraud charges arising out of an investigation into the trafficking of Chinese migrants into the USA. This was the second time in less than nine months that a senior US migration officer in Hong Kong was implicated in corruption related to migrant trafficking.[66] An immigration inspector of Kennedy Airport in New York was convicted of smuggling irregular migrants from the Dominican Republic for $6,500 each.[67]

As irregular immigration erodes the moral values and economic integrity of the receiving society and as it becomes increasingly associated with criminality, illicit activities and violence, it tends to generate an anti-immigrant feeling among the public. The poorer segments of the society feel threatened by the decline in labour and social standards. As a report submitted to the Commission of the European Communities in 1991 noted, 'acceptance of low wages and low standards of social security by the irregular migrants is...the source of a growing xenophobia on the part of those who – being on the lowest step of social hierarchy – feel their own interests are being threatened'. Interested political parties and lobbies soon seek to exploit the situation by raising populist anti-immigration slogans. Social tension, racial intolerance and xeno-

---

[60] *Migration News*, Vol. 3, No. 1, January 1996.

[61] *Migration News*, January 1996, op. cit.

[62] *The Independent*, 16 May 1992.

[63] *El Pais*, 7 September 1994.

[64] R.A. Mahmood, 'Clandestine foreign workers and domestic labour market: Process of integration and implications', 1996. Paper presented to the IOM/UNFPA workshop on emigration dynamics in South Asia, Geneva (mimeo).

[65] *La Libre Belgique and Le Soir*, 10 February 1993, *El Pais*, 15 April 1991.

[66] *International Herald Tribune*, 7 April, 1997. The INS expects 1.7 million naturalisation applications in 1997, up from one million in 1995 and 592,000 in 1994.

[67] *Migration News*, Vol. 4, No. 2, 1997.

phobia gain increasing ground. When this happens on a large scale, social peace and stability can be seriously threatened.

A negative upshot of the situation is that it often rebounds to the discredit of the legal immigrants, including permanent settlers, belonging to the same ethnic groups. This may be an important reason why legally resident immigrants arc generally supportive of measures taken by the receiving state to curb irregular or clandestine immigration, as recently exemplified by the results of an opinion poll in France on its 1993 Immigration Act. In the United States, the recent (1994–95) campaign in California against illegal immigrants seems to have created a climate in which legal immigrants, too, felt stigmatized – a development which may have contributed to a sudden increase in the number of legal immigrants applying for US citizenship.[68]

It is not suggested that irregular migrants are themselves more prone to criminality and lawlessness than regular immigrants or the local population. Nor is there any conclusive evidence that the rate of crimes is necessarily higher among irregular immigrants than among the others. Indeed, irregular immigrants would normally be more reluctant to be involved in criminal activities for fear of being apprehended and thrown out of the receiving country. And yet, it cannot be denied that extreme economic despair and vulnerability can ruthlessly drive them towards criminality and even violence. It is not without significance that when informed of a deportation order, many irregular migrants deliberately commit offences to avoid immediate deportation. In Spain, for example, it was reported that many of them tried to sell a small quantity of drugs, break a shop window or do just about anything to get arrested instead of being expelled.

Clearly, irregular migration presents particularly difficult problems of integration. It condemns individuals to some of the worst forms of exploitation and insecurity and makes them the most vulnerable victims of an anti-immigrant feeling in the receiving society. Many of these problems tend to persist since given their illegal status, irregular migrants cannot be easily integrated into the receiving society. The facilities provided under its various integration programmes may not be available to those who are not recognised as legal immigrants. Even if they are, the irregular migrants, fearful of apprehension and harassment, especially in times of high anti-immigrant feeling in the receiving country, may themselves be reluctant to come forward and take advantage of the facilities. In the USA, for example, the fact that irregular immigrants could not be subjected to mandatory vocational training and other work requirements that would help them obtain employment served as an impediment to their full integration (further discussed in Chapter 4).

The irregular immigrants thus continue to work in the underground economy, live in ghettos or in places of hiding and enjoy few human rights; as they are consequently trapped into a situation in which their marginalisation and

---

[68] *International Herald Tribune*, 4 April, 1995.

lack of social protection tends to increase rather than decrease over time. They become easy prey to gangs involved in crime and violence. It is this vulnerability and economic despair of most irregular migrants, combined with the growing control of these movements by gangs of traffickers, that largely account for a considerable, and possibly rising, part of criminality among these migrants.

Such exclusion can have seriously negative consequences both for the migrant and the receiving country, and over time it may affect social cohesion and stability, economic progress and even security of the receiving state. The situation could also entail certain immediate risks. For example, recently in France, an immediate danger of exclusion of irregular immigrants from public health assistance became a focus of attention following an initiative taken by 20 voluntary associations. As many of the sick irregular immigrants do not go to public hospitals for fear of being denounced, an ordinary infection may become an urgent case and thus very expensive to treat; and in the case of a contagious disease it can become a health hazard for many others in the community.

3.4. Irregular migration, national sovereignty and inter-state relations

Irregular migration has already become an important source of irritation and conflict in inter-state relations. Zealous about their sovereign rights, most migrant-receiving states find it difficult to cope with new exigencies of migration as a powerful global process. Irregular migration makes the situation more sensitive. As these movements take place in defiance of established national laws and practice, they tend to be perceived as a challenge to state sovereignty. In some cases, irregular immigrants could be an instrument of political subversion or can be perceived to be so. Experience in Africa, for example, shows that the presence of large numbers of irregular immigrants who may be discontented or may be desperate to earn their livings by any means provides a ready reserve of recruits for public disorder or other subversive activities. The riots in Kano, Nigeria, in 1980 and 1982 in which illegal immigrants from five West African countries were allegedly involved has been cited as an example of the security risk involved.[69]

In some other instances, they may seek to use the neighbouring receiving country as a base to mount armed operations against those in power in their country of origin. In an atmosphere of increasing sensitivity about the issue, the receiving country can be easily swayed to interpret irregular and unwanted immigration as an unfriendly act by the sending country that violates the established norms of inter-state relations. The latter, on the other hand, is apt to feel aggrieved and slighted when the irregular immigrants are abused and exploited in the receiving country. This often includes harsh or even inhuman

[69] Aderanti Adepoju, 'Undocumented Migration in Africa: Trends and Policies', *International Migration* Vol. XXI, No. 2, 1983, p. 212.

treatment of irregular immigrants as they try to cross the border of the destination or the transit country.

New trends in trafficking in which, as already noted, powerful international criminal gangs, supported by wide extensive networks across countries, organise large-scale human smuggling through international air, sea and land routes are adding a new urgency to this security dimension of irregular migration. In the summer of 1993, when a series of smuggling ships with irregular Chinese migrants entered the USA, President Bill Clinton declared that the tactic posed a threat to national security and authorised the National Security Council to direct the response.[70] Although primarily aimed at restoring democracy in that country, the threat of US invasion of Haiti in September 1994 was linked to the potential unauthorised immigration flows into the United States. In his speech on 15 September 1994, President Clinton cited the 'threat of a mass exodus (the number was estimated at 300,000) of Haitian refugees and its constant threat to stability in our regions and control of our borders' as a major justification of US action.[71]

The involvement of international crime syndicates in human trafficking, alongside smuggling of drugs and arms and laundering of funds, often as interlocked activities, poses a particularly serious threat for smaller countries and areas.[72] They have limited resources and staff to enforce immigration control and protect their borders. Their easily permeable sea shores and in many cases the scattered location of many constituent islands over a wide area, make border protection extremely difficult. A number of them, including the Bahamas, Belize, Bermuda, British Virgin Island, Dominica and Gibraltar have already been facing, in one form or another, problems of drug trafficking and money laundering. Many of the powerful syndicates which are involved in these activities are well informed and well equipped to take full advantage of the lax immigration regulations and inadequate border control of these small countries/areas and use them as transit points or bridgeheads for smuggling migrants.

Irregular immigration, as is well known, has long been a delicate and controversial subject in the bilateral relations between the USA and Mexico. The recent initiative in the US state of California to make the undocumented aliens ineligible for state education facilities and non-emergency health care has been seriously resented in Mexico. Its foreign ministry complained of 'racist and xenophobic' overtones in the California initiative and warned that the improvement in the commercial and economic relations brought about by the North American Free Trade Agreement (NAFTA) could be at risk.[73] Further

---

[70] Luis Freedber, 'Immigration Now A Security Concern: Smuggling Forces White House to Bring Intelligence Agencies', *San Francisco Chronicle*, 23 June 1993, p. A1.

[71] New York Times, 16 September 1994, A.16.

[72] Bimal Ghosh, 'Uncontrolled Immigration into Small Countries', 1996. Paper prepared for the International Organization for Migration, Geneva, p. 6 (mimeo).

[73] *Financial Times*, 21 October 1994.

south, in the Caribbean and Central America, the Bahamas' relations with Haiti and Cuba remain strained due to the large inflows of irregular immigrants from the latter countries. Belize's relations with Guatemala, already tense due to other reasons, have not been helped by the influx of refugees who were initially in an irregular situation.[74]

Similarly, over the past few years the treatment of irregular migrants has often strained the otherwise friendly relations between the states in Western Europe and North Africa. In Morocco, for example, there were widespread discontent and protests against Spain in July 1993 over the treatment meted to 47 Moroccans, who together with about 100 other North Africans, were refused entry at the port of Algecirac as they were allegedly carrying false Italian residence and work permits.[75] Earlier, in 1991, Spain, for its part, had expressed its displeasure to the Moroccan Government about the increasing number of irregular Moroccan immigrants.[76] Subsequently, however, an understanding was reached between the two governments and joint measures were planned to combat clandestine migration. To cite another example, in January 1991 when feelings were already running high over the Gulf War, Morocco warned the Belgian authorities about the possible repercussions of the manner in which they were planning to expel large numbers of irregular Moroccan immigrants.[77] In August 1993, relations between Spain and China were strained over incidents involving the deportation of Chinese irregular immigrants.[78]

3.5. Irregular migration as a challenge to orderly movements of people

As noted above, one of the worst consequences of irregular migration is that it breeds intolerance of foreigners and inevitably builds up resistance to movements of people, including legal and orderly migration, across countries. As irregular migration expands with its attendant ills, it tends to overshadow the manifold positive contributions that orderly flows can make for the benefit of human society – by strengthening national economies, encouraging interchange of skills and knowledge and enhancing enrichment of culture.

It is not difficult to see how irregular migration adversely affects the prospects of orderly movements of people. Irregular migrants may be less visible, but when they are in large numbers the corrosive effects of their presence on living conditions, business ethics and moral values are likely to be soon felt in the receiving society. When irregular immigration becomes linked with criminal activities, and law and order is threatened, the resentment of the local popula-

---

[74] Bimal Ghosh, 'Uncontrolled Immigration into Small Countries', 1996, op. cit., p. 5.

[75] *El Pais*, 20 and 22 July 1993.

[76] *El Pais*, 29 September 1991.

[77] *La Libre Belgique* 17, 19/20 and 22 January 1991, *Le Soir*, 18,23,24 January 1991; and *Migration News Sheet*, February 1991.

[78] *El Pais*, 4 January 1994.

tion turns into growing intolerance of all aliens which can soon explode into xenophobic violence. Since irregular immigration by its very nature reflects a lack of government control, it enhances the anxiety of the government over inflows of foreigners. As noted above, the situation is often exploited by extremist political elements to stir up further anti-immigrant feeling as part of the electoral campaign. In such a setting, it becomes difficult to maintain or develop a sound, balanced and pro-active immigration policy, based on the real needs and conditions of the country.

There is another important reason why the presence of irregular migrant workers can inhibit or delay the formulation of an active and transparent national policy on immigration. As noted in Chapter 2, the experiences of Japan and several East Asian countries show that as long as the pressing labour market needs for unskilled workers are satisfied through an inflow of irregular immigrants, the pressure from industry or other sections of the community may not be sufficiently strong to impel the government to take a clear (and often difficult) policy decision on labour immigration or other, alternative measures. And, for similar reasons, reforms in migration and economic policies may not be given a high priority or handled with a sufficient sense of urgency in the sending countries. The tough policy decision may thus be postponed. But the long-term costs – social, human and economic – of such policy vacillation could be high.

CHAPTER FOUR

Recent policy trends and practical measures: A variegated landscape

In so far as irregular migration is a challenge to the established laws and regulations of the receiving or the sending country, or both, it would be natural for the governments concerned to strive to curb or totally eradicate it. Remedial measures are of course no less important when the irregularities, as discussed in Chapters 1 and 2, occur due to deficiencies in existing institutional arrangements rather than as a result of the migrant's deliberate defiance of the established regulatory system.

National action against irregular migration has taken various forms, and has often been reinforced by bilateral agreements. Despite its relatively short history, multilateral, including regional and sub-regional, cooperation has been intensified in recent years to foster, sustain and harmonise national measures as irregular migration itself has become a global phenomenon. The present Chapter briefly reviews, on a selective basis, recent policy and practical measures adopted at the national, regional and international levels to address irregular migration. The discussion should provide insights into the wide variety of the measures adopted and serve as a useful background against which to design a comprehensive and balanced strategy to deal with irregular migration (discussed in Chapter 5).

4.1. Trends in industrial countries

The measures adopted in industrial countries generally concern border interdiction and punitive action against irregular entry, including aiding and abetting, forgery of documents, smuggling of migrants, irregular hiring of foreigners and transportation of irregular migrants. A synoptic overview of the legal provisions in different industrial countries concerning the punitive actions is provided in Table 4.1.[1]

---

[1] For a description of the legal provisions on irregular immigration in countries listed in the table, see: IGC 'Summary Description of Legislation of Aliens Trafficking', Secretariat of the Intergovernmental Consultations on Asylum, Refugee and Migration Policies in Europe, North America and Australia, Geneva, December 1995.

Table 4.1. Legislation on irregular migration in selected industrialised countries: a range of penalties, 1995

Participating state	Alien smuggling	Aiding and abetting: Transporting	Aiding and abetting: Harbouring	Illegal entry	Fraudulent documents	Employer sanctions	Carrier sanctions: Local currencies	Carrier sanctions: US $	Forfeiture
Western European Countries									
Belgium (5/96)	1–5 years & fine: Bfr100,000–5 million Organised crime: 10–15 years forced labour Bfr 200,000–20 million	8 days–3 months and/ or fine: Bfr 340,000–6 million	8 days–3 months and/ or fine: Bfr 340,000–6 million	8 days–1 year and fine: Bfr 5,200–200,000	Minor offence: 1 month–1 year Major offence: min. 5–15 years prison/forced labour	1 month–1 year and fine: Bfr 1.2–6 million or admin. fine: Bfr 500,000	Penal fine: Bfr 600,000 Admin. Fine: Bfr 150,000	5,000	Yes
Denmark	2 years	2 years	2 years	6 months	8 years	6 months	Fine: DKR 8–10,000	1,500	Yes
France	5 years & fine: FF 200,000	5 years & fine: FF 200,000	5 years & fine: FF 200,000	1 year & fine: FF 20,000	?	3 years & fine	Fine: FF 10,000	2,000	yes
Finland (5/96)	2 years	2 years	2 years	(usually fined)	4 years	1 year	No	–	Yes
Germany (5/96)	5 years Organised network: 10 years	5 years	5 years	1 year (3 years proposed)	5 years	5 years	fine: DM 20,000	13,200	Yes
Italy	2–6 years & fine: Lira 10–50 million	up to 2 years or fine: Lira 2 million	up to 2 years or fine: Lira 2 million	up to 2 years or fine: Lira 2 million	1–5 years	3 months–1 year &/ or fine: Lira 500,000–10 million	Fine: Lira 200–500,000	225	Yes, according to provision in Penal Code
Netherlands (5/96)	1 year (4 to 8 years proposed)	1 year or fine	1 year or fine	6 months	4 years	1 year or fine	Imprisonment up to 6 months; fine of approximatley Dfl 5,000	3,000	No specific legislation but Code of Criminality Procedure may be used
Norway	2 years	2 years	2 years	6 months	5 years	2 years	Yes (pending implementation)	–	Yes
Spain	Fine: Ptas 2 millions	fine: Ptas 2 millions	fine: Ptas 2 millions	No	Yes	6 months & Fine: Ptas 15 millions	max fine: Ptas 150,000,000 trafficking by sea	approx. 1.19 million	No
Sweden (5/96)	2 years	2 years	2 years	No	2 years	1 year or fine	Fines	–	Yes
Switzerland (5/96)	6 months & fine up to Sfr. 10,000 Organised network/crime: 3 yrs & fine up to Sfr. 100,000			6 months & fine max. Sfr. 10,000	6 months & fine max. Sfr. 10,000	fine Sfr. 3,000–5,000 and/or max. 6 months	Under study	–	?
UK	7 years	6 months	6 months	6 months	6 months	No	Fine: £2,000	3,000	Yes

Continued.

Table 4.1. (cont.) Legislation on irregular migration in selected industrialised countries: a range of penalties, 1995

		Aiding and abetting					Carrier sanctions		
Participating state	Alien smuggling	Transporting	Harbouring	Illegal entry	Fraudulent documents	Employer sanctions	Local currencies	US $	Forfeiture
				Other Industrial Countries					
Australia (5/96)	2 years	A$ 10,000 or 2 years	2 years	Fine: A$ 10,000	2 years	No specific legislation, can be charged with aiding and abetting	Fine: A$ 2–10,000	1,600–7,900	Applies only to proceeds from crimes which are indictable offences
Canada	5 years	5 years	5 years	2 years	14 years	2 years	Administrative fee of C$3,200	2,300	Yes
USA	10 years–life imprisonment or death penalty	5 years	5 years	4–20 yrs for aggravated repeated offences	10 to 15 years	6 months	Fine: $3,000	3,000	Yes

Source: Secretariat of the Intergovernmental Consultations on Asylum, Refugee and Migration Policies in Europe, N. America and Australia (IGC), 1995.
Note: Cut off date: 1995, unless otherwise indicated. Legislative measures taken after 1995 are not included in the table, but selected references to them are made in the text of the chapter.

United States of America

In the USA, public concern over irregular immigration became particularly pronounced in the 1970s when border interdiction, which was then the main instrument to prevent irregular immigration, was found ineffective to arrest the continuing rise in the number of irregular immigrants. There was a growing fear that large inflows of irregular immigrants would intensify competition at the lower end of the labour force and thus help create a permanent underclass of impoverished people in US society, composed of both immigrants and domestic groups. The rapid increase in the inflow of the Spanish-speaking population through regular and irregular channels was another source of concern in certain quarters. And at least some state and local governments were afraid of the rising demands on social services from the irregular (and regular) immigrants.

To address the rising concern and complement border control measures, the US Labour Department introduced in the late 1970s, the 'Special Targeted Enforcement Program' (STEP) which aimed at reducing the attractiveness of hiring irregular immigrants through stricter enforcement of labour standards, notably those concerning minimum wages, overtime and child labour, in industries and areas that normally employed large numbers of irregular immigrants. As STEP focused attention on conditions of employment in agriculture, the garment industry, construction, laundries, restaurants and certain other services especially in south-western United States, it was believed that the new measures, combined with border interdiction by the Immigration and Naturalization Service (INS), would curb irregular inflows while improving the working conditions for all workers in these sectors.[2]

The STEP proved to be less effective than expected. Its weakness stemmed from several sources. First, it was too narrowly designed, only focusing on punitive measures to diminish the influence of pull factors. Even within this punitive approach it was confined to enforcement of labour laws rather than covering a full range of laws whose stricter enforcement could have reinforced the STEP's effectiveness – for example, better enforcement of immigration laws in the interior of the country and of tax laws affecting employers that used clandestine workers to avoid fiscal obligations. Its scope was further restricted by the fact that many irregular immigrants were engaged in activities – such as those run by family businesses or in the underground economy – which were outside the reach and competence of labour laws. Finally, the lack of adequate enforcement resources resulting from budgetary constraints impeded the effective functioning of the STEP even within its narrowly designed scope.

Employer sanctions and stricter enforcement of labour laws were also given particular emphasis in the recommendations made in 1981 by the Select Commission on Immigration and Refugee Policy to combat illegal immigration.

---

[2] John Fraser, 'Illegal immigration in the United States and the limits of sanctions against employers' in *Migration and Development*, OECD, Paris, 1994, p. 75.

However, despite several efforts at new initiatives, nothing much happened until the enactment of the Immigration Control and Reform Act (IRCA) of 1986.

Although, like STEP, IRCA focused on reducing the influence of the pull factors through employer sanctions and stricter border control, it also provided for legalisation by according legal residency status to certain categories of former illegal immigrants. Another important feature of the new Act was sanctions against employers who discriminated against regular immigrants, although these sanctions were less severe than those against employing irregular immigrants. Employer sanctions were probably the most important and the most controversial feature of the new legislation.

Several years after IRCA went into force, indications were that its success in stemming irregular inflows was limited. True, average annual border apprehensions had come down during the first few years, but this was perhaps mainly due to the legalisation of formerly irregular immigrants which led to a decline in illegal cross-border traffic. Although the level of border apprehensions may be influenced by several factors, including the degree of effectiveness of control measures, it is none the less of some significance that since 1989 the number of border apprehensions has climbed to nearly pre-IRCA levels.

Employers were generally aware of IRCA's requirements and their new responsibilities, and its labour market effects on those who were able to qualify for legal status were positive. But it did not have an appreciable impact on the numbers of irregular immigrants, compared to the pre-IRCA levels; nor did it reduce the availability of the kind of jobs – in small and family enterprises and in the underground economy – where irregular immigrants generally find employment. While employers' compliance levels were relatively low, the fear of sanctions did lead to some negative social consequences, notably in the form of employment discrimination from which even legally admitted Asian and Hispanic workers suffered. As a 1990 report by the General Accounting Office (GAO) observed, many employers stopped hiring job applicants whose foreign appearance or accent led them to suspect that they might be unauthorised aliens.[3] Many others applied the employment eligibility verification system only to persons who had a 'foreign' appearance or accent. These practices represented 'new' national origin discrimination that would not have occurred without IRCA.

Another negative consequence was the proliferation of fraudulent and counterfeit documents that thwarted the system of employment eligibility verification. The availability of false or fraudulent documents also imposed higher administrative costs on those employers who tried to verify employment eligibility of their workers.

---

[3] US General Accounting Office, *Report to the Congress: Immigration Reform: Employer Sanctions and the Question of Discrimination*, Washington DC, March 1990, pp. 5–6.

These and other shortcomings of the system led to calls by several employers and labour groups and Hispanic and Asian minorities for the repeal of employer sanctions and related provisions of IRCA. Although both Reagan and Bush administrations supported employer sanctions, a number of measures were soon recommended (and some of them implemented), to remedy the perceived weaknesses of employers sanctions as provided for under IRCA. In its 1990 report, the GAO, for example, recommended several new lines of action, including increased efforts to educate employers on how to comply with IRCA's anti-discrimination provision; and simplification of employment eligibility verification by reducing the number and variety of relevant documents and making the remaining work-authorising documents more counterfeit-resistant. A special task force, which was subsequently appointed to review the matter, supported these recommendations. It also called for statutory changes in IRCA's anti-discrimination provision and a broader role for the Department of Labour in enforcing employers' responsibilities concerning employment eligibility verification.[4]

The government took action to implement many of the recommended administrative and operational measures, while the new Immigration Act of 1990 included several of the task force's legislative recommendations and established increased penalties for document fraud. It was also believed that employers' new access to immigrant workers through increased admission of permanent and employment-based immigrants under the new 1990 Act would reduce the influence of pull factors in encouraging irregular immigration. Events have however proved otherwise. Except for a short-term decline in the years immediately following legalisation, the number of irregular workers, especially in low skill, low wage jobs has continued to increase.

In 1994, budgetary difficulties in meeting rising social welfare costs, alongside a growing anti-immigrant sentiment, led the state of California to take a major initiative (Proposition 187) that would deny irregular aliens social services and non-emergency medical care as well as public education (see Chapter 3). In February 1994, the US Attorney-General announced the administration's 'comprehensive response' to immigration. This included a plan to curb irregular immigration that envisaged allocation of additional funds on matters such as improved border control, expulsion of criminal aliens, speedier processing of asylum applications and better enforcement of employer sanctions in 'high violator' industries such as agriculture, construction, garment-making, and janitorial and similar services. As part of a wider reform of the US immigration system, the issue was also addressed by the Commission on Immigration Reform in the interim report which it released in September 1994. Meanwhile, several bills were introduced in US Congress to reduce the level of legal immigration and discourage irregular immigration. As the implementation of the main provisions of California's Proposition 187 remained blocked by

[4] Fraser, op. cit.

adverse court decisions mainly on the grounds that they usurped federal authority, the focus of the debate shifted to Congress.

Even as US Congress was grappling with the issues of immigration, in October 1995 President Clinton, in the face of an increasing threat of irregular immigration, signed a 'presidential decision directive' ordering government agencies to use creatively all legal means to combat international organised crime, including trafficking in migrants. In December 1995, a report submitted to President Clinton by an interagency working group on alien smuggling considered official corruption and lax law enforcement in several countries as facilitating these flows. It recommended a strategy, based on use of diplomacy and increased law enforcement, to deal with migrant smuggling at its source as well as in those transit countries through which migrants are moved to the USA. Although Congress had turned down INS requests for funds to augment US enforcement capability abroad and expand training programmes in foreign countries, the agency was considering at the end of 1995 some internal shifts of budgetary resources to add about 15 more agents to offices abroad.[5] As evidence of the Clinton administration's resolve to fight irregular immigration, the National Democratic Committee recently claimed that the administration has increased border patrols by 40 per cent. According to the latest available information, the INS budget has doubled from $1.5 billion in the 1993 fiscal year to $3.1 billion in the 1997 fiscal year. It should have a permanent staff of 26,000 by the end of 1997.[6]

By May 1996, both the US House of Representatives and the Senate had passed their respective versions of a new, immensely complicated immigration bill, and the two versions were to be reconciled through joint discussion. Both versions included a pilot project to test a more reliable system of employee verification. It would require selected firms to ascertain the legal status of any potential employee, using the social security records, including new standardised birth certificates and a more comprehensive database to be compiled by the INS. The provision, however, continued to be vehemently opposed by some legislators on the grounds that it added to the burden on businesses and was the first step on the slippery path to a national identity card system.[7] There was less controversy about the other provisions to combat irregular immigration, envisaged in both the versions. These would double the number of guards on the border with Mexico, deny welfare and other social benefits to irregular immigrants and increase penalties for trafficking immigrants and document fraud. The final version of the bill, which was adopted in September 1996 retained most of these provisions (see Box 4.1).

---

[5] *The Washington Times*, 3 November 1995; *Washington Post*, 28 December 1995.

[6] *Migration News*, Vol. 4, No. 2, February 1997.

[7] *Financial Times*, London, 3 May 1996.

Box 4.1. The US Illegal Immigration Reform and Immigrant Responsibility Act of 1996

Unlike previous legislation, the 1996 Illegal Immigration Reform and Immigrant Responsibility Act did not create new nonimmigrant categories. It does however, contain important procedural changes to existing nonimmigrant provisions in the United States. One of the most significant changes implemented by IIRIRA provides that a nonimmigrant visa is void as soon as the nonimmigrant alien overstays his or her period of authorized stay, even if by only one day. Thereafter the alien may only be readmitted to the US as a nonimmigrant on the basis of a visa issued in the country of his or her nationality, reapplying in third countries such as Mexico or Canada is no longer allowed and only 'extraordinary circumstances' may constitute exceptions. Among other provisions outlined below which went into effect on April 1 1997, IIRIRA also restricts the ability of federal courts to overturn Immigration and Naturalization Service's (INS) decisions.

A total of 16,000 INS staff at US border posts have been retrained and 75 forms revised in order to implement IIRIRA.

The most significant provisions regarding illegal immigrants are as follows:

Admission

According to IIRIRA the longstanding notion of 'entry' in immigration law will be replaced by 'admission'. From April 1, 1997 onward, whether an alien is charged with inadmissibility or deportablility depends not on whether the alien 'entered' but on whether he or she was 'admitted'. For removal proceedings, aliens who have been 'admitted' to the US will be charged with grounds of deportability while aliens who have not been 'admitted' will be charged with grounds of 'inadmissibility' (formerly 'exclusion'). The difference has implications for the procedure to be followed in removing irregular immigrants.

Inadmissibility and Deportability

Aliens who are 'unlawfully present' in the US for more than 6 months but less than one year after 1 April 1997, who then voluntarily depart from the US, and later seek admission to the US, are inadmissable for three years. Likewise, those aliens who are unlawfully present in the US for one year or more after implementation of IIRIRA and who depart and then seek admission are inadmissable for 10 years. 'Unlawfully present' means that the alien is present after overstaying an authorised period of admission, or without being admitted or paroled. Further, all aliens who enter the US without inspection (EWI) or who 'arrive in the US at any time or place other than as designated by the Attorney General' are inadmissable. Those aliens who are unlawfully present but not 'inadmissable' may be deported.

Removal

The 1996 Act establishes a single 'removal' hearing in place of the current separate deportation and exclusion hearings. The Act also changed two current methods of relief from deportation, INA§212 (c) relief and suspension of deportation to 'cancellation of removal'. Regarding former 'relief of deportation', INS may grant 'cancellation' to an alien who: (a) has been a lawful permanent resident for not less than 5 years; (b) has resided in the US continuously for seven years after having been admitted in any status; and (c) has not been convicted of any aggravated felony.

Likewise, as regards 'suspension of deportation', the INS may cancel removal of an alien who: (a) has been physically present in the US for a continuous period of not less than 10 years immediately preceding the date of such application; (b) has been a person of good moral character during such period; (c) has not been convicted of an offence under INA§§212(a)(2) or 237(a)(3); and (d) establishes that removal would result in exceptional and extremely unusual hardship to the alien's US citizen or permanent resident spouse, parent or child. These are stricter conditions than in the past whereby, foreigners who had lived illegally in the US for seven or more years were quite often granted legal residency – the so-called seven year amnesty. The 1996 Act also placed a numerical limit (4000) on suspension of deportation/cancellation grants.

Further, the IIRIRA saw the implementation of a new system of Expedited Removal which took effect on 1 April 1997 at ports of entry and toughened the consequences for individuals arriving in the US without proper documents. Except for Cubans, all aliens arriving at US ports of entry who are found inadmissable under the INA§§212(a)(6)(C) (misrepresentation) or 212(a)(7) (no valid documentation) grounds of inadmissability will be subjected to the expedited removal procedure. An immigration officer at the port of entry will screen each member of this class of arriving aliens to determine possible asylum intentions or fears of persecution. If the officer finds neither of the above, he/she can order the alien summarily removed from the US. In the case of genuine asylum seekers or a credible fear of persecution, the individual alien is permitted to pursue his/her claim which, according to IIRIRA, must now be filed within one year upon his/her arrival in the United States. The 1996 Act also mandates denial of asylum if the INS determines that the alien may be removed, pursuant to a bilateral or multilateral agreement, to a country (other than the alien's own country) in which the alien's life or freedom would not be threatened. For the immediate future, the expedited removal procedures will only be applied to aliens at ports of entry or interdicted at sea.

Penalties

In keeping with its aim to curb illegal immigration and strengthen penalties, IIRIRA nearly doubles the size of the border patrol forces along the 2,000 mile frontier with Mexico by adding 1,000 agents a year for the next five years. The legislation also increases the penalties for trafficking of migrants and raises the maximum penalty for document fraud to 15 years imprisonment.

Public benefits and affidavits of support

The Personal Responsibility and Work Opportunity Reconciliation Act of 1996 (Welfare Act) has also had implications for irregular immigrants. See Box 4.2 on welfare changes in the United States.

Sources: *Interpreter Releases – report and analysis of immigration and nationality law*, Vol. 74, No. 7 and No. 11, 24 February and 24 March 1997; Migration News, Vol. 4, No. 4 and No. 5, April and May 1997.

It is clearly too early to evaluate the impact of the various specific provisions of new legislation in combatting irregular immigration. Since, however, the report of the Commission on Immigration Reform (1994) served as a basic framework for the new law and is likely to continue to influence the debate on irregular immigration in the coming years, a brief review of some of the Commission's main proposals on irregular immigration could be useful.

The Commission's wide-ranging recommendations concerning irregular immigration include the following: Better border management, enhanced capacities to combat organised smuggling for commercial gain; improved work site enforcement through a more efficient system of verification of work authorisation; anti-discrimination strategies; and more effective enforcement of employer sanctions and labour standards.

Additionally, a major recommendation of the Commission was that illegal aliens should not be eligible for any publicly-funded services or assistance except on an emergency basis or for similar compelling reasons to protect public health and safety (e.g., immunisations and school lunch and child nutrition programme) or to conform to constitutional requirements. The Commission further recommended that future federal legislation should clearly permit states and local authorities to limit benefit eligibility on the same criteria as the federal government. This was to avoid the cost of any restrictions on illegal alien use of federal assistance being shifted to states and localities. The Commission believed that irregular aliens would thus be unable to benefit from any public assistance programmes – federal, state or local and that for all those irregular aliens requiring such assistance, the only recourse would be to return to their countries of origin.

In order to improve procedures for ensuring that only authorised persons receive public benefits, the Commission recommended improvements in the system of identification and verification of alien (regular or irregular) status and the use of the same system for both work authorisation and verification of benefit eligibility. It also recommended pilot programmes to test the efficacy of the proposed new verification procedures. In still another recommendation concerning irregular immigration, the Commission suggested that in the case of mixed households – in which some members are citizens and/or legal residents and others were irregular aliens – only the authorised members should receive public benefits.

The US experience shows that employer sanctions can play a useful, albeit partial, role in discouraging irregular immigration, provided that they can be effectively enforced, and that they are combined with non-discriminatory fulfilment of employers' verification obligations. But, as already noted, this presents difficult choices. Stricter enforcement of the employment eligibility verification system, for example, entails high financial costs and the social costs may be even higher. While simplification of the system through the development of a universal identification document might seem to provide at least a partial solution to some of these problems, it stirs up deep-seated civil liberties concerns.

Previous discussion has also revealed that since irregular immigrants are largely employed in small-scale and family enterprises and in the underground economy, the ability of labour enforcement agencies to reach these enterprises and sectors is severely restricted both by law and due to the limitation of resources. In such a situation, better enforcement of employer sanctions is likely to divert the flows of irregular immigrants into activities in the informal sector. Significantly, at a recent hearing of the US Civil Rights Commission on racial and ethnic tensions, a Chinese-American labour union representative testified that the employer sanctions provision of IRCA is known in New York city's Chinatown as the 'slave law' since it pushed low-wage workers to illegal sweatshops and encouraged the most exploitative employers to bring in thousands of Chinese aboard 'slave ships'.[8] Employer sanctions thus need to be combined with prevention or control of employment of irregular immigrants in the underground economy through other appropriate means and approaches (further discussed in Chapter 5).

As for the denial of public benefits to irregular immigrants, there is little doubt that although the legal difficulties to which reference is made above can be overcome through new legislation, the implementation of such measures could be onerous and expensive for several reasons. First, the verification system as now used under the Systematic Alien Verification for Entitlement (SAVE) programme to determine the benefits eligibility relies mainly on the INS data base which is not always kept up to date. Additional verifications by hand are time-consuming and costly. Second, as in the case of work authorisation, care needs to be taken to ensure that the verification system avoids discrimination and differential treatment of foreign-looking or foreign-sounding applicants, and that it does not infringe upon civil liberties and privacy of information. Whether or not these and other difficulties can be overcome by adopting the new procedures proposed by the Commission remains to be tested.

Finally, the existence of mixed or multiple status households presents several administrative problems and social dilemmas. Especially so since the eligibility unit varies according to programmes of assistance, and may be an individual, a family, a household, or other. To illustrate, irregular immigrants' children born in the USA are entitled to benefits in the form of cash payments under AFDC (Aid to Families with Dependent Children), but the undocumented parents are not. However, as legal care-takers, the parents receive the benefit on behalf of the children. Given that as irregular immigrants the parents are, by law, prohibited from taking up jobs, they have no legal means of supporting the children. Nor could such parents be subjected to mandatory training and work requirements that could help them obtain employment and eventually get off the assistance programme.

---

[8] *Daily Labour Report*, 21 September 1994. *Migration News*, Vol. 1, No. 9, October 1994.

The issue becomes even more complicated in the case of eligibility for housing. The Housing and Community Development Act of 1980 defines the eligibility unit in a broad sense as a family or household. This broad definition makes it difficult to introduce the migration status as an eligibility criterion when the living unit consists of both legal immigrants or citizens (who are eligible to benefits) and unauthorised aliens (who are ineligible). It is not unusual to find households where one parent is a legalised immigrant, the other is an irregular alien and the children are US citizens. There are also families in which one or both parents and possibly one or more children are irregular aliens, while other children are born US citizens. In the words of the Commission itself "the relationship between the eligibility unit and the living unit is a complex aspect of eligibility determination ...'.[9]

Two main conclusions can be drawn from the above analysis. First, even with appropriate legal enactment it would not be easy for the USA to enforce a policy of denial of public benefits to irregular immigrants on an effective and non-discriminatory basis. Achieving this will entail additional administrative effort and financial outlay. Second, even if the measures might provide some fiscal relief for the federal, state and local authorities, it can hardly be relied upon as an effective or adequate deterrent to irregular immigration; nor is it likely to spur any large-scale return of irregular immigrants to countries of origin. The Commission itself seemed hesitant to place full reliance on such measures as an adequate deterrent to irregular immigration as it observed, "... better enforcement of the borders and of the work authorisation procedures also should help to prevent and deter the entry of unauthorised immigrants in the first place ...".[10]

Against the backdrop of the recommendations of the Commission on Immigration Reform and the wide public debate on fiscal deficits alongside rising welfare costs especially for specific groups such as regular and irregular immigrants and unmarried mothers, the US has just decided to embark on a new welfare policy. In August 1996, marking a significant departure in its welfare policy since the New Deal under the Roosevelt administration, it adopted a new welfare bill (The Personal Responsibility and Work Opportunity Reconciliation Act of 1996, see Box 4.2). The new legislation changes the relationship between the federal government and the states, giving state capitals more control over welfare spending. At the same time, it reduces lifetime welfare assistance to a maximum of five years for each family, require recipients to return to work after two years of benefit and place limits on funding for the food stamps and income support programmes for the poor. President Clinton claimed that the new legislation would make 'welfare what it was supposed to be – a second chance, not a way of life.'[11]

---

[9] US Commission on Immigration Reform, *US Immigration Policy: Restoring Credibility*, Washington DC, 1994.

[10] Ibid.

[11] *Financial Times*, London, 1 August 1996.

Box 4.2. United States:
Welfare changes and irregular immigration

The US welfare law (The Personal Responsibility and Work Opportunity Reconciliation Act) signed on 22 August 1996 should have a significant impact on the lives of numerous immigrants in the United States. While former policy made immigrants generally eligible for welfare benefits, the new law makes them generally ineligible. Two major factors led to this decision: society's anti-immigrant feelings as demonstrated by the vote to approve Proposition 187 in California in November 1994; and the need to find savings in order to balance the federal budget. While the law focuses on legal immigrants, it has implications for illegal immigrants as well. First, it excludes almost all noncitizens (legal or illegal) from receiving two significant federal programmes: Food stamps and Supplementary Security Income (SSI), the cash assistance programme for low-income persons who are aged, blind or disabled. Second, by curbing benefits for legal immigrants in general, the law serves to decrease the incentive of people who may migrate illegally in order to receive social services and welfare assistance. At the time of writing, bills seeking to reverse the part of the 1996 welfare law regarding non-citizens are before Congress and immigrants have filed suits in several states against it. Under the budget compromise reached on May 16, 1997, Congress and President Clinton agreed to modify the 1996 welfare law to maintain Supplemental Security Income and Medicaid for disabled legal immigrants who entered the US before August 23, 1996, and those in the US before August 23, 1996 who are disabled or become disabled in the future.

Sources: *Migration News*, Vol. 4, No. 4, 5, 6 April, May and June 1997; *The Economist*, 1–7 March 1997.

Although the new bill is not directly focused on immigration, and far less on irregular immigration, several of its provisions can be expected to have an impact on immigrants including irregular immigrants. First, to the extent that the new legislation provides for reduced welfare for nationals and regular immigrants, there will also be less scope for alleged abuse of the welfare system by irregular immigrants. Second, since under the new bill the state governments are constrained only by a few, and somewhat vague federal standards, they may in the future try their own welfare schemes. And, given that the poor in general, and irregular immigrants in particular, have little political power, at least some state governments may try to further reduce public welfare for the poor, with possible adverse effects on regular and irregular immigrants as well. Third, since the bill envisages a ban on most welfare benefits to legal immigrants who have not yet become US citizens, the welfare cost of regularisation can be further deferred and possibly reduced (through lower welfare usage).[12] Finally, with the devolution of much of the responsibility for designing welfare programmes to the states, the on-going debate (discussed in Chapter 3) concerning the sharing of welfare costs for (regular and irregular) immigrants between the federal and state authorities will no longer have the same relevance. About 44 per cent of the projected savings in welfare costs – $24 billion out of the $54 billion over six years – is expected from cutting benefits to immigrants, regular and irregular.

Western Europe

The rise, both actual and potential, in the numbers of irregular immigrants and the growing links between migrant trafficking and smuggling of arms and drugs have led the West European states to deal with irregular immigration with a new sense of urgency. For the European Union member states, the urgency stems also from their commitment to free movement of persons within the community – an objective that cannot be fulfilled without controlling irregular immigration at the external border.

The measures taken to fight irregular immigration include punitive action such as penalties for illegal entry; sanctions against employers and intermediaries involved in trafficking, employing irregular immigrants or otherwise encouraging irregular immigration; enforcement of legal norms and practices governing immigrant workers' employment and residence; border control through inter-country cooperation and mutual assistance; and dissemination of information in the sending countries on the risks involved in irregular immigration.

Penalty for irregular entry is generally light in Europe. However, in several countries it is punishable by imprisonment for up to six months, and there is a marked trend towards new legislation providing for detention of an apprehended irregular immigrant prior to deportation. Measures against those who work illegally include withdrawal of temporary residence permits, deportation, and in some countries, penalties for irregular workers themselves in the form of imprisonment and/or fines. In a number of Western European, countries the employer is subject to criminal sanctions for illegal employment of foreigners if he/she fails to ascertain that the foreigner is in possession of a valid work permit. A stricter application of these measures in recent years has meant allocation of additional resources, improvement of technology for control and vigilance, introduction of new legislation and, as noted above, closer inter-country cooperation.

In Italy, the Martelli Law on immigration, introduced in 1990, provided the general framework for two main approaches to irregular immigration: regulari-

---

[12] It is worth recalling that irregular immigrants legalised under the 1987–88 programme were not entitled to most welfare benefits until after five years (1993).

sation and expulsion. Following the unexpected landing of thousands of Albanians in March 1991, the perceived 'threat of an invasion' by unwanted immigrants has been gaining ground in the country. In 1992, the tasks of employee welfare inspectorates were widened to include checking on the certificates furnished by non-EC workers when applying for renewal of their residence permits. The checks carried out in different sectors and regions revealed several forms of irregularity – forged employment contracts, fictitious firms and work permits that did not correspond to the sector in question.[13] In August 1993, a new Act was adopted to facilitate the expulsion of immigrants convicted of illegal activities and a decree was issued in the same year to prohibit irregular seasonal employment of foreign workers from developing countries.

However, in the face of the seemingly increasing numbers of irregular immigrants, residing or transiting through Italy, and growing political sensitivity over irregular immigrants, especially of non-European origin, existing measures were considered inadequate. A new urgency to tighten border control also stemmed from the difficulties the country was facing in meeting the March 1995 deadline for giving effect to the Schengen Accord.[14]

As part of a more vigorous move against irregular immigration, a new bill was introduced on 18 November 1995, and pending its adoption by parliament, the new measure was introduced as a cabinet decree. It was designed, *inter alia*, to tighten control measures relating to entry of temporary workers and expulsion of irregular immigrants, while setting into motion a third regularisation programme.

Temporary immigrants mostly from North Africa are brought into Italy to meet labour demands in agriculture, but helped by ineffective controls many of them stay on as they are afraid of not being allowed back into the country. As for expulsion, except in the case of serious crimes, existing procedures allowed 14 days to elapse between a court order and its execution. However, during this intervening period many of the irregulars destroyed documents and disappeared, swelling the ranks of irregular immigrants. In 1995, for example, although 56,015 expulsion orders were issued, no more than 7,417 were executed. The figure for 1994 was 6,139 out of a total of 56,583 expulsion orders.[15]

To deal with these and other aspects of irregular immigration, the new bill includes a number of measures such as: an identity card for those with work permits; immediate expulsions for illegal immigrants; a certificate from the sending country attesting that the job-seeker has not spent more than 30 days

---

[13] OECD, *Trends in International Migration (SOPEMI)*, Paris, 1993.

[14] The Schengen group originally comprising Belgium, France, Germany, the Netherlands and Luxembourg signed in June 1985 what is known as the Schengen Agreement, designed to abolish controls on movement of persons between their territories and harmonise controls on immigration from their countries. These countries were joined by Italy in 1990 and Spain and Portugal in 1991. The Convention on the Application of the Schengen Agreement, which was signed in 1990, covers a wide range of migration issues, including irregular migration.

[15] *Financial Times*, London, 8 February 1996.

in prison for any crime; severe punishment for trafficking in immigrants (carrying a sentence of up to 15 years); heavy sanctions against employers using illegal labour; and refusing family reunification (i) before a minimum of two years' employment, and (ii) in the absence of reliable evidence of the immigrant's financial capacity to support the new members.

The new initiative, sponsored by the right-wing political parties, notably the National Alliance, was not free from criticism. The centre-left political parties were concerned about its negative implications for the protection of human rights. For example, under the bill immediate expulsions allowed no appeal, and the requirement of a certificate from the sending country for those seeking work permits ignored those fleeing oppressive regimes. There was also criticism that the underlying approach was far too simplistic and that more careful attention needed to be given to regulated inflow of temporary labour which was essential for agriculture, while strengthening border controls against illegal flows.

The new measure was, on the other hand, also criticised on the grounds that it was still not tough enough to curb irregular immigration. According to a statement made in February 1996 by Mr. Giovani Rinaldo Coronas, interior minister in the government of Mr. Lamberto Dini, of the 1,973 expulsion orders issued under the new legislation, probably none had been carried out. Unless a person was accused of a serious crime (which would permit immediate deportation) immigrants still had a minimum of 10 days before expulsion orders were executed. The orders were open to challenge in administrative courts, and the immigrants could use the 10 days to evade control, while the problems of obtaining funds to carry out repatriation continued to create additional loopholes.[16]

Meanwhile, however, the police have tightened up border control and their surveillance of immigrant groups and have dismantled several irregular immigration networks. But a major continuing problem lies in the fact that while for purposes of regularisation the law requires the irregular immigrants to enter the regular job market, in most cases they can find employment only if they remain undeclared in the underground economy (further discussed under regularisation).

Spain launched a new drive in 1993 against irregular employment of foreign workers by increasing the frequency of work site inspections and establishing stricter control of social security registrations. In 1992–93, Portugal adopted a number of decrees to better regulate immigration flows and reinforce the fight against irregular immigration through improved control of entry, stay and expulsion of foreigners in an irregular situation.

With such exceptions as the United Kingdom and Ireland, most EU countries as previously noted had already adopted legislation which makes it a criminal offence to employ illegal immigrants. Recently, as part of its drive

---

[16] Ibid, 8 February 1996.

against irregular immigration, the United Kingdom Government, too, decided to move in the same direction by including in the Immigration and Asylum bill a provision which would sanction employers who hire irregular immigrants with penalties running up to £5,000 (US$ 8,000) per illegal worker hired. In addition, the United Kingdom Government has decided to track down irregular immigrants through checks on people seeking social security benefits, council houses and places in schools for their children.

The employer sanction measure, according to the Government, was mainly designed to check the use of illegal immigrants in sweatshops at 'slave labour rates', and would not require the employers to verify the validity of national insurance or other work documents but only to check that they have such documents. The employers were nonetheless unhappy that they were made responsible for policing immigration and that failure to make the checks would be a criminal offence. The Confederation of British Industry, the Association of British Chambers of Commerce and the Institute of Directors have furthermore complained that the proposed legislation would add to the burdens on business. Concern has also been expressed that the measure would have a discriminatory effect on ethnic minorities as companies would concentrate checks on black or Asian workers or might simply exclude them from consideration for employment. Another concern was that it would virtually oblige schools and hospitals to report suspected irregular immigrants. An independent body, led by Sir Ian Glidewell, a former senior member of the judiciary, expressed the view – rebutted by the Government – that the bill would have little chance of achieving its objectives and that its implementation would be expensive and have dangerous implications for race relations.[17] More severe critics maintained that these (and other measures in the bill) "are addressed less at the country's social problems than at the governments electoral problems" – and that "by promoting anti-immigration policies the government risk encouraging racism and undermining liberty".[18] The new bill was passed in1996 and went into effect on 27 January 1997.

In Belgium, since a 1990 measure against the supply of unauthorised labour, workers in the construction sector have been required to have a valid personal identification document. In order to prevent the use of irregular migrant labour under sub-contracting arrangements, the lead contractor is required to inform the National Social Security Office prior to commencement of work on the site; he/she must also keep a list of all workers involved, including those engaged by the sub-contractors.

France has also strengthened its arsenal of legislation intending to curb irregular immigration. An Act of 31 December 1991 introduced new, and tightened up existing, penalties for those guilty of smuggling, transporting, or providing accommodation for undocumented foreigners. It increased the exist-

---

[17] Ibid, 17 April 1996.

[18] *The Economist*, London, 8–15 December 1995.

ing penalties for foreigners who ignore or evade a ban on their entry into the country, an expulsion order or a deportation procedure. The conditions were also tightened up for issuing accommodation certificates required of certain foreigners for a family or private visit to France.

The sanctions against employers of irregular workers have been made more severe and new penalties have been introduced. Employers are now required to be more strict about notification of the hiring of employees. At the same time the definition of undeclared employment has been widened; and in the case of subcontracting arrangements, all the operators involved are made jointly liable for the use of undeclared labour. Also, inter-ministerial coordination to combat irregular immigration and employment now extends to the departmental level. Under different rules and regulations, a number of measures (e.g. withdrawal of a short-stay visa issued to a foreigner if the person takes up an employment without authorisation and checking of students' visas) have been taken to speed up action against irregular immigration and unauthorised employment.[19]

While hiring undocumented aliens was already punishable through imprisonment, a new law introduced in December 1994 stipulated that anyone helping illegal immigrants would also be liable to imprisonment. The Government has sought to justify these measures on the grounds of rising numbers of irregular immigrants and the spread of migrant trafficking and terrorism. But there has also been criticism about the severity of some of these measures. The Protestant Federation of France, for example, announced in October 1995 that it would defy the 1994 Law by continuing to help aliens in need, whether they had valid documents or not.

The publication in April 1996 of the report of an all-party Parliamentary commission on irregular immigration – the so-called Sauvagio report, named after the deputy who acted as secretary to the commission – created sharp political divisions.[20] The report contained 46 proposals to limit the entry and stay of foreigners and reduce irregular immigration though a series of tough measures. These included: an extension of the period of administrative detention from 10 to 45 days; systematic recording of finger prints to facilitate the identification of irregular immigrants who destroy their identity documents; denial of medical assistance to those classified as illegal except in cases of emergency and contagious diseases; withdrawal of French nationality from employers of foreign origin who employ clandestine workers; restrictions on educational facilities for children of foreign parents without authorisation of residence; and suppression of the ban on expelling children of foreigners in an irregular situation. Even the government seemed divided on the whole issue: Mr. Xavier Emmanuelli, minister for humanitarian assistance, for example, commented that the report contained 'unacceptable and scandalous' ideas.

---

[19] OECD, *Trends in International Migration (SOPEMI)*, Paris, 1993.

[20] *Financial Times*, 20/21 April 1996; *Migration News Sheet*, May 1996.

While the adoption of a new general law is not very likely, the government had made known its intention to amend and 'complete' the existing laws on immigration even before the publication of the report.

The new government in France, led by Mr. Lionel Jospin, has announced its intention to present in August 1997 an Immigration Bill aimed at amending the laws passed in 1993 and early in 1997, (the so-called Pasqua and Debré laws). Meanwhile, it has issued a new decree permitting a re-examination of the conditions governing the issuance of residence permits for foreigners. This would affect eleven categories of foreigners who were without valid residence permits and were thus in an irregular situation.[21]

In 1991, the German government reaffirmed its intention to continue its efforts both on the national and international levels to effectively combat illegal practices connected with entry, residence and employment of foreigners in the country, including through the abuse of the asylum procedure.[22] On 1 July in the same year, it introduced a new rule requiring all dependent workers to be in possession of a social security card with a photograph, to be presented to an employer on request. An employer engaging a foreign worker has the obligation of informing the social security authorities of the appointment date and a foreigner receiving unemployment or sick pay must deposit the social security card at the paying-out office. In some industries such as construction, janitorial services and restaurants, workers must carry their cards at work. The authorities are empowered to check on employers and ask them to produce their workers' social security cards.

The labour ministry which is responsible for enforcing laws against employment of irregular foreigners and unlawful use of employment and other social benefits by foreign (and German) workers, carries out these tasks by comparing payroll tax and employment data, by verifying information on foreign worker employment against a central register of data on foreigners and by visiting workplaces.

In the Netherlands, new employer sanctions were introduced in 1991. The employers have been made responsible for the cost of expulsion of foreign irregular workers. Additional inspectors have been recruited to help detect the employment of undocumented workers and step up the frequency of checks.[23] New legislation (1993) concerning identification obligations specifies the places and situations in which all persons are required to identify themselves. Border control has been tightened and immigration officials are now stationed at the airports to identify those suspected of overstaying their tourist visas. Norway has established a special bureau to centralise information collected by different agencies, including the police, airline companies and embassies as part of its

---

[21] *Journal Officiel*, 26 June 1997, *Migration News Sheet*, July 1997.

[22] Federal Ministry of the Interior, 'Survey of the policy and law regarding aliens in the Federal Republic of Germany', 1991 (mimeo).

[23] OECD, *Trends in International Migration (SOPEMI)*, Paris, 1992.

Table 4.2. Amnesties for illegal immigrants, in selected countries and areas

Country or area	Year	Numbers regularized/applicants
Argentina	1984	142,330
France	1981/82	124,101
Italy	1987/88	105,176
Italy	1990	216,000
Italy	1996	N/A
Malaysia	1992	320,000
Netherlands	1975	13,930
Netherlands	1992	70,000
Portugal	1992/1993	38,364
Republic of Korea	1992	61,000
Spain	1985/86	43,815
Spain	1991	108,848
Taiwan, China	1991/1992	22,579
United States	1986	2,483,348

Sources: Stalker, *The Work of Strangers*, 1994; *SOPEMI*, OECD, Paris 1990 and 1976; *Corriere della Sera*, 18 January 1996; *Migration News Sheet*; January and December 1992; January 1994

reinforced efforts to check irregular immigration. In Greece, concern about the rise in irregular immigration prompted the minister of public order to announce on 21 February 1994 that a specially trained, 400-strong police force would use jeeps and electronic devices to deter irregular entrants.[24]

Regularisation, expulsion and carrier sanctions in Western Europe As discussed above, stricter border control, increasingly stringent punitive measures against traffickers (further discussed below) and any one who promotes irregular immigration and employer sanctions are among the most common approaches adopted by the governments in Western Europe to combat irregular immigration. Since most of them also rely on regularisation and, increasingly, on expulsion and carrier sanctions it is useful to briefly review the application of these latter measures.

In the past, many West European governments, including France (1981/82), Italy (1987/88, 1990 and 1996), the Netherlands (1975, 1992), Spain (1991), and Portugal (1992/93) have used *regularisation* as part of their approach to deal with irregular immigration (Table 4.2). A few of them have announced further regularisation programmes for the coming years. But, in general, there is a growing reluctance to rely on regularisation especially in dealing with future situations so that the irregular aliens may not have the feeling that their status would be regularised simply with the passage of time.

The response to most regularisation programmes in the past has generally been rather limited. An important reason for this limited response relates to

[24] 'Public Order Minister announces formation of special border police', BBC, 23 February 1994.

the regularisation rules and the method of implementation. In the case of the Netherlands, for example, it has been observed that the requirements stipulated in the ministerial circular of 18 March 1975 (which provided for the regularisation of the immigrants in an irregular situation) were such that they were practically inapplicable to immigrants who did not already have valid papers. But those who could meet these requirements were hardly likely to enter the country in a clandestine manner.[25]

Similarly, the requirement under the French Act of 17 October 1981 that the applicant must be holding a steady job since before 1 January 1981 could not be met by many applicants; and the notion of a 'steady' job was itself subject to varying interpretations. Clearly, immigrants may be prevented from holding a steady job for reasons of illness or pregnancy. On the other hand, the requirement of a pre-working contract for regularisation may lead to an underground market for selling such contracts issued by fictitious firms. This was experienced, for example, in Spain during the 1991 regularisation exercise when large numbers of false work contracts were reported to have been sold to Moroccan irregular immigrants.[26]

This apart, a risk inherent in regularisation, even when it exempts employers of any punishment for their misdeeds in the past, is that they might get rid of the irregular immigrant workers – because of the fear of being identified for future surveillance. The fact that they may have to meet obligations arising from employment of irregular immigrants and that they would no longer be able to benefit from cheap and docile labour may also lead employers to fire irregular immigrant workers before the initiation of the regularisation process. The potential danger of losing jobs may in turn discourage irregular immigrants from seeking regularisation and induce them to accept still more precarious jobs, defeating one of the main purposes of regularisation. The French experience suggests the wisdom of uncluttering the eligibility rules from restrictions that are unfair to the irregular immigrants or are counter productive.[27]

The experience of Italy is equally revealing. Under its 1996 regularisation programme, the irregular immigrant and his/her employer (who must be an Italian) must declare a regular job and pay at least six months' social contributions in arrears. By 31 March 1996 (the cut-off date for submitting applications), 248,950 applications had been received, about 54,000 less than the number of permits that had expired since the second regularisation (i.e. between 1991 and the end of 1994).[28] Many among the group that refrained from applying thought that they would gain more by remaining in an irregular situation. This

---

[25] Marta Peletier, 'Regularisation and Obligations of Unauthorized Immigrants in the Receiving Countries. Protection of the Fundamental Rights of Unauthorized Immigrants', *International Migration* Vol. XXI, No 2, 1983, p. 179.

[26] *El Pais*, 3 September 1991.

[27] J.P. Garson and Y. Moulier, 'Clandestine immigrants and their regularisation in France 1981–82', ILO, Geneva, May 1982 (mimeo).

[28] OECD, 'Irregular immigration in Italy', Note by the Secretariat, 5 June 1995, Paris (mimeo).

is because many employers who live off the underground economy would hire them only if they were undeclared.

Regularisation also raises other practical problems. These include fixing the effective date from which regularised immigrants should have the status of lawfully admitted foreigners in countries where foreigners must spend a specified period of time before qualifying for security of stay and free choice of employment. If the actual date of entry is recognised as the starting point, it would be discriminatory against regular immigrants and is likely to encourage future irregular immigration. On the other hand, should the regularisation date be reckoned as the starting point, the danger of being refused permission to work for some time following regularisation may make some irregular immigrants reluctant to reveal themselves.[29]

An additional point that deserves attention is that legalisation of irregular immigrants often opens door for multiple immigration benefits. In the United States, for example, the IRCA regularisation programme bestowed temporary legal status to 2.3 million Mexicans, of which 2.1 million were expected to become US permanent residents. Should permanent residency confer immigration petition rights for the spouses and children of principal immigrants, it would be logical to anticipate that in most cases these rights would be fully used. In the United States, a provision of the Act of 1 October 1991 had the further effect of allocating most immigration visas for spouses and children of lawful US permanent residents. This implied that, within the country-specific numerical limits, Mexicans (and others) in the category of legalised permanent residents would be in a position to make quicker use of their family reunification rights.

Other entitlements or benefits could also follow as an upshot of the regularisation process. For example, in the USA, after having remained in the status of a permanent legal resident for 5 years, an alien may become a naturalised citizen; citizenship in turn bestows on the person additional immigration rights – such as petitioning rights for *immediate* reunification with their parents, spouses and minor children and also for reunification (with delays) with their unmarried adult children and siblings. Thus, to the extent that illegal immigration is motivated by the urge for family reunification, the new immigration opportunities may be expected to reduce the pressure for irregular inflows. At the same time, entry through family reunification may have important implications for the labour market, for example, in terms of the skill and ethnic composition of the labour force, and may therefore need to be harmonised with the country's labour market policies.

Deportation or expulsion, a direct opposite to regularisation, has been used by most Western European countries, and in recent years it has indeed become one of their important means to deal with the problem. Recent legislative changes in the Netherlands, for example, reinforce the detention and expulsion

---

[29] W. R. Böhning, 'Regularising the irregular', *International Migration*, Vol. XXI, No. 2, 1983, p. 165.

of illegally resident foreigners. The basic legal provisions of almost all states guarantee the right of foreigners to apply to the courts to challenge an expulsion order issued by the competent administrative authorities. But, as in the case of Italy (discussed above), the changes introduced or contemplated in immigration laws to maximize the authorities' control over foreigners in an irregular situation may fail to give adequate recognition of this right; or even if recognised, it may not be always fully respected. Human rights groups and migrant-serving associations have been vocal in criticizing these trends and have maintained that in many instances the government follows a policy which is tougher and less humane than legislation provides.

In the absence of the relevant documents such as a valid passport or an identity card showing the nationality of the irregular migrant and the cooperation of the country of origin to facilitate readmission, the receiving countries find it difficult to implement deportation measures. This often adds to the political sensitivity of the situation. Many receiving countries are now trying to overcome this difficulty by signing readmission agreements on a bilateral or multilateral basis (further discussed later in this Chapter).

Carrier sanctions Like the USA, a number of Western European countries, including France, Germany, the Netherlands and the United Kingdom impose fines on airlines carrying passengers who are without the papers required for admission. The Netherlands is the only country where imprisonment for up to six months is allowed if the person concerned failed to carry out their checking duties properly or to maintain necessary records.

In France, when a passenger is refused entry, the carrier must take the person back to the port of boarding or if this is impossible to the country which issued the travel document used or to any other place which will accept the person. Finland and Switzerland are among the countries which do not have carrier sanction laws, while Norway has the necessary legislation that permits carrier sanctions in the form of fines, although it is hardly applied. The Spanish law (27/1992 of 24 November) on Seaports and Mercantile Marine contains provisions for fines in the case of trafficking by sea.

It is of course not always very easy for carriers to detect travel documents that are not genuine. Several West European governments therefore provide training to the airline staff to help them carry out this task, following the example of Canada where cooperation and mutual assistance between the government and the airline carriers are well advanced and are based on a memorandum of understanding.

Heavy penalties on carriers, especially in the case of sea vessels, can sometimes create most awkward situations and even human tragedies. The problems were highlighted by an incident which took place in 1992 when six Ukrainian sailors were brought to trial by the French authorities and charged of killing eight African stowaways to avoid paying hefty fines and the obligation of maintaining the stowaways on board the ship until their eventual repatriation to the country of origin.[30] It is reported that some ships have had the experience of carrying on board their stowaways for several years and that even the presence of a single stowaway can devalue the price of a ship on sale.

Australia and Japan

Although in Australia the problem of irregular immigration has not assumed the same proportion as in Europe or North America, the government recently introduced a set of measures to toughen control of irregular residence and employment of foreigners. The amendments to the Migration Act which came into effect on 1 September 1994 facilitate the deportation of foreigners illegally residing in the country. At the same time the inspection of workplaces has been reinforced as well as the penalties for fraud associated with irregular immigration, although the punishment for illegal entry has been reduced from 2 years' imprisonment to a fine.

In Japan where, as noted in Chapter 1, despite strict border control irregular immigration has become a serious problem, an amendment was introduced in 1989 to the 1951 Immigration Control Act providing for heavy fines and terms of imprisonment for employers and agents recruiting irregular immigrants. At the same time a committee has been set up to better coordinate the efforts of the Ministry of Labour, the Ministry of Justice and the immigration authorities to curb irregular immigration. Other measures include a reinforcement of the immigration inspection service, use of improved techniques for identifying fraudulent documents and increased deportation of foreigners, including numbers of irregular foreign workers.

4.2. Central and Eastern Europe

To curb irregular immigration, Central European countries which are used by irregulars both as final destinations and more often as transit points have recently adopted various measures. The Czech Republic and Slovakia, for example, are seeking a solution to the problem through more intensive border control, close collaboration with neighbouring countries and improved legislation concerning the entry and stay of foreigners.[31]

In addition to strengthened border control and improved immigration legislation, including revision of non-visa agreements with other countries, Hungary has relied on expulsion and repatriation to deal with irregular immigration, including trafficking. To illustrate, from 1 October to the end of December 1991, about half a million irregular immigrants were expelled from the country; another half a million were expelled in the first ten months of

---

[30] *Le Monde*, 16 November 1995; *Liberation*, 29 November 1995; and *Migration News Sheet*, December 1995.

[31] OECD, *Trends in International Migration*, 1993, op. cit., p. 126.

1992. Control of overstayers has also been strengthened, although expulsion and turning back have been the most frequent form of action against irregular inflows. Experience suggests however that the latter is not the most effective method and that it is extremely expensive, costing on average over $1,200 per person.[32] On 22 March 1996, Hungary adopted a regularisation programme, which became effective on 30 April and should last until 30 August 1996. It was targeted on those who entered and resided in the country as regular immigrants but subsequently became irregular due to the stricter rules under the new Aliens Act which became effective on 1 May 1994.[33]

In Poland, employers can be fined zl 5000 ($1,850) for each irregular worker, but as in most other countries of the region, lack of staff and resources make it difficult for the authorities to locate irregular foreign workers. In June 1992, Romania adopted new laws to reinforce border control against irregular immigration. Illegal entry is punishable by imprisonment ranging from three months to two years and migrant trafficking is subject to heavy fines and imprisonment.

In general, legislation on employers sanctions is less developed in Central and East Europe than in western industrial countries; and in those countries where such legislation exists, the sanction takes the form of fines rather than imprisonment of the employer.[34]

4.3. Developing Countries

Some developing countries have used regularisation programmes as a means of tackling the problem of irregular immigration. Argentina, for example, has used this method several times during the past few decades involving several hundred thousand persons, mainly from Bolivia. The 1984 programme led to the regularisation of 142,230 persons. Venezuela has used both regularisation and expulsions to address the problem. Its 1980 regularisation programme involved 267,000 persons, of which 46 per cent were women.[35] Around the same period it deported thousands of irregular immigrants, mainly from Colombia. Some Latin American governments are also tightening up employer sanctions. The Argentine Government, for example, recently proposed to increase fines to $100,000 and prison terms up to six years, for employers who hire illegal foreign workers.[36]

Other developing countries/areas that used regularisation include the Republic of Korea (1992), Malaysia (1992), Taiwan, China (1991/92) and

---

[32] Ibid.

[33] *Migration News Sheet*, May 1996.

[34] 'Harmonization of Legislation to Combat Trafficking in Aliens', paper prepared for the third meeting of the Budapest Group (set up by the Budapest Conference of Ministers to Prevent Uncontrolled Migration) Zurich, September, 1995, p. 21.

[35] United Nations International Research and Training Institute for the Advancement of Women, *The Migration of Women*, Santa Domingo, 1994, p. 78.

[36] *Agence France Presse*, 14 February 1996.

Thailand (1996). The new Thai regulations approved by the Cabinet allow irregular workers from Cambodia, Laos and Myanmar who entered the country before 25 June 1996 to be legalised for two years in two sectors – waterways transportation and manufacturing. Thai employers are required to register them as illegal workers with the local police, bail them out, and then register them at the local labour office between July 1996 and June 1997.[37]

Some developing countries have imposed heavy penalties on irregular immigrants. In Singapore, for example, the penalties for irregular immigration were recently stiffened; since March 1989, foreigners entering the country illegally and those convicted of overstaying 90 days or more shall receive, in addition to a mandatory jail term of three months, three strokes of the cane. A new law, which came into effect in March 1996, makes the general contractor responsible for all violations of immigration laws on construction sites. In April 1994, Malaysian Parliament took a new initiative to increase fines on employers who hired irregular immigrants from M$5000 (US$ 2,500) to M$ 50,000 (US$ 25,000), and subject them to be caned as in Singapore.[38] In Hong Kong, irregular workers are subject to a mandatory prison sentence of 15 months and a fine. Employers, too, are liable to imprisonment for up to three years and may be required to pay a fine, while sub-contractors are black-listed by the government and principal contractors and are debarred from future sub-contract work.[39]

In Taiwan, China under the new Act of 1992, employers engaging irregular workers face sanctions which include fines or a three-year jail sentence.[40] Sanctions against irregular employment have also been strengthened in Thailand, where a revised law which came into force in 1991 provides for increased fines or up to one year's jail sentence or both for employers who are found to illegally employ foreign workers for the first time. For repeated offences the sanctions become heavier and include mandatory jail sentences of up to one year, in addition to the stipulated fines.[41] The National Security Council is hopeful that stepped up border control and sanctions would reduce irregular entry and plans to force all irregular workers out of the country by 1998. In Bangladesh, severe punitive actions, including death penalties, are being considered for those involved in trafficking of women and children for sexual and commercial exploitation. Labour recruiting agents involved in irregular migration run the risk of losing their official licenses and are now also subject to prosecution on criminal charges.

---

[37] *Migration News*, Vol. 3, No. 8, August 1996.

[38] 'Caning, stiffer fines to stop influx of illegal immigrants', *New Straits Times*, 18 March 1994, *Migration News*, Vol. 1 No. 3, April 1994.

[39] Anthony Gar-on Yeh, *Foreign Labour in Hong Kong: Trends, Impacts and Implications*, 1990; OECD, *Migration Trends in Some Asian Countries*, 1993, op. cit, p. 21.

[40] Roger Mark Selya, 'Illegal Migration in Taiwan: A Preliminary Overview', *International Migration Review*, Vol. 26, Fall 1992.

[41] OECD, *Migration Trends in Some Asian Countries*, 1993, op. cit, p. 21.

In Africa, mass expulsions have been used as one of the main measures by states to deal with situations created by irregular inflows. Ivory Coast expelled Beninese irregulars in 1964, Senegal expelled Guineans and Cameroon expelled Nigerians in 1967. About half a million irregular aliens, who were without residence permits as of 2 December 1969, from Nigeria, Upper Volta (now Burkina Faso) and Niger were expelled by Ghana. In 1971, Zambia ordered all alien workers without valid permits to leave the country; and Zaire (now Congo), Gabon, Niger and Ethiopia have used expulsion at one time or another to deal with irregular immigration. A widely known example of mass expulsion of undocumented aliens is the deportation order issued by Nigeria in January 1983 to aliens without residence permits (discussed in Chapter 1). Despite some relaxation subsequently introduced in its application, the expulsion order was estimated to have led to an exodus of 1.5 to 2 million persons, of whom some 700,000 were from Ghana.[42] Another expulsion followed on 15 April 1985 when the Government ordered that undocumented immigrants who could not obtain valid residence permits by 10 May of the same year must leave the country. It was estimated at that time that around 700,000 immigrants (300,000 from Ghana) would be affected.[43] More recently, in March 1994, the government announced that irregular immigrants in Nigeria must obtain residence permits by June 1994, and that after that date all irregular immigrants would be deported. At the same time border controls have been tightened to prevent irregular immigrants from entering the country.[44]

Recent measures against trafficking As discussed in Chapter 1, trafficking in migrants is not new, but over the past few years it has expanded in scale and gained in complexity and sophistication. Its growing links with trafficking in drugs and arms and its frequent involvement in women prostitution and child abuse have turned it into a most menacing form of irregular migration. Although the discussion above makes brief references to the subject, the legal measures being taken against human trafficking merit some further discussion in this Chapter.

While legislation against illegal entry has long existed in most receiving countries as part of their immigration control, laws targeting specifically against the traffickers of migrants were previously confined to a few countries. However, with the recent expansion of human trafficking, most industrial states and several states in Central and Eastern Europe have adopted specific laws against alien trafficking. Australia and Spain are among the notable exceptions (Table 4.1). However, in Australia, prosecution for alien trafficking is possible

---

[42] Aderanti Adepoju, 'Expulsion of Illegals from Nigeria: round two', *Migration World*, Vol. 14, No. 5, 1986, pp. 21–24.

[43] Aderanti Adepoju, 'International Migration in Africa South of the Sahara, *International Migration Today*, Vol. I, UNESCO and University of Western Australia, 1988.

[44] 'Nigeria: Illegal immigrants to be deported', Inter-Press Service, 17 March 1994.

under the Migration Act; and in Spain, a decision was recently taken to include alien trafficking as a specific crime in the new Criminal Act. In most countries, existing criminal codes and other relevant laws make it possible to punish human trafficking when related to other criminal activities.

In relation to its 1996 decree on the regularisation of immigrants without resident permits, the Italian government introduced a new provision designed to help fight trafficking of women into prostitution. The new legislation enables any third country immigrant who provides the police with information about forced prostitution, arms or drug trafficking, extortion or Mafia involvement, to receive a special residence permit. This provision aims at dismantling the networks which traffic African and Albanian women into Italy for prostitution. The special residence permit is granted for as long as the cooperating immigrants is required to stay in Italy, and in certain circumstances may be withdrawn by the police.[45]

A number of the industrial countries are currently reviewing their anti-trafficking statutes either to enhance the penalties or toughen the legislation in other ways. Under the new US legislation, for example, the usual sanction has been raised to 10 years' imprisonment. Maximum penalty can reach 20 years' imprisonment when human trafficking entails bodily injury or places life in jeopardy; and where death results, life imprisonment or death penalty is permitted. At the same time the US has also taken several new operational measures against trafficking such as Operation Global Reach (see Box 4.3).

A new law in Belgium makes alien trafficking a criminal activity punishable by 15 years' forced labour. In Denmark, the penalty has been raised to two years under a new Act of 18 January 1995 and in the Netherlands the possibility of raising the imprisonment from one year to 4 to 8 years was under consideration.

Several countries in Central and Eastern Europe have also tightened their anti-trafficking legislation and in most of them human trafficking is considered a criminal act. In a few countries (e.g. Poland), where legislation concerning criminalisation of trafficking is lacking, alien smuggling is treated as an act aiding and abetting the crime of illegal border crossing.

Clearly, the definition of trafficking is critically important as it determines the scope of the law and the action that can be taken under it. National laws seem to diverge on whether the criminal offence of trafficking relates only to the foreigners' entry into the country or whether it also covers their residence in, and exit from, the country.[46] A related, and equally important, definitional issue concerns the geographical scope of the anti-trafficking legislation – whether the criminal offence of trafficking covers deeds both inside and outside

---

[45] *Trafficking in Migrants* (Quarterly Bulletin), No. 13, IOM, Geneva, December 1996.

[46] See in this connection, 'Harmonization of Legislation to Combat Trafficking in Aliens', 1995. Paper presented to the third meeting of the Budapest Group, Zurich 14–15 September 1995 (mimeo).

Box 4.3. Operation Global Reach:
A new anti-trafficking initiative in the United States

Under a new initiative called *Operation Global Reach*, the Immigration and Naturalization Service (INS) of the United States has decided for the first time to establish a permanent presence of US criminal investigators and intelligence analysts overseas to work on deterring migrant trafficking in source and transit countries. The premise behind Global Reach is that it is much less expensive to prevent people from migrating illegally outside the US than it is to expel or deport them once they are in the country. The new Global Reach staff will focus on: (1) training foreign law enforcement and airline officials to identify fraudulent documents; (2) improving liaison and cooperation with host country officials to deter migrant trafficking; (3) developing information for the successful persecution of alien smugglers in the US and host countries; and (4) strengthening cooperation of host country migration and law enforcement officials in investigating and persecuting smugglers. The new staff will also work with State Department officials to provide 'enhanced immigration services' to qualified applicants in each host country. Changes implemented by Global Reach include the opening of 13 new overseas offices and the assignment of 45 additional officers to counter international trafficking of migrants. These officers are all 'highly trained INS officers – many of whom already have overseas experience and speak two or more languages. All are trained to detect document fraud'. The 45 officers will be supervised by the office of International Affairs and the three INS overseas district offices in Rome, Bangkok and Mexico City.

Source: Interpreter Releases, Vol. 74, No. 24, June 30, 1997.

the country, or only those that take place inside the country. Article 23 of the Swiss Aliens Law probably provides one of the broadest definitions on both these counts by stipulating: "Who, in Switzerland *or abroad*, facilitates or helps to prepare an illegal *entry or exit or an illegal stay* is punished ...". The Austrian legislation (Article 80 of the Aliens Law) is also quite wide in scope, although it does not go as far as the provision in Swiss law: "Trafficking is facilitating illegal entry or exit of an alien, irrespective of whether this occurs before or after the crossing of the border or during the foreigners' stay in the country".

The prospects of a harmonised approach to anti-trafficking legislation are being explored by the states belonging to the so-called Budapest Group, consisting of 40 European states.[47] An expert group which was set up by the

[47] The group was set up by the Budapest Ministerial Conference to Prevent Uncontrolled Migration, held in February 1993. It now comprises some 40 states in Western, Central and Eastern Europe, with Canada and the USA as observers.

Table 4.3. Anti-trafficking legislation in selected countries: the geographical and operational coverage of criminalisation clauses

	Entry	Stay	Exit	Abroad (other states)
Austria	×		×	×
Czech R.	×	×		
Germany	×	×		
Hungary	×			
Slovak R.				
Slovenia	×			
Switzerland	×	×	×	×

Source: 'Harmonisation of legislation to combat trafficking in aliens'. Paper prepared by Belgium (Schengen Presidency), Austria and ICMPD for the third meeting of the Budapest Group, Zurich, 14–15 September 1995

participating states to examine this and other issues, recently made a comparative analysis of the scope of the national laws in terms of their geographical and operational coverage. Some of the differences in the scope of national laws of selected countries, as identified by the group are encapsulated in Table 4.3.

The discussion at a recent meeting (September 1995) of the states participating in the Budapest Group led to a recognition of the importance of broadening the geographical scope of national legislation, for example, along the lines of the Swiss law. Under the Budapest Process consideration was also being given to the possibility of an anti-trafficking convention for the European region as a whole. It is worth noting that the Schengen agreement already envisions a wider geographical scope of anti-trafficking legislation by creating a common anti-trafficking area in which all member states are to penalise the planning and carrying out of trafficking operations directed towards any of the member states, irrespective of where the planning take place. This is reflected in Article 92A concerning the crime of trafficking of the revised German Aliens Law.

As indicated in Chapter 1, trafficking encompasses many operations, and there are a variety of ways in which it can be aided and abetted. In most countries where migrant trafficking is a criminal offence, the punishability also covers acts such as transporting and harbouring and other related activities. In fact, as shown in Table 4.1, legislation on aiding and abetting generally (but not always) carries the same penalty as the trafficking itself. A notable exception is the legislation in the United Kingdom where a trafficker can be sentenced up to seven years' imprisonment but the maximum penalty for aiding and abetting a trafficker is only 6 months. A possible change in the latter provision was under consideration. In the USA, the maximum penalty for aiding and abetting is five years imprisonment which is less than for trafficking. Many countries including Belgium and Denmark, which recently increased the penalty for trafficking, have done the same for activities that aid and abet it.

Almost all traffickers in migrants use fraudulent documents and some of the larger syndicates often produce them. Penalties for possession of fraudulent documents are generally less severe than for producing them. Most countries have laws providing for penalties for the production of fraudulent documents. In some of them, the laws are of a general nature to cover crimes of forgery and falsification of documents, and they cover fraudulent travel documents produced or used for migrant trafficking. In other cases, there are specific laws applicable to fraudulent documents produced or used to facilitate human trafficking. For the countries listed in Table 4.1, the maximum penalties for production of fraudulent documents range from 6 months to 15 years. The wide differences in the maximum penalties are partly due to divergence in the scope of the national laws.

An important deterrent to human trafficking concerns the forfeiture of the traffickers' income and the means of transport used in trafficking. Most industrial countries and a number of countries in Central and Eastern Europe have legal provisions for confiscation of income gained and/or property used in connection with human trafficking. Several of them (e.g. the USA) have specific provisions on alien smuggling and forfeiture; others, including Italy and the Netherlands, make use of the general provisions included in the penal code that covers a wide range of criminal offences.

As regards action against trafficking in women, a significant recent trend lies in treating them as victims rather than criminals. Under this approach, they should have access to medical, financial and legal assistance and be assured police protection during and after the trials of suspected traffickers. Indicative of this trend is the recent EU declaration on guidelines for measures to combat trafficking in women (see Box 4.4).

Three additional points need to be briefly mentioned. First, the efficacy of action against human trafficking is not just a matter of legislation; much depends also on how effectively the legal provisions are applied. Second, meaningful action against trafficking cannot be isolated from other complementary and supporting measures that enhance the effectiveness of pre-entry and border control and increase the risks for traffickers and potential immigrants, serving as deterrents both to traffickers and those seeking to use their services. Third, given that human trafficking is being increasingly organised through global networking, traffickers are likely to exploit those states that have inadequate legislation and less efficient instruments to deal with the operations.

4.4. International rules and norms

Under the auspices of the United Nations, the ILO and various regional bodies such as the Council of Europe and the European Community/Union, an array of international and regional instruments have been adopted in recent years that are of relevance to irregular migration, including trafficking and employment of irregular migrants. Broadly speaking, international and regional instru-

Box 4.4. European Union Protection for Trafficked Women

The European Union has agreed on a plan designed to protect foreign women trafficked and forced into prostitution. During a Ministerial conference in the Hague in April 1997, the members of the European Union adopted a declaration on European guidelines for effective measures to prevent and combat the trade. The Hague conference was also attended by ten Central and Eastern European countries in view of the fact that female nationals of these States are frequently victims of trafficking. Among other things, conference members agreed to grant temporary residence to foreign women without valid papers, a measure already followed in the Netherlands and Belgium. This move intends to encourage the women to provide evidence against pimps and traffickers. The women will therefore be allowed to stay in the host country, at least until the suspects have been tried. With respect to granting residence permits, the only limit is that such a move must be compatible with national legislation on the matter.

The Conference especially emphasized that trafficked women should be viewed and treated as victims rather than criminals. They should have access to appropriate social, medical, financial and legal assistance and should be assured of police protection both during and after the trials of suspected traffickers. Further, the EU ministers agreed to increase the exchange of information through Europol and to cooperate closely to expose international networks of trafficking in women. All of the above guidelines emerging from the conference are not binding and each country has the liberty to decide what methods will be used to implement the proposals.

Source: *Trafficking in Migrants – Quarterly Bulletin*, No. 15, IOM Geneva, June 1997.

ments deal with two major aspects of the issue: the protection of certain basic rights of migrants in an irregular situation and measures to combat irregular migration. In the earlier stages the emphasis was on the eradication of clandestine immigration, but gradually a more balanced approach has emerged, with protection of irregular migrants receiving due attention alongside preventive measures. More recently, however, at least in some of the regional instruments the preventive measures are again receiving special attention, possibly at the expense of the protection aspects.

Many of the international instruments (e.g. the Covenants on Civil and Political Rights and on Economic, Social and Cultural Rights, the International Convention on the Elimination of all Forms of Discrimination), adopted during 1960–70, relating to human rights apply to all persons within the territory of a ratifying state and thus cover irregular immigrants. However, since the early

1970s, irregular migration has been the focus of attention in various international and regional organisations.[48] In some cases, the instruments are specifically concerned with the migrants in an irregular situation. In other instances, they have dealt with the issue under instruments of wider scope covering all migrants. Examples of these two groups of instruments include ILO Conventions no. 97 concerning migration for employment and no. 143 concerning migration in abusive conditions and promotion of equality of opportunity and treatment of all workers, as well as the International Convention on the Protection of Rights of All Migrant Workers and Members of Their Families, adopted by the UN on 18 December 1990.

One of the first initiatives in this area was taken by the ILO when in 1939 – just before the outbreak of the Second World War – it adopted an international Convention (no. 66) and a Recommendation (no. 62) on migration for employment. The instruments were primarily of a preventive nature, designed, *inter alia*, to arrest false and misleading propaganda in favour of irregular migration and regulate measures for recruitment and placement of migrant workers, including supervision by competent authorities when the operations were carried out by private agencies. In 1949, when labour shortages especially in Western European countries had already been encouraging large-scale migratory movements, the ILO adopted a new Convention (no. 97) and a new Recommendation (no. 86) in order to broaden the scope of the previous instruments and formulate detailed standards covering preparation for migration, recruitment and placement, with an emphasis on the supervisory role of public services. Activities of private agencies were sought to be strictly regulated and penalties against misleading propaganda were increased and those for encouraging irregular migration specified in detail.

By the early 1970s the situation had changed again. With a sharp rise in labour migration and increasing problems of irregular migrants, alongside growing signs of economic slowdown in Western Europe, international attention turned to the treatment of regular migrants, on the one hand and the social and human problems created by irregular migration, on the other. The outcome was the adoption in 1975 by the ILO of a Convention (no. 143) and a Recommendation (no. 151) concerning migration in abusive conditions and promotion of equality of opportunity and treatment of migrant workers. The provisions of the Convention dealing with irregular migration urge the ratifying states to determine whether any irregular flows arrive or pass through its territory and to take all necessary steps to suppress clandestine movements of migrants for employment. Also, provisions are made for the prosecution of both the traffickers of clandestine migrants and the employers of such irregular migrants. An interesting feature of the Convention is that the "authors of

---

[48] For a brief historical review (up to the early 1980s) of international regulations on illegal migration see, G. Bertinetto, 'International Regulations on Illegal Migration', *International Migration*, Vol. XXI, No. 2 1983.

manpower trafficking can be prosecuted whatever the country from which they exercise their activities" (Article 5). The provision is of relevance to the issue of the geographical scope of national laws on migrant trafficking, as discussed above.

The second element of the Convention seeks to protect the basic human rights of all migrant workers and to ensure in particular equality of treatment as regards the rights acquired through past employment in relation to remuneration, social security and other benefits. In case of disputes concerning these rights, the irregular immigrant is entitled to present his/her case to a competent body. Finally, to ensure effective application of both parts of the Convention, it emphasized the importance of collaboration between governments and the social partners (employers and workers) and between the countries of origin and of employment.

Although the Convention does not specify the human rights applicable to all (including irregular) migrant workers, it is considered that the reference is not to an entire body of human rights as codified by the UN, but only to the most fundamental ones or those which cannot be withheld from an individual even when he/she is in an irregular situation such as, for example, "the right to life, to protection against torture, and cruel, inhuman or degrading treatment or punishment, the right to liberty and security of person and protection against arbitrary arrest and detention and – if criminal proceedings are brought prior to expulsion – the right to fair trial".[49] As regards the fate of immigrants in an irregular situation, the Convention includes a declaratory provision allowing ratifying states to regularise their situation. No guarantee is given to the irregular immigrant against expulsion, but the Recommendation provides for the right of appeal before an administrative authority or judicial authority, and the right to legal assistance and an interpreter. The Convention does not specify who should bear the cost in the case of expulsion of the worker or his family but rules out the cost being met by them.

The two main parts of the Convention were conceived to be interdependent and complementary. Eradication of irregular migration and consequent non-availability of cheap and unprotected labour to employers was regarded as a vital condition for protection of migrants' basic rights and promotion of social justice. Although several of the ILO's earlier instruments aim at ensuring non-discrimination or equality of opportunity and treatment between national and non-national workers, the 1975 ILO Convention was probably the first attempt at the international level to secure certain rights for immigrants in an irregular situation and to fight clandestine migration and employment. By 1995, 40 countries were parties to Convention 97, and only 17 had ratified Convention 143.

Since 1972, the United Nations, alongside the ILO, has been concerned with the problems of irregular migration. That year as the UN Economic and Social

---

[49] G. Bertinetto, 1983, op. cit, pp. 194–195.

Council (ECOSOC) was meeting in Geneva, a sealed truck which was supposed to be carrying sewing machines, broke down in a near-by site. It was then discovered that the truck was clandestinely transporting 35 workers from Mali who were travelling from Tunisia through Italy and Switzerland to France. The incident was not an isolated one, but it spurred the UN into action against irregular migration and trafficking. The ECOSOC adopted a resolution (No. 1706) urging the governments to prevent and combat exploitation of migrant workers and clandestine trafficking in migrants. The same year the United Nations General Assembly suggested that the Commission on Human Rights should as a matter of priority examine the question of exploitation of labour through illicit and clandestine trafficking.

In the years that followed, both the ECOSOC and the General Assembly adopted a series of resolutions on irregular migration. In 1974–75, a study was carried out on behalf of the Sub-Committee on Prevention of Discrimination and Protection, which included a number of recommendations dealing, *inter alia*, with the elimination of clandestine trafficking, the protection of the fundamental human rights of irregular migrants and official control of all migratory movements. As in the ILO, the discussion in the General Assembly revealed a shift towards a more comprehensive approach to the problem of irregular migration. It was not enough to concentrate on illegal trafficking in migrants; clandestine employment which often entails exploitation of labour must also be stopped and the basic human rights of all migrant workers and their families upheld.

Despite the progress made in international action against irregular migration through the UN, the ILO and various regional bodies in the 1970s, many sending and receiving countries – no doubt for different reasons – were dissatisfied with the existing international instruments, and the pressure for further international action was building up. Some developing countries, notably Mexico, was particularly anxious to ensure additional protection for the long established communities of irregular migrant workers which, though tolerated, remained illegal in the receiving country. These countries felt that the situation needed greater legislative and political attention and to that end decided to push the idea of a new instrument to cover all migrant workers and their families under the auspices of the UN itself. Although there were doubts in certain circles about the wisdom of the initiative, especially in relation to the competence of the ILO in this field,[50] the General Assembly adopted a resolution in December 1978 requesting the Secretary-General of the UN to explore the possibility of drawing up a Convention to protect the rights of all migrant workers and their families. The following year, based on a report by the Secretary-General, the General Assembly decided (resolution 34/172) to

---

[50] Bimal Ghosh, 'Movements of People: The Search for a New International Regime' in *Issues in Global Governance*, Kluwer Law International, London, The Hague and Boston, 1995, p. 414–416.

establish at its Autumn 1980 session an open-ended working group to prepare a draft convention.

Twelve years later and after long and protracted negotiations between and among the various parties concerned, the UN General Assembly finally adopted the International Convention on the Protection of All Migrant Workers and Members of Their Families in December 1990. As in the case of the 1975 ILO Convention, a basic idea underlying the UN instrument is that in as much as effective protection of irregular immigrants means that employers can no longer benefit from cheap and docile labour, it eradicates one of the main causes of irregular migration

The UN Convention applies to all migrant workers and members of their families, while maintaining a distinction between those who are in a regular situation and those who are not. Fundamental human rights (in civil, political, legal, economic, social and cultural areas, as elaborated in existing basic human rights instruments of the United Nations), are extended to all migrant workers. It establishes the principle of equality of treatment with nationals for all migrant workers in a number of areas such as before the courts and tribunals, and regarding remuneration and social security. It also upholds the right to transfer earnings, savings and personal effects and belongings upon termination of stay and prohibits measures of collective expulsion. Expulsion may only be in pursuance of a decision by the competent authority in keeping with the law, and the person shall have a reasonable opportunity before or after departure to settle any claims for wages. The Convention makes it clear that provision of these and other rights do not imply the regularisation of a migrant worker or a family member who is in an irregular situation.

As noted, under the instrument, protection of irregular immigrants goes hand in hand with combatting irregular migration. It thus enjoins state parties concerned to cooperate in adopting measures for the orderly return of immigrants in an irregular situation and urges them to end irregular situations (and mentions the possibility of regularisation). The state parties are at the same time required to collaborate to prevent illegal or clandestine movements and employment of migrant workers in an irregular situation. Such action may include measures against the dissemination of misleading information; measures to detect and eradicate illegal or clandestine movements of migrant workers; and effective sanctions on persons or entities who organise such movements and on irregular migrants themselves.

A concern has been expressed that the addition of the new UN instrument parallel to the ILO 1975 Convention, encumbers the international normative system by creating two parallel sets of standards, each with its own supervisory and compliance mechanism.[51] The concern is not entirely unjustified. But more

---

[51] M. Hasenau, 'Setting Norms in the United Nations System: The Draft Convention on the Protection of Rights of All Migrant Workers and Their Families in Relation to ILO Standards on Migrant Workers, *International Migration*, Vol. XXVIII, No. 2, June 1990.

worrying is the fact that to date only a few countries have either ratified or acceded to the instrument. As of 1 November 1996, the Convention had been ratified by Morocco and the Philippines, acceded to by Egypt, Colombia, Kuwait, Seychelles and Sierra Leone, and signed by Chile and Mexico.[52] It requires the commitment, in the form of ratification or accession, of at least 20 countries before coming into force.

A detailed description of the international organisations' advisory assistance and operational activities relating to irregular migration is beyond the scope of the present study. It is important however to note that in recent years several international organisations have initiated or expanded their advisory and operational activities in dealing with irregular migration. The International Organization for Migration, for example, organised in October 1994 an international seminar on international responses to trafficking in migrants and the safeguarding of migrant rights. In June 1996, it organised jointly with the European Union a European conference in Vienna to help design common instruments to combat trafficking in women. In the same year (May 1996) the organisation held, jointly with UNHCR and the Organization for Security and Cooperation in Europe (OSCE), a conference in Geneva to examine issues of population movements in the CIS countries. The programme action adopted by the conference contains a number of elements of special relevance to irregular migration.[53]

The organisation's voluntary return programmes are also being used to facilitate the return of rejected asylum seekers and other migrants in irregular situations to their country of origin in conditions of dignity. These include programmes for the return of rejected asylum-seekers and irregular migrants including those stranded in transit as well as stranded students in the CIS countries. At the same time it is helping several governments in Eastern Europe to improve their policies, structures and information programmes to deal with migration, including irregular flows. Its activities in this area are closely linked to its wider concern to make migration more orderly, manageable and humane within a harmonised global framework.

Aside from its extensive normative work, the ILO, for its part, has been active in helping governments to develop sound labour migration policies, and

---

[52] United Nations, Economic and Social Council, Commission of Human Rights, 'Measures to improve the situation and ensure the human rights and dignity of all migrant workers', E/CN.4/1997/65, 16 December 1996. According to the information received from the UN in August 1997, the following countries have also acceded to the instrument: Bosnia and Hercegovina, Sri Lanka and Uganda.

[53] See 'Programme of Action', CIS Conference on Refugees and Migrants, CISCONF/1996/PA/5. 20 May 1996. The programme including the basic principles and the action strategy contains several important elements both to prevent and remedy irregular migration. See also 'UNHCR/IOM Joint Operational Strategy in the Countries of the Commonwealth of Independent States', Years 1996–2000' CISCONF/1996/CRP/2/Rev 23 May 1996.

reduce pressures for irregular migration through promotion of training and employment.

4.5. Regional initiatives

Alongside international action, there have been a number of regional initiatives to address the problems of irregular migration, including trafficking. In the European region, the Council of Europe took one of the earliest initiatives. At its Conference of Ministers of Labour, held in Rome in November 1972, it recommended sanctions against trafficking and exploitation of immigrant labour. Several years later, in 1978, it adopted a detailed resolution recommending the adoption by member states of a set of preventive and punitive measures to curb irregular immigration and employment. These included: severe penal and administrative sanctions against traffickers, employers and intermediaries, measures against misleading propaganda and close cooperation between the member states. Repatriation was a possibility, but it should preferably be arranged through international agreements. Member states could also consider the possibility of regularising the status of irregular immigrants on humanitarian grounds and in the light of the job market situation, but this must not undermine the fight against clandestine migration.

As by the early 1990s irregular migration, especially trafficking, became an issue of mounting concern, exacerbated by the new flows from and through Central and Eastern Europe, the Council of Europe once more focused its attention to the problem. The final Communiqué issued by the Ministerial Conference, organised by the Austrian Government with the assistance of the Council of Europe (Vienna, 1991), included a special reference to the need for closer cooperation on measures against illegal immigration, as well as agreements on readmission of illegal migrants by the states of origin or transit.

Later in the same year, another Ministerial conference was held in Berlin (October 1991) on East–West migration which recommended the adoption of a series of practical measures to combat irregular migration. These included tighter and harmonised control procedures at certain key points; requiring carriers to check their passengers' transit and residence permits; arrangement for the return to the country of departure or origin of persons who have illegally entered another country; conclusion of bilateral or multilateral readmission agreements; and harmonisation of visa policies in a spirit of mutual cooperation. Acceleration of joint East–West action to combat illegal inflows meant that the Central and Eastern European countries would need to bring their immigration laws and control measures in line with those of Western European countries. In exchange, the latter was to offer more short-term work contracts and training courses for nationals of Central and Eastern European countries.

Continuing attention to the problem led the Ministers responsible for migration in 35 European states (including those from Central and Eastern Europe) to adopt, at its conference in Budapest (15–16 February 1993) a recommendation calling for collective action to prevent mass movement of irregular migrants from east to west. Agreement was reached on readmission of irregular migrants (further discussed below) and on provision of economic assistance to those countries which were major sources of irregular migrants due to widespread poverty. In order to prevent and combat illegal trafficking and employment, several measures were to be taken – such as the confiscation of the means of transport used by the traffickers; creation of special units and forces; imposition of stricter control measures at the borders and organisation of new types of border patrols; and regular exchange of information and mutual assistance among the member states.

The Vienna Group (established after the 1991 Vienna conference referred to above) discontinued its activities in September 1994. Action initiated by the Ministerial Conferences in 1991 and 1993 is now being followed up by the so-called Budapest Group, with its secretariat services provided by the Vienna-based International Centre for Migration Policy Development (ICMPD). At the time of writing, the Budapest Group was examining several specific steps to improve control of irregular migration, including the compilation of an inventory of the needs of the Central and Eastern European (e.g., training, computers, vehicles, and communication equipment) and of possible offers from Western European sources and exploration of possibilities of additional financial assistance to improve border control and facilitate return programmes. The emphasis is thus shifting towards measures to combat migrant trafficking, border control and readmission agreements.

More recently, the Council of Europe has also provided some practical assistance on immigration control through specific projects such as police training in Poland, and its programme for 'Assistance for the Development and Consolidation of Democratic Security' and Themis Plan for the Development of Law.

The European Community/Union has also been an important actor since the 1970s when its irregular migrant workers had reached the level of 600,000 or 10 per cent of its total foreign workforce. In a programme of action in favour of migrant workers, adopted in 1974, the EC denounced the exploitation of clandestine workers. This was followed by a resolution, adopted on 2 February 1976, which listed three objectives as the basis for its policy against irregular migration: increased collaboration between member states; adequate sanctions against trafficking; and employers' obligation to protect workers' rights, especially those gained through past employment, regardless of the other consequences of the workers' irregular status.

In keeping with these objectives, which were broadly similar to those of the ILO Convention No. 143, a draft directive on irregular migration was prepared as a first step towards harmonisation of national legislation and practice on entry, residence and employment of non-EC workers. The European Parliament suggested some amendments to the draft dealing, for example, with the protection of irregular workers' rights acquired through previous employment and regularisation of the status of irregular migrants. In 1978, some of these and other suggestions were incorporated by the Commission in a revised draft. However, in view of the continuing differences among the member states on a number of issues, the European Council decided in November of the same year to set aside the whole proposal. The decision also reflected a cautious attitude among the member states on the whole migration issue at a time when economies in Western Europe were in the midst of a deep recession. Notwithstanding this negative outcome of the initiative, the basic principles and objectives of the draft directive on irregular migration were generally upheld in most member states.

Recent policy trends in the EU on irregular migration are largely reflected in the report submitted by EC ministers responsible for immigration to the Maastricht meeting of the European Council in 1991. The Ministers recognised that, as long as the restrictive admission policy of the EU failed to eliminate migratory pressures, an increase in illegal immigration would be inevitable. They then addressed the question: To what extent can illegal immigration be effectively curbed without infringing the democratic principles of the member states?

Strict surveillance both at the borders and within member states was considered essential, although given the long sea borders of member states it would not completely eradicate illegal immigration. Ministers reiterated the importance of close collaboration between member states as envisaged in the EU Convention (agreed but not signed) on the crossing of external borders. Checks within the territory of member states on persons entering illegally were considered important, although these should be carried out without infringing individual freedom.

In addition, the ministers advocated a four-point approach against irregular immigration. First, social measures from which illegal residents could benefit on humanitarian or emergency grounds must not serve as an invitation to irregular immigration. Second, policies for reducing illegal employment should be intensified mainly through employer sanctions. Third, an extremely reserved position should be taken regarding large-scale regularisation in order not to undermine the prospects of political integration of legally resident immigrants. Fourth, a flexible and humane, but effective policy of expulsion should be implemented, while exploring solutions of the problem in the country of origin or in a third country of emigration. The Ministers recommended a gradual approach to harmonisation of policy on irregular immigration. A common acceptance of basic principles along the above lines should be the first step.

Restrictive admission, freer movement within the Union, and stricter checks and controls of external borders and irregular residents are the main features of current EU policy. Under the Maastricht I Treaty on European Union, (Article K.1(3)(c)) irregular migration is listed as an area of 'common interest' and is thus amenable to inter-governmental as well as Community-level action.

Included within the inter-governmental (Council of Ministers) structure is the Centre for Information, Discussion and Exchange on the crossing of frontiers and immigration (CIREFI), an informal forum which brings together officials from national ministries of justice and home affairs to assist member states in preventing illegal migration and unlawful residence, combatting immigration crime, detecting forged documents and improving expulsion practice.

The Working Group on Migration, which also operates as part of the inter-governmental structure, has drafted two instruments of relevance to irregular migration. The first one is entitled *Recommendation concerning checks on and expulsion of third country nationals working without authorisation.* The document indicates which categories of illegal immigrants, and under what circumstances, should be checked and expelled. The second draft instrument is called the *Joint Action on harmonising means of combating illegal immigration and illegal employment and improving the relevant means of control.* As a Joint Action, the proposed instrument dealing with control measures through identity verification, checks on social security applicants and improvement of the reliability of residence permits, is of greater legal force than a Recommendation. As of 1995, the draft was still under discussion with member states.[54]

Another working group – on External Borders – which is concerned with checks and controls at external borders is preparing relevant legislation based on the Draft of External Borders Convention whose principles were agreed upon in June 1991 but, as noted above, remains to be signed. The European Commission, for its part, has prepared a Communication on Immigration and Asylum Policies (February 1994) which included an outline approach for fighting irregular immigration. Already approved by the European Council, the Communication should provide a basis for future EU legislation on the subject.

Meanwhile, in December 1995, the Council of the European Union adopted a recommendation on concerted action and cooperation in carrying out expulsion measures. The instrument which *inter alia* supplements the recommendation adopted on 30 November 1992 (and the addendum thereto of 1–2 June 1993) concerning transit for the purposes of expulsion, lays down principles of cooperation in the procurement of the documentation necessary for expulsion and in facilitating the transit for purposes of expulsion as a concerted effort.

Under the EU's Maastricht II Treaty (June 1997), immigration issues were moved from the treaty's third to first pillar. This implied that the EU Commission may initiate immigration proposals, that the European Parliament has a right of overseeing these issues and that cases involving immigration can be brought to the European Court of Justice.

Mention may be made of another intergovernmental body, the TREVI Group, which operates outside the EU framework. It was initially set up to coordinate efforts to combat terrorism, but has expanded its activities to deal

[54] IGC, *Illegal Aliens: A Preliminary Study*, 1995.

with issues of police cooperation, including those involving irregular immigrants. Alongside these and other measures, European states have been pursuing the question of irregular migration through other regional and inter-regional fora such as the Geneva-based Inter-governmental Consultations on Asylum Refugee and Migration Policies in Europe, North America and Australia (IGC) and the Vienna-based International Centre for Migration Policy Development.

Outside Europe regional initiatives to combat irregular immigration have remained limited so far, although many of the regional cooperation arrangements include provisions concerning movement of workers. The Andean Pact in Latin America is one of the few exceptions, its member states being committed to cooperate in efforts to suppress trafficking of illegal migrant workers and to regularise the status of undocumented migrants. In Africa, an *ad hoc* committee was charged by the Organisation of African Unity to draw up a basic agreement on migrant workers, one of the aims of which was to reduce illegal migration.

Readmission agreements as a form of bilateral and multilateral cooperation

Readmission agreements which can be bilateral or multilateral in scope require a state to readmit to its territory specified categories of persons at the request of another contracting state. Although such agreements generally cover different categories of persons, they are increasingly being used as a means of dealing particularly with irregular migrants, including rejected asylum seekers, in cooperation with source and transit countries. The European Union, for example, has placed special emphasis on readmission agreements, and, as indicated above, has adopted several instruments on the subject to promote concerted action. The discussion in this Chapter will therefore remain incomplete without some further reference to these agreements.

Readmission agreements are not new, but since the mid-1980s they have received special attention from the European governments, which are now involved, in some 60–70 bilateral readmission agreements (Tables 4.4(A) and 4.4(B)).[55] Readmission obligations are also included in several multilateral agreements such as the Schengen Agreement, the Nordic Passport Union Agreement and the Benelux Agreement, as well as in agreements concluded between the Schengen countries and Poland (1991) and between the Benelux countries and Slovenia (1992). In addition, provisions concerning readmission are included in, or linked to, certain agreements dealing with other subjects of bilateral or multilateral interest. The EU has concluded a number of such agreements as indicated below.

Several specific reasons explain the increasing or renewed interest in readmission agreements in Europe. First, when large numbers of irregular immigrants and rejected asylum seekers reside on the territory of a country, as has been

[55] For a detailed discussion of the subject, see: Secretariat of the Inter-Governmental Consultations (IGC), 'Working Paper on Readmission Agreements', Geneva, August 1994.

Table 4.4A. Readmission agreements: selected industrial countries, 1995

	Austria	Belgium	Bulgaria	Canada	Czech Republic	Denmark	Estonia	Former Yugoslavia	France	Germany	Hungary	India	Italy	Latvia	Lithuania	Luxembourg	Morocco	Netherlands	Norway	Pakistan	Poland	Portugal	Romania	Slovak Republic	Slovenia	Spain	Sri Lanka	Sweden	Switzerland	USA	Vietnam
Australia																															
Austria		√			√				√	√	√		√			√		√			√		√	√	√				√		
Belgium	√				×				√	√		×	√			√	√	√		×	√			×	√				√		
Canada																														√	
Denmark							√			√				√	√																
Finland																															
France	√	√								√			√			√	√	√			√	√			√	√		√	√		
Germany	√	√	×		√	√			√		×					√		√	√		√		√					√	√		
Italy								√													√				×						
Netherlands	√	√							√	√						√	√				√				√						√
Norway										√					√																
Spain									√								√				√	√									
Sweden									√	√											×		×								
Switzerland	√	√							√	√							√		√				×				√				
UK																															
USA				√																											

× Under negotiation
√ Existing
Source: IGC Secretariat, *Consultations on Asylum, Refugee and Migration Policy (IGC)*, 1995.

Table 4.4B. Readmission agreements: selected Central and European countries, 1995

	Austria	Belarus	Belgium	Bulgaria	Croatia	Czech Republic	Denmark	France	Germany	Hungary	Italy	Netherlands	Norway	Poland	Romania	Slovak Republic	Slovenia	Spain	Sweden	Switzerland	Ukraine
Bulgaria									×					√							
Belarus														√							
Croatia										√											
Czech Republic	√								√	×				√	×	√					
Estonia							√														
Former Yugoslavia											√										
Hungary	√				√	√									√	√	√				√
Latvia							√														
Lithuania							√						√								
Poland		√		√		√									√	√					√
Romania	√					×			√	√				√					×		
Slovak Republic	√					√				√				√							√
Slovenia	√		√					√		√		√									
Ukraine										√				√		√					

× Under negotiation.
√ Existing.
Source: IGC Secretariat, *Consultations on Asylum, Refugee and Migration Policy (IGC)*, 1995.

the case in most of Western Europe in the past few years, the agreement can facilitate their readmission to the country of origin. In the absence of an agreement, such cooperation may not be available, or the procedure may be cumbersome and the negotiation time-consuming. The situation can also add to the political sensitivity of the repatriation process and provoke adverse reaction. Second, as noted in Chapter 1, in recent years taking advantage of their relatively lax immigration control, large numbers of third country nationals have been travelling through Central and Eastern European countries to reach Western Europe and North America for the purpose of remaining illegally or seeking asylum there. By inducing such transit countries to tighten their immigration laws and control measures, readmission agreements can restrain the migratory flows through (or from) their territories to the destination countries in the west.

In the case of asylum-seeking, a third reason that has encouraged the Western European countries to enter into readmission agreements stems from their shared concern to contain the growing problem of asylum shopping – that is, the practice of seeking asylum in several countries at the same time or of re-applying in one or several countries after rejection. A readmission agreement can allow a receiving country to return an asylum-seeker to a country through whose territory the person has already passed and where he or she could have requested asylum. The concept of burden-sharing (a better distribution of the burden of providing asylum) has also been advanced in this connection, although in practice this has proved to be somewhat elusive. Finally, increased freedom of movement of persons within the European Union has also enhanced the need for the EU countries to agree on readmission arrangements between themselves and also with surrounding countries.

Although seemingly of less direct interest to the source and transit countries, the readmission agreements can also yield certain advantages to them. The risk of return or readmission can serve as a powerful deterrent against the use of the country as a transit point by irregular migrants from third countries. Without such accords, as the Czech Interior Minister noted in 1994 in the context of a Czech-German agreement, the republic "could turn into a rubbish pool for the countries participating in the Schengen agreement". Cooperation in readmitting its own citizens can help a state to maintain and foster friendly relations with the other contracting state and secure other benefits as part of the agreement itself or otherwise. Aside from enhancing the standing of the source/transit country's regular immigrant community in the host country, the readmission agreement can offer specific advantages to the former. For example, in return for a readmission agreement with Schengen countries, Poland secured for its citizens exemption from the visa requirement for entry and less than three months' stay in the Schengen countries. Belgium negotiated a similar readmission agreement with Morocco in return for simplifying the issue of entry visas for Moroccans. In some cases, the agreements – for example those concluded between Germany and individual Eastern European countries (e.g.

Bulgaria, the Czech Republic and Romania) – provide for financial aid to the source/transit country in order to improve its migration management systems and institutions. Advantages in the form of trade concessions and/or development aid may also serve in some instances as a compensation for accepting the readmission obligation by the source/transit country.

A significant number of trade and cooperation agreements concluded between the European Union and its member states and third countries thus contain references to the need for cooperation to prevent irregular entry and presence of the nationals of one contracting party on the territory of another, in keeping with the principles and practices of readmission. Such references are found in agreements with Armenia, Azerbaijan, the Baltic states, Belarus, Georgia, Kazakstan, Kirgyzstan and Russia. The agreements with several countries including Egypt, Jordan, Lebanon, Morocco and Tunisia foresee, among other matters, cooperation for resettlement of the readmitted migrants. The recent discussion in the EU Council on this subject seems to suggest that the readmission clauses are likely to be included in many of the EU's future 'mixed agreements' with third countries.[56]

Meanwhile, as indicated in Table 4.4(B), a number of Central and Eastern European countries have already concluded agreements between themselves and with countries of Western Europe. Parallel to the EU action, an initiative launched by the Budapest Group aims at encouraging such bilateral agreements between countries of Western and Eastern Europe. As part of this exercise, Central and Eastern European states jointly elaborated in 1995 a set of basic principles for concluding such agreements on a uniform basis. This was then compared with the principles embodied in a draft specimen of a bilateral agreement prepared by the EU states. Despite certain differences between the two documents, shared concern and commonalty of approach to the basic objectives seem to suggest that it should soon be possible for countries of Eastern and Western Europe to agree on a common text of general principles for all such bilateral agreements. This might even lead to the elaboration of a multilateral model for Europe as a whole in the future.[57]

Since the obligation for a state to readmit its own nationals is already recognised under international law, is it really useful for a host country to conclude readmission agreements? There are at least two important reasons why it could be so. First, the readmission obligation of a state under international law does not extend to third country nationals, although it is accepted under customary international law. Second, the main purpose of a readmission agreement is not to create a new obligation, but to facilitate its implementation.

---

[56] *Migration News Sheet.*

[57] 'Overview of the mandate and activities of the Expert Group and of its recommendations', Doc. BG3/5. Third meeting of the Budapest Group, Zurich, 14–15 September 1995 (mimeo). The two documents were similar on basic principles with the exceptions mainly of those relating to the circumstances under which third country nationals should be readmitted and which party should ensure the escort of the third country nationals.

The implementation of this obligation may be avoided or delayed by the source/transit country in the absence of established procedures for issuing necessary travel documents for the person to be readmitted. Readmission becomes a particularly difficult and time-consuming problem, when irregular immigrants destroy their passports and other identity papers making it difficult to establish their nationality or country of origin. A readmission agreement can minimise these difficulties by specifying the formalities required and simplifying them so as to make the process of readmission more expeditious. Germany's agreement with Romania, for example, ensures that Romanians who entered Germany illegally will be readmitted to Romania without particular formalities even if they do not have valid personal documents.[58] From this perspective, even those agreements in which the states' obligations are limited to their own nationals serves a useful purpose.

Experience shows that a source or transit country, even when a signatory to a readmission agreement, may not always be very cooperative in issuing the papers that are necessary for repatriation – either because of its doubts about the nationality or status of the immigrant or simply to avoid being overflooded by returnees. Some agreements allow the host country itself to establish, if necessary, the nationality of the immigrant by following a specified procedure of its own. The EU Recommendation of 21 December 1995, referred to above, provides a set of guidelines for member countries in dealing with situations which present repeated difficulties in procuring the necessary documentation for repatriation.

Admittedly, a proliferation of readmission agreements can create a climate in which a state may feel that in the absence of such an agreement it can refuse to readmit its own citizens. However, one consequence of such a situation could be that countries which have not concluded such agreements might see a diversion of irregular flows into their own territories. This in turn may place them under increasing pressure to conclude readmission agreements with the source countries.

Nonetheless, without the genuine cooperation of the source or transit country, readmission programmes can hardly be successful. And such cooperation is unlikely to be forthcoming if the country feels that the agreement has been imposed upon it. To ensure its smooth functioning, not only should the agreement be freely negotiated, but it must also be fully transparent. In France, a riot that took place at Geispolsheim, near Strasbourg, in 1994 involving 12 Algerians confined in a detention centre there, was widely attributed to the application of a Franco-Algerian readmission agreement, that had been signed in the summer of 1994, but not made public before.[59]

---

[58] Federal Ministry of the Interior, 'Survey of the policy and law regarding aliens in the Federal Republic of Germany', 1993, p. 46 (mimeo).

[59] *Le Monde*, 22 October 1994.

A state may have the internationally recognised obligation to accept its own nationals, but except when it is on a voluntary basis, repatriation of immigrants, even if in an irregular status, will always be politically sensitive for both host and source countries. It makes it particularly important to implement the readmission agreements with care and circumspection. Upholding the human dignity of the person concerned is a most essential element of such an approach.

The discussion in this Chapter gives an indication of the wide range of measures that have been taken or advocated at the national, regional and international levels to combat irregular migration in its different forms and dimensions. It also reveals that irregular migration, like migration itself, is a global phenomenon, and that the involvement of international crime syndicates in human trafficking is making it even more so. The concern over the problem is widely shared, even if the degree of such concern varies between regions and countries. The question that remains to be addressed is: What should be the most effective policy approach to the issue? This is discussed in the light of the experiences to date in the next Chapter.

CHAPTER FIVE

Looking ahead: A comprehensive approach

Designing an effective strategy to combat irregular migration calls for more circumspection than is generally considered necessary. The discussion in Chapter 4 has revealed that the policies so far followed by the sending and receiving countries have been far from adequate or fully effective in combatting irregular migration. In general, the sending countries have taken a somewhat relaxed attitude towards irregular emigration of their nationals. Despite the increasing sensitivity of the issue in most industrial receiving countries, their policies in the past have often failed to demonstrate a sense of firm conviction or achieve the degree of coherence needed to combat irregular immigration effectively. As to the cooperation between sending, receiving, and transit countries, much remains to be done.

As discussed in Chapters 1 and 2, in the past, especially during periods of labour shortages, irregular immigration was often allowed in most industrial countries, with the connivance, if not active encouragement, of the government, to help meet the shortages. In more recent years, the spectacular expansion of the informal sector offering job opportunities for irregular workers and labour demand from non-competitive industries that largely depend on cheap, irregular immigrant workers has fuelled the irregular inflows, constraining the capacity of the governments to curb them. Clearly, policy ambivalence or, worse still, contradictions in policies, notably those affecting migration and trade, have only served to detract from the effectiveness of action against irregular migration.

A central point that has emerged from the previous discussion is that when there are powerful push factors in sending countries or pull factors in receiving countries and especially when the two fully converge, restrictive measures alone cannot arrest migratory flows; they are simply diverted to irregular channels. In such circumstances, a direct trade off can be envisaged between legal exclusion (migration restriction) and illegal or irregular immigration. (This is further discussed in Appendix II).

To be effective, a strategy to combat irregular migration therefore needs to be comprehensive enough to address both the push and the pull factors in a coherent manner. Indeed, the experiences in both Western Europe and North America over several decades have clearly demonstrated that there is no easy or uni-dimensional solution to irregular migration since it is influenced by a complex set of factors, often in combination with one another.

Irregular migration, as the discussion in Chapters 1 and 2 has shown, can take different forms, caused or shaped by a wide variety of factors. An effective strategy to combat it must take due account of these various causal factors and attendant circumstances. It must combine and balance between punitive measures and protection of basic human rights, between stricter border control and removing root causes of irregular movements, and as far as possible, it must also harmonise measures of the sending and the receiving countries, including those taken within each group.

There is at the moment a real danger that in their anxiety to curb irregular migration as quickly as possible, the receiving industrial countries might attach a disproportionate importance to a set of narrow and *ad hoc* measures, focusing on short-term cures through border control and punitive action. It would be unfortunate if in the process preventive action to remove the root causes is neglected or receives only scant attention.

The present Chapter briefly refers to the relative effectiveness (or lack of it) of the various measures which are already in place (discussed in Chapter 4), and puts forward a set of proposals to be woven into a coherent and comprehensive strategy to combat irregular migration.

A comprehensive strategy should combine three types of action: (a) punitive and remedial measures against current irregular migration; (b) preventive measures to attenuate the immediate pressure for irregular migration and redress the root causes; and (c) legal and institutional measures to sustain and help implement remedial and preventive action and remove those direct causes of irregular migration that are linked to existing legal and institutional deficiencies.

5.1. Punitive and remedial measures

Punitive measures, such as border control and apprehension, as well as employer and carrier sanctions, are primarily designed to combat the current or immediate threat of irregular migration. They are expected to have a quick impact on the situation. The same applies to the remedial measures such as regularisation, expulsion and voluntary return in as much as they all focus on a prompt solution to a problem that already exists, rather than addressing the root causes of it or its possible future recrudescences. In other words, these are more curative than preventive measures, with a narrow temporal horizon.

Border control, employer sanctions and other punitive measures

Although, as noted above, stricter *border control* and related punitive measures are potent instruments to combat current irregular flows (with some dissuasive effect also on future movements), their limits need to be recognised. Countries with long and porous borders – such as the United States which has a 2000-mile long southern border to control – find it difficult to insulate themselves. For these countries, effective control of irregular entry would often imply deployment of a large, well-trained border police force equipped with sophisticated technology. Other accessory measures may include the installation of fences (as in San Diego in the USA) to reduce border violence and facilitate enforcement, consistent with protection of human rights. All this could be a costly affair especially in times of budgetary constraints. It is worth recalling that although more stringent border control was envisaged at the time when the 1986 US Immigration Reform and Control Act was adopted, the government in the past had never delivered the necessary funds for this purpose. Notwithstanding the recent relative improvement in the situation in the United States as in most other industrial countries, the problem will probably continue to exist.

The problem is much more serious for the countries in Central and Eastern Europe, including those in the CIS, and for many migrant-receiving developing countries, especially the small island economies. Many of the Central and Eastern European countries, for example, have long and porous borders, and are overwhelmingly exposed, as noted in Chapter 1, to large-scale transit migration. The efforts being made by these countries, with the financial and technical support under the various bilateral, regional and international arrangements, to improve border control are clearly a move in the right direction, but for most of them resource constraints will remain a major problem.

There are also limits that the political culture and tradition of a receiving country may place on some of the internal control measures such as identity checks. A country with strong libertarian traditions that place high values on privacy, civil liberties and non-discrimination is likely to face public resistance towards initiatives for strict enforcement of national identity checks. True, even in countries like the United Kingdom and the United States, which have traditionally placed high values on civil liberties, governments are now moving towards increasingly strict control measures, but the political cost of such policy options in terms of intrusion on civil liberties cannot be overlooked or underestimated.

As for the *punitive measures*, in order to be effective as a deterrent to future inflows, they need to be exceedingly onerous so that the human and financial cost of irregular entry may outweigh the anticipated benefits. But such draconian measures inevitably raise issues of human and civil rights in modern democracies. What is worse, instead of reducing irregular immigration, tougher preventive and punitive measures, taken in isolation, may drive the potential migrants to turn to professional traffickers. It is difficult to indicate precisely the extent to which the recent tightening up of restrictive control and punitive measures against irregular immigration in industrial countries has contributed to the rise of organised trafficking in migrants. But there is enough evidence to suggest that there are close links between the two.

The need for anti-trafficking measures is now widely recognised, and there is a clear trend towards tightening up anti-trafficking legislation. As noted in Chapters 1 and 2, a good many of the trafficked migrants, especially children and women, are victims of trafficking, and not deliberate actors or perpetrators of crimes. It is therefore important that the anti-trafficking legislation not only makes a clear distinction between victims and criminals, but also provides for protection of the victims while punishing the traffickers themselves. The discussion in Chapter 4 has underscored the need for a clear and wide definition of trafficking in national legislation (as under the Swiss law) so that action can be taken against the crime whether it is committed inside or outside the country concerned. It is equally important for anti-trafficking measures to cover not just the core offences, but also the operations that are conducive or ancillary to it, such as document forgery, extortion and instigation, exploitation of trafficked migrants through sexual abuse and coercion into illegal activities.

Finally, regional and international cooperation must be regarded as an essential element in enhancing the efficacy of anti-trafficking measures. This is because, as already emphasised, migrant trafficking has now become a global operation, often planned and executed through multi-country networking. Apprehension and punitive action cannot therefore be expected to be fully effective without inter-state cooperation at the global and regional levels. A related reason is that if one country cracks down heavily on traffickers and makes the activity particularly risky, traffickers will simply shift to another country which may be more vulnerable. Regional efforts aimed at harmonising legal penalties and sanctions and enhancing the efficacy of operational measures though mutual support and assistance, as undertaken, for example by the Budapest Group (discussed in Chapter 4), can be immensely valuable in this connection.

Employer sanctions, as discussed in the preceding Chapter, can be a useful deterrent provided that they can be effectively enforced, that the penalties are high enough so as not to be considered by employers just as an additional cost of doing business, and that they are combined with non-discriminatory fulfillment of employers' verification obligations. But this presents difficult choices, as verification through, for example, identity checks impinges on civil liberties and privacy of the individual. Even more important, employer sanctions can hardly be effectively applied in small and family enterprises and firms in the underground economy, which account for a large proportion of irregular immigrant workers.

This, however, does not mean that the dissuasive control and punitive measures, including employer or carrier sanctions, have no role to play in combatting irregular migration. These are an essential, though not an adequate, condition of reducing irregular migration, and in many areas, such as organised trafficking they need to be strengthened. However, as already noted, by and large these measures are taking hold especially in most Western industrial countries, and inter-state cooperation is growing fast.

In stepping up these measures, three sets of conditions need to be met. First, care must be taken that they do not encourage any discrimination against regular immigrants belonging to ethnic minorities. Similarly, while employers and transport companies involved in illegal entry and employment of immigrants must be duly punished, it is important to ensure that such measures do not become unnecessarily harassing or burdensome for them. Equally important, the employers and transport companies should not be required to undertake responsibilities that belong to the border police and immigration control staff.

Second, the measures must be consistent with the human dignity of the migrants even when they are in an irregular situation and their rights must be duly protected. This is not just a matter of equity and social justice, important though they are. This is also a most effective means of removing one of the principal sources of attraction (demand-pull) of irregular immigrant labour in the receiving country. These protective measures are thus closely correlated to remedial and preventive action. As recognised in the major international instruments on the subject, this correlation is one of the most critical elements in a balanced and comprehensive approach to irregular migration.

Third, the restrictive and punitive measures must be complemented by medium and longer-term programmes capable of relieving over time emigration pressures (due to economic, political and ecological factors) in sending countries and the demand-pull in the receiving ones which are among the root causes of irregular immigration (further discussed below).

Regularisation

Regularisation has an immediate effect on the numbers of irregular immigrants in the receiving country at a given point of time. The main argument against regularisation is that it tends to encourage new irregular inflows and may thus be largely self-defeating if the impression is created that similar amnesties will be repeated in the future. As the European Commission observed in 1991, schemes to give legal resident status to illegal residents as carried out by certain member states make the responsibility to control irregular immigration weigh even heavier since this "tends to make illegal residence a long-term route to legal immigration".[1]

Even so, in certain circumstances regularisation can be an important element in a sound, comprehensive strategy to combat irregular migration. One of the main justifications of regularisation is to end the human suffering and exploitation of irregular immigrants and improve their general working conditions. By removing an important source of cheap and docile labour, it encourages the

[1] Commission of the European Communities, *Commission Communication to the Council and the European Parliament on Immigration*, Sec. 91, 1855 Final, Brussels, 23 October, 1991, p. 14.

process of industrial upgrading and structural change in the economy. It also brings orderliness to the migration situation, helping the country to start on 'a clean slate', with enhanced social stability and cohesion and improves the general credibility of the government in managing immigration. The case for regularisation is particularly strong when irregularity is due to legal and administrative deficiencies in the sending or receiving country or both, rather than the result of a deliberate decision of the migrant to defy established laws in pursuit of unlawful gains or activity. Regularisation also helps in reducing loss in public receipts in the form of taxes and social security contributions, although raising public revenues may not be a primary purpose of the measure.

However, these positive gains from regularisation cannot be achieved unless there is a large-scale response from the irregular immigrants. The eligibility rules and criteria should therefore be formulated in a manner that is flexible and fair to both regular and irregular immigrants, care being taken that irregular status is not especially rewarded leading to further irregular inflows. Enlisting the support and cooperation of the migrants' ethnic associations and migrant-serving non-governmental organisations is often a valuable means of securing a maximum response from the potential beneficiaries.

As the receiving countries tighten their measures against irregular immigration, they need to explore at the same time the possibility of regularising the situation of existing clandestine immigrants in a fair, orderly and transparent manner. In so doing, the countries should not necessarily limit regularisation to those foreigners who are already holding a steady job. Since regularisation would often imply additional payments to the workers, the employer may be inclined to get rid of the irregular immigrant workers before regularisation takes effect. As discussed in Chapter 4, the requirement of holding a regular job may also raise questions of equity and encourage corruption in the form of transactions in bogus job certificates.

Regularisation of some of the irregular immigrants may also be based on their selection for the new opportunities that may be opening up under bilateral programmes (e.g. recent agreements between various West and Central-East European countries) for fixed-term employment and training of foreigners from neighbouring countries. The regularised immigrant may be given the option of staying on in the country or returning home after the termination of the job or training. The success of such an approach requires that the irregular immigrants must not be afraid to reveal themselves and participate in the selection process. Possibilities of linking regularisation to voluntary return are further discussed below. To this end, immigrants and their employers must be convinced that information contained in regularisation applications will never be used for any purposes other than to decide legalisation eligibility.

For the reasons already discussed in Chapter 4, in adopting regularisation programmes, governments should take careful account not only of their immediate impact, but also their longer-term implications in terms of future inflows through, for example, family reunification and their impact on the labour market.

Voluntary return in conditions of dignity

Irregular migration is not just a one-sided problem. Many irregular migrants, disillusioned and disheartened by the lack of suitable job opportunities, poor housing and living conditions, long separation from the family, and insecure and marginalised existence in the receiving society, are anxious to return home. But the fear of apprehension in the receiving country and an uncertain future in the country of origin often hold them back. A significant number of rejected asylum seekers are in a similar situation, except that they may also be afraid of political repression as they return home. Many others who are under the clutches of traffickers and crime syndicates may have lost all their freedom of action. There are other special cases such as the stranded migrants including students in the CIS countries who now find themselves in a precarious and often irregular situation (discussed in Chapter 1). True, the individual's own choice plays a determinant role in voluntary return. But, without assistance from the receiving and sending countries, many irregular migrants would find it difficult (even more than those who have entered legally) to return home, although they might be willing, even anxious, to do so. While the kind of support needed would vary from one situation to another, some general principles can be underlined.

As the irregular immigrants reveal themselves for purposes of returning home, they need to be treated as humanely as possible. States have a responsibility to readmit their own nationals and persons with permanent residence on their territory, who may be illegally present in a foreign country. Bilateral and multilateral cooperation, including readmission agreements, could help solve some of the problems encountered in arranging smooth return of irregular migrants, including those in transit, to the source country. It is important, however, that the readmission agreements are freely negotiated, without any direct or indirect coercion, and that they remain transparent at all times. Nor should it be forgotten that, except when it is on a voluntary basis, repatriation of immigrants will always be a delicate operation for both host and source countries, and must therefore be handled with care and circumspection.

The experience of several West European states since the mid-1970s shows that providing the immigrants (regular or irregular) with certain amounts of cash money as an inducement to return home is a poor substitute for real motivation to return. While the importance of such support is not questioned, it is essential that potential returnees are genuinely convinced that the return programme holds a positive future for them and their families.[2] In addition,

---

[2] For example, in Germany despite the financial incentives provided for returns under the government decision of July 1982 and even with the additional measures taken under the Act of 28 November 1983 to Promote the Preparedness of Foreign Workers to Return, the impact was minimal.

they must be sufficiently motivated to make it a success. Psychological orientation is an important part of the process.

Assistance should *inter alia* include vocational training of the potential returnees both before departure and upon arrival in the country of origin; counseling and guidance about housing, jobs and economic opportunities; technical and financial assistance in setting up small enterprises, cooperatives and other self-help projects; and follow up support. Much of this can be effectively done when the return programmes are closely related to job creation and other development projects as an integral part of local and regional or national development of the country of origin.[3] Such an approach would not only ensure the sustainability of the projects, but should also make it easier to include the local populations as beneficiaries. The latter is particularly important to avoid discrimination, whether real or perceived, between the returnees and the local populations.

Action along these lines would call for active collaboration between the sending and receiving countries, at the governmental as well as the non-governmental level. Migrants' associations and migrant-serving voluntary bodies in both countries can play a most valuable role in ensuring the success of such programmes. Joint commissions consisting of the representatives of sending and receiving countries and the migrants' associations could be useful. At the international level, assistance from organisations such as the IOM and the ILO which already have extensive experience in return programmes may be usefully mobilised for the purpose.

Return programs could also suffer if the returnees, including rejected asylum seekers, remain vulnerable to continuing political instability and civil strife. The home country government may be unwilling or unable to extend adequate protection and assistance to the returnees. The legal and practical problems that the situation creates apply even to the return of legally recognised refugees. At the international level, the problem becomes complex because of the non-applicability of international refugee law for protection of persons inside their national territory; and because humanitarian laws primarily apply only to situations of armed conflict.

True, the refugees recognised under the 1951 United Nations Convention are in a somewhat different position since at least the UNHCR carries a residual responsibility for their reintegration following return. Also, in certain specific cases (e.g. in Iraq and the former Yugoslavia), it has been mandated

---

[3] *Le Monde*, 1 March 1995. In some countries, a small beginning has been made along these lines linking legalisation of irregular immigrants and their subsequent return to their country of origin. In France, for example, under a recent initiative supported by the Ministry of Interior, a small number of irregular immigrants from the African Sahel were being regularised and trained on the understanding that they would return home when the training was completed. Training is tailored to the job opportunities and development needs in the local communities of the sending countries so that the returnees can have a gainful activity linked to local development.

by the UN General Assembly or the Secretary-General to take *ad hoc* action in favour of the victims of civil strife inside their own countries. But these are fragile and fragmentary arrangements. As far as rejected asylum seekers and other irregular migrants are concerned, there is hardly any international legal or institutional arrangements to extend protection and assistance to them following their return.[4] An exception can be found in cases where the IOM has been actively involved in the return programmes; in such instances, based on arrangements with the sending and receiving countries, the organisation has provided assistance and a degree of indirect protection for returning irregular migrants as well as rejected asylum seekers.

As things stand now, there is clearly an important vacuum in the international legal and institutional arrangements for the protection and assistance of the rejected asylum seekers and other irregular migrants following their return to the home country. To make the return programmes a success this needs to be remedied as a matter of high priority.

Expulsion and protection of basic rights

Aside from voluntary return, a country which has large numbers of irregular immigrants on its territory and which does not opt for either regularising them or ignoring their presence, has a fourth choice – deporting or expelling the irregulars. But expulsion is an extreme measure; enforcing it humanely and effectively is not easy; and it almost invariably raises sensitive issues of human rights. Mass expulsion in particular is hardly consistent with respect for fundamental human rights.

On the other hand, expulsion or deportation measures that respect human rights are often time-consuming and costly; their effective follow-up requires large outlays of financial and human resources. Readmission agreements such as those being signed by countries in Western Europe with those in Eastern Europe and elsewhere could to some extent soften the image of harshness that expulsion usually projects among the public. In fact, expulsion of irregular immigrants should not be conceived as a unilateral measure. Bilateral consultations should ensure proper arrangements for their reception in the country of origin and as far as possible they should be linked to well-designed return programmes as discussed above.

But even with all possible safeguards, expulsion remains a temporary and *ad hoc* solution to the problem of irregular immigration. A sovereign state may find it necessary to use it in exceptional circumstances, but it would be unwise and impractical to rely exclusively on expulsion – or even as a principal instrument of action – to tackle the problem of irregular immigration. Clearly,

---

[4] See in this connection, Bimal Ghosh, 'International population movements and global governance: A select list of key issues', Geneva, 1993 (mimeo). Paper prepared for the Commission on Global Governance.

it cannot be a substitute for increased surveillance and control at the frontiers and other measures to prevent irregular entry: prevention is certainly better than subsequent expulsion.

5.2. Preventive measures: Immediate pressures and the root causes

Legal entries as relief points

As discussed earlier, lack of opportunities for legal entry, on the one hand, and a compulsive urge to migrate in order to reunite with the family or escape poverty, unemployment and political oppression, on the other, account for much of the current irregular migration. It can therefore be expected that to the extent that these emigration pressures could be relieved, even if temporarily, through authorised outlets and lawful entries, there would be less need for individuals to migrate clandestinely. Such relief points could be accommodated within the framework of short to medium strategies to combat irregular migration. One way of doing this is to keep the existing family reunification channels open and apply the procedure both humanely and efficiently. Admittedly, there is a risk that family reunification and, especially, family formation may widen the network for new irregular flows. But, humanitarian considerations apart, the risk of illegal entry may even be greater should the family reunification channels remain completely suppressed. Nor should it be forgotten that the receiving states have the possibility of defusing the risk by following a comprehensive strategy comprising a whole range of both preventive and pro-active measures against irregular immigration as discussed in this Chapter.

In addition to family reunification entries, potential receiving countries should explore several other possibilities of providing legal channels for temporary or fixed-term immigration, even when they are unable or unwilling to accept foreigners on a permanent or long-term basis. These can take many forms such as: project-tied employment, training-cum-short-term employment, seasonal and cross-border employment, and fixed-term employment, based on labour market needs. Such arrangements for fixed-term employment and/or training are not new, but following the massive East–West migration in 1989–90, several new bilateral agreements were signed between different states in Western Europe (e.g. Germany, Belgium, France and Switzerland) and those in Eastern Europe, (e.g. Poland, Hungary, the Czech Republic and Slovakia).

Experience suggests that the implementation of these schemes is not without risks. In Germany, for example, there is a growing concern that fixed-term training, project-tied work and temporary employment schemes for nationals of Eastern Europe might turn out to be a convenient device to use cheap immigrant labour, substituting a proper labour immigration policy. In some other cases, such as cross border and seasonal employment programmes, the concentration of immigrant labour may have a wage depressing effect in the border areas and seasonal industries. More importantly, there is a possibility, as revealed by the experience in Germany, that some of these schemes might open the way for irregular migration through, for example, illegal lending of temporary workers and unauthorised extension of stay. At the same time, the schemes can well be a source of cheap and exploited foreign labour.

These problems are difficult but not insurmountable. They can be largely overcome or at least reduced through appropriate planning and effective monitoring as well as inspection and supervision. Measures already introduced by some Western European states (e.g. Belgium and Germany) in the case of subcontracting work are illustrative of such action. Close cooperation with, and active support from the sending countries are important in reducing the risks of such 'leakage' from these schemes while enhancing their intrinsic value to both countries.

As noted earlier, in the absence of legal channels for entry, pressures for irregular migration also stem from the urge of millions of people to escape from political oppression, violation of human rights, civil war and generalised violence and environmental degradation. Many of these victims are in a refugee-like situation. However, in the present restrictive climate it is unrealistic to expect that many states would be inclined to widen the definition of the 'refugee' as inscribed in the 1951 UN Convention on the status of refugees and the corresponding national laws. And yet, most industrial states, especially in Western Europe, have from time to time relaxed their laws and accommodated, as in the case of war refugees from the former Yugoslavia, at least some of those categories of persons who are in a desperate, refugee-like situation. But the approach has often been arbitrary and unpredictable.

From the perspective of combatting irregular migration, it is important that provisions be made for temporary safe havens for people in these categories, consistent with the genuine needs in each case. The arrangements need to be transparent, predictable and internationally harmonised so as to enhance the credibility of the system, on the one hand, and facilitate equitable burden sharing among the receiving states, on the other. Rather than improvising in a slipshod manner, as was seen especially during the early stages of the exodus from the strife-torn areas of former Yugoslavia, the states would have a built-in capacity to respond to situations of emergency. The opening up of such additional channels, if clearly defined and well regulated, will lessen the strain on the asylum-seeking procedure under the 1951 UN Convention on refugees, while reducing the pressure for irregular entry.

Addressing the root economic causes

The medium and long-term measures to fight irregular migration must focus on the root causes of irregular migration. The root causes are primarily economic and political, although other factors – environmental degradation and demographic pressure, for example – also play an important part. Generally, both economic and (if to a lesser extent) political factors work through a combination of push and pull effects involving the sending and the receiving countries, respectively. As discussed in Chapter 2, economic factors often play a particularly important part in the build-up of emigration pressure in the medium to long term. Given this and the special significance of interlinkages between human movements on the one hand, and the movements of goods, services and capital on the other, particular attention is given in this section to trade policies and foreign investment. Many of the economic measures discussed in this section are complex, and, at least in some cases, controversial. Underlying these controversies there is the general issue of the nature of the relationship between development and migration. A brief review of the latter is included in Appendix I, but a detailed discussion of the various specific aspects of the issue is beyond the scope of this study. Rather than taking up such a discussion, this section basically seeks to flag a number of economic areas which closely interact with migration and in which new or more dynamic initiatives would help in addressing irregular movements. As in other sections of this Chapter, the focus is on policy aspects rather than on technical details.

Economic policies and reform Few people take the decision to leave their country lightly, and fewer people would take the risk of entering and living in a foreign country unlawfully. When they do so for economic reasons, they are often pushed by poverty and unemployment, low wages and poor working conditions and an overwhelming sense of economic despair. People flee, primarily, not to wealth, but from poverty – an observation made by an interdepartmental study group set up by the Swedish Ministry of Labour in 1990.[5] This is certainly true of the majority of the irregular migrants, although a few may be driven by opportunity-seeking in a more affluent country.

An active and comprehensive strategy must therefore address these long-term causes of irregular migration by promoting broad-based economic and social development of the sending countries. To this end, the sending countries need to be encouraged and enabled to adopt employment-oriented development policies, consistent with dynamic economic growth. Alongside macro-economic stability, special emphasis must be laid, as key elements of the strategy, on demographic planning, human resources development and poverty alleviation, targeting the areas and groups of populations that are the principal sources of irregular flows.

The short-term effects of economic reform, such as structural adjustment and liberalisation – however important for longer-term growth – can be harsh. And they are often harsher for the poor and low-income workers and other

[5] Swedish Ministry of Labour, *A Comprehensive Refugee and Immigration Policy*, Stockholm, 1990, p. 6.

vulnerable groups. Social safety nets could remove some of these economic strains and sufferings, which could otherwise be destabilising and may well lead to the build up of disruptive and irregular migratory pressures. Equally important, the reform programmes themselves should be so designed that the burdens of adjustment and fiscal austerity fall less heavily on the poorer groups. In other words, the relief for the poor should as far as possible be built into the reform strategy, and not serve merely as an additive measure.

Trade policies Broad-based development policies, with a focus on employment creation and expansion of exports, need to be largely outward-looking, but with a strong domestic base. For many migrant-sending developing countries which are late-comers in the world market, it would be difficult to achieve success in such a strategy without the support of congruent trade, aid and investment, as well as debt-relief policies of industrial countries. To illustrate, it has already been noted how trade protectionism in favour of a number of less competitive industries in industrial countries encourages them to survive by using cheap and docile irregular immigrant labour, while depriving many migrant-sending countries of the possibility of creating jobs and raising foreign exchange earnings through expansion of labour-intensive exports. The 1990 report of the US Commission for the Study of International Migration and Cooperative Economic Development cites the well-known example of arrangements for the protection of the sugar industry in that country. A 75 per cent reduction in the imports of sugar from the Caribbean area deprived these countries of much of the benefits envisaged under the Caribbean Basin Initiative. As a result, between 1982 and 1988, the countries may have lost 400,000 jobs.[6] A recent estimate by the Washington-based International Council on Agriculture, Food and Trade indicates that the losses incurred by developing countries due to the policies of the European Union, the United States and Japan amount to over $2 billion a year, or approximately one-third of their entire export earnings from sugar.[7]

According to an UNCTAD study, over two-thirds of developing countries' commodity exports are affected by the trade distorting subsidies under industrial countries' agricultural policies.[8] In recent years, developing countries have been losing $100 billion annually in lost revenues for farm products and a further $50 billion for textiles and clothing alone due to such trade protection-

[6] Commission for the Study of International Migration and Cooperative Economic Development, Unauthorized Migration: An Economic Development Response, Washington D.C. July 1990.

[7] International Policy Council on Agriculture, Food and Trade, *Sugar Policy in the Post Uruguay Round Era*, Washington DC, 1996.

[8] UNCTAD, documents submitted to the commodities Committee, Geneva, 1995. See also *The Financial Times* (London), 20 October 1995.

ism.[9] Estimates also suggest that in the absence of such trade barriers, poverty in these countries could be lower by two percent on average.[10]

For Central and Eastern Europe, too, the effects of trade expansion on unemployment could be significant because of the labour-intensive composition of their exports. A recent estimate shows that if, as a result of removal of trade barriers and other constraints, an eastern country were able to export 20 per cent of its GNP to the European Union (compared to an average of 3.2 per cent in 1988) the employment effect, under a reasonable set of assumptions, including a rise in eastern wages, would be equivalent to the potential outmigration of 8 per cent of the work force. And, if the wages do not rise in proportion, trade can make a more substantial difference to unemployment, thereby slowing down migratory movements from eastern countries, especially those driven by poverty and unemployment, through regular or irregular channels.[11]

The fall and fluctuations in the primary commodity prices is another source of concern (a loss of US$ 80 billion in 1980–88 for these countries).[12] In several cases the volatility in commodity prices has in the past created terms-of-trade shocks equal to the loss of several percentage points of the gross domestic product. An UNCTAD study (1995) reveals that the real value of commodity export earnings of African countries was halved in the past two decades.[13] Despite the rise in dollar prices of most commodities between 1994 and 1995, IMF calculates that in real terms, commodity prices continued to fall in 1996 and are expected to do so in 1997.[14]

Another trade policy-related problem that particularly affects primary goods-producing countries concerns tariff escalation – increase in tariffs with the degree of product processing. In order to offset these negative effects of the fall and fluctuations of commodity prices, these countries have endeavoured to diversify their exports through product processing; however, the efforts have been constrained by the problem of tariff escalation. In most industrial countries, despite significant reduction in overall tariffs and tariff escalation under the Uruguay Round trade accords, the average tariff for processed imports

---

[9] UNDP, *Human Development Report 1992*, United Nations, New York, 1993.

[10] Depending on the pattern of growth and the degree of income inequality, the decline in the level of poverty in individual countries may vary between 1.5 and 3.5 per cent. UNCTAD, 'Note on international trade and poverty alleviation', (mimeo) June 1991.

[11] Richard Layard et al., *East West Migration: The Alternatives*, The MIT Press, Cambridge, Mass. USA, London, England, 1992, pp. 53–55; Bimal Ghosh, 'The Future of East–West Migration', in Solon Arditti (ed), *The Politics of East West Migration*, op. cit, pp. 240–241.

[12] See in this connection UNCTAD/IOM, *Foreign Direct Investment*, Trade and Migration, United Nations, Geneva, 1996. Current Studies Series No. 29; and UNCTAD, 'A preliminary analysis of the results of the Uruguay Round and their effects on the trading prospects of developing countries: report by the UNCTAD secretariat', United Nations document No. TD/B/WG.413, 10 June 1994.

[13] UNCTAD, documents submitted to the Commodities Committee, Geneva, 1995, op. cit.

[14] IMF, *World Economic Outlook 1996*, Washington DC. See also, 'No better harvest forecast', *Financial Times* (London), 27–28 April 1996.

under the most-favoured nation (MFN) arrangement have remained significantly higher than tariffs for raw products.[15]

As already noted in Chapter 2, the industrial country policies thus contribute to irregular immigration in a two-fold way – through their pull as well as push effects. The result is that their trade policies and immigration policies often run counter to each other. Clearly, on balance such trade protectionism is also harmful for the industrial countries themselves as their consumers are obliged to pay more and their economies suffer from distorted allocation of resources. Changes in these trade policies should be accompanied by planned, anticipatory assistance to help replace the wasteful, non-competitive industries, or restructure them through technological upgrading while at the same time minimizing the transitional social cost. Without such assistance, political resistance and social unrest will make the policy changes difficult to achieve.

A reorientation of trade policies can make a particularly important contribution towards reducing irregular migration. This is because the poverty-driven migrants who constitute the majority of irregular migrants and who are mostly low-skilled and at the lower end of the labour force would be the major beneficiaries of the expansion of employment and trade in labour-intensive products.

The Uruguay Round trade accords have no doubt marked some progress in this direction. But, on the other hand, the accords also imply erosion of trade preferences so far enjoyed by a number of developing countries under various preferential schemes. As tariffs are lowered and the preferential schemes themselves are scrapped or modified in keeping with the provisions of the Uruguay Round accords, these groups of countries are likely to face economic difficulties leading to increased migratory pressures. True, the preferences such as those accorded under the Caribbean Basin Initiative and the Lomé Convention have remained somewhat limited for many of the labour-intensive products in which these countries have an actual or potential comparative advantage. Likewise, the Association Agreements signed between the European Union and the transition economies in Central and Eastern Europe and various neighbouring developing countries have also been somewhat restrictive in granting market access for several of the labour-intensive products which are considered 'sensitive'. But the erosion of even these limited preferences can only impel the unemployed and low-income workers to migrate through regular or irregular channels.

Migratory pressures are also likely to be increased in some of the same developing countries which will need to pay higher food import prices as a result of farm trade liberalisation under the Uruguay Round accords.[16] Special

---

[15] UNCTAD, *Trade and Development Report 1991*, United Nations Publication, Sales No. E.91.II.D.15., Geneva, 1991 and UNCTAD, Poverty Alleviation Programme (UNCTAD-PAP), 'Note on international trade and poverty alleviation', June 1994 (mimeo).

[16] See in this connection, Bimal Ghosh, 'Foreign direct investment, trade and international migration', Geneva, 1994. Paper jointly commissioned by United Nations and IOM. Chapter V.

aid to the food importing countries enabling them to increase food production and extend social safety nets to those severely affected during the transition should therefore receive urgent attention. Equally important is to extend assistance to the low-income countries, especially the least developed ones, so that they, too, can actively participate in, and benefit from the trade liberalisation process and do not fall by the wayside. Also worthy of consideration is a specific proposal – put forward by the WTO Director-General on the occasion of the June 1996 summit meeting of the Group of 7 in Lyon, France – that the tariffs on the exports of the LDCs to industrial countries be scrapped. The proposal may however lead to a degree of conflict of interest between the LDCs and other developing countries – at least to the extent that for certain export items the two groups of countries directly compete with each other in the international market. An additional problem stems from the possible transshipment of goods from third countries.

Mention may also be made of a recent United States initiative – at the time of writing it was before the US Congress – to help economic recovery in sub-Saharan Africa through increased trade and investment, but with a shift away from development aid. The basic premise underlying the proposed African Growth and Opportunity Act is that those nations willing to pursue growth policies by opening their economies and liberalising their markets are likely to be the engine of growth in the region. What must be emphasised, however, is that such economic reforms need to be complemented by an effective and judicious use of aid (discussed later in this chapter), so that the low-skilled, low-income groups, too, can be empowered to actively participate in the development process and can have an equitable share of the benefits of economic reform. Unless this is done, a real risk exists that there will be a further worsening of the situation of these disadvantaged groups, adding to the pressure for emigration through irregular channels. Policy shifts to economic openness sharply enhance the importance of development aid for poor countries and disadvantaged groups.[17]

Trade-related labour mobility Another avenue which holds considerable potential for reducing the pressure for regular and irregular migration, especially among skilled and professional workers, concerns trade in services.[18] For a variety of reasons, developing countries have so far somewhat neglected the development of the modern services sector, including business and producer services. There has been a general feeling among the policy makers in many developing countries, as was revealed, for example, during the earlier stages of

[17] See in this connection, Bimal Ghosh, 'Just as effective aid gets easier, support for it is dwindling', International Herald Tribune, Paris, 21 May 1997.

[18] For a detailed and most recent discussion on the subject, see Bimal Ghosh, *Gains from Global Linkages: Trade in Services and Movements of Persons*, Macmillan Press, London, St. Martin's Press, New York, 1997.

the Uruguay Round trade negotiation, that these countries have little comparative advantage in the world market for service industries. Available balance of payments statistics indicate however that many developing countries have a revealed comparative advantage (RCA)[19] in a wide variety of service industries, especially those that are labour (including skill or knowledge) services. These include engineering, accounting, legal, management consulting, medical, nursing, software development, data processing and cleaning.

As the experience of industrial and newly industrializing countries shows, services can be a most dynamic sector for creating new and better jobs and promoting growth. Also, closer inter-linkages between services and other sectors of the economy can put the whole economy on an upward swing, while contributing to further expansion of the services sector itself. Increased emphasis on the development of the modern services sector, including skill- and knowledge-intensive services, can thus reduce the pressures for irregular migration, whether driven by unemployment or opportunity-seeking. The gains could be further increased as the developing countries increase their participation in world trade in services by making a dynamic use of their actual and potential comparative advantage in this sector. A recent estimate shows that by contesting only those skill and knowledge intensive services for which developing countries have a comparative advantage and which can be delivered mainly through telecommunications and computer systems, developing countries can over time create anywhere between 6 and 30 million new jobs and increase their foreign exchange earnings by $210 million.[20]

An important condition enabling developing countries to fully benefit from their increased participation in world trade in services is freer temporary movement of service-providing personnel. For pure labour service contracts, a mainstay of the service exports of many low-income countries, the movement is in fact inseparable from the content of the service itself. Even for the skill-intensive, long-distance services, which are mostly delivered through telecommunications and computer systems, a degree of interaction with the customer is often critically important – to secure the contract, hold technical consultations, provide post-delivery services and the like. The General Agreement on Trade in Services (GATS) has opened a new window of opportunity in this direction by providing for liberalised trade-related temporary movements of persons. However, the actual commitments made by the industrial countries under the GATS have basically remained limited to the movement of executive

---

[19] The revealed comparative advantage (RCA) index is the ratio of exports of a given export item to a country's total exports divided by a similar ratio for the world. An index ratio above unity suggests that the country has a comparative advantage in the item resulting from its relative specialization. See Bernard Hockman and Guy Karsenty, 'Economic development and relative specialization in service', *Development Policy Review*, 10 September 1992, pp. 211–236.

[20] See, Bimal Ghosh, *Gains From Global Linkages Trade in Services and Movements of Persons*, op. cit.

and other senior level personnel in the form of intra-company transfers, with little opening for self-employed professionals or unskilled workers. The resistance to further liberalisation stems at least partly from the fact that trade-related temporary movements are often confused or equated with long-term migration, although the GATS (Article XVI and Annex) makes a clear distinction between trade-related mobility and longer-term migration. In reality, the former, on balance, can be a partial substitute for the latter. True, there is a risk of some 'leakage' in the form of temporary service providers becoming longer-term immigrants in an irregular manner. But the risk is limited and can be further reduced through effective monitoring, including, in particular, the use of an internationally harmonised special visa regime for trade-related movements.[21]

Further liberalisation of temporary movement of service-providing personnel could thus be an important factor in reducing the urge or need for skilled and unskilled workers to migrate through irregular channels. As, helped by such liberalisation, developing countries increase their participation in services trade, the importing industrial countries could benefit from easier access to the services at lower costs, and the world economy could gain through improved efficiency. Industrial countries should also benefit from an increased demand for their exports, although bold and imaginative adjustment assistance programmes will be needed to help meet the transitional social cost of the structural change in their economy. Intensification of international efforts for such liberalisation in the coming years would be worthwhile, especially since under the provision of the GATS the subject would come up for further negotiation in the year 2000.

Foreign direct investment: Why it is shy to flow to poor and stagnant economies[22] Although the direct contribution of foreign direct investment to employment creation is known to be rather limited, it can nonetheless be an important source of economic growth and technological upgrading, while contributing to indirect job creation through its multiplier effect. Given a sound policy environment that avoids increasing income inequality, it can also help in creating a new optimism about the future of the home country economy, thereby reducing the urge to emigrate.

Despite its scarcity in poor, migrant-sending countries, and its relative abundance in rich migrant-receiving countries, capital does not seem to flow to the former countries – at least to the extent that the factor cost equalisation process under classical economic theories would suggest. Poor countries typically attract only a small proportion of total investment capital, whether in the

---

[21] Ibid.

[22] This section is largely based on: Bimal Ghosh, 'Economic migration and the sending countries', October 1994 (mimeo). Paper presented to the 15th conference of the Belgian-Dutch Association for Post-Keynsian Economics, University of Antwerp, pp. 18–19. See also Keith Griffin and Azizur R. Khan, 'Globalisation and the developing world: An essay on the international dimension of development in the post cold-war era'. UNDP, New York, 1992.

form of foreign direct investment or portfolio investment. Even more paradoxically, for several consecutive years in the past, developing countries had witnessed a reverse transfer of resources in the form of capital flight. True, inflows of foreign direct investment into developing countries surged from $31 billion in 1990 to $100 billion in 1995, but most of it went to a few newly industrialising and dynamic economies; and the flow to the developed countries ($215 million in 1995) was more than twice as large.[23] Indeed, the entire net outflow of investment from developed to developing countries during the period of 1990–93 had the effect of reducing the rich world's stock by a mere 0.5 per cent from what it would have otherwise been.[24]

There are several economic and non-economic reasons for this seemingly paradoxical situation. An important economic reason is that the returns to capital in developed countries are comparable to, or even higher than in most migrant-sending developing countries. For example, published data on US foreign direct investment for the five-year period 1985–1989 has revealed that the rate of return was 14.1 per cent on investment in developing countries and 16.9 per cent in the developed ones. Another study shows that the average rate of return on non-residential capital stock in seven major industrial countries has been 17 per cent in recent years, compared to 12 per cent in developing countries. This was confirmed in an analysis made by the International Finance Corporation of the rate of return of 200 investment projects in different regions: it was found that the return on investment in developing countries was generally lower than in industrial countries.[25]

How can developed countries have a higher return of capital, despite its relative abundant supply? The assumption that the rates of return to capital should be lower in capital-rich countries rests on a two-fold hypotheses: that labour is homogeneous and has the same production function in both rich and poor countries, and that returns to capital diminish as its supply increases. However, a closer and more careful look at the situation will reveal that both these general assumptions may need to be qualified in the light of the real world situation.[26]

Labour productivity is certainly not the same everywhere. It is much higher in rich (including the dynamic, newly industrialising) countries because of the large expenditure made on the development of human capital in the form of health, education and training. Higher human capital embodied in the labour

---

[23] UNCTAD, *World Investment Report 1995*, United Nations, Geneva and New York, 1996.

[24] P. Krugman, 'Does Third World growth hurt First World prosperity?', *Harvard Business Review*, July-August 1994.

[25] International Finance Corporation, 'Development impact of IFC operations 1990', cited in *UNDP Development Report 1992*, op. cit.

[26] See in this connection, Robert Lucas Jr., 'Why doesn't capital flow from rich to poor countries?', *American Economic Review*, May 1990. Keith Griffin and Azizur R. Khan, 'Globalisation and the developing world: An essay on the international dimension of development in the post cold-war era', op. cit.

force of these countries leads to higher efficiency per unit of labour and ensures its superior production function. Nor is it certain that deepening of capital in these countries necessarily implies lower or diminishing returns. On the contrary, there is evidence that many industries in the manufacturing and service sectors in the industrial countries benefit from economies of scale, access to advanced technology based on research and wider effects of the learning-by-doing process. It is widely known that although developing countries as a whole account for about 80 per cent of the world population, they are responsible for only 4 per cent of global expenditure on research and development. Continuing technical change in the form of new methods of production and new, higher value-added goods and services, coupled with improved productivity of human capital and its positive externalities, sustain a higher return to capital in a dynamic and innovative economic environment. At the macroeconomic level, higher rates of return to capital stimulate increased investment and a faster rate of capital accumulation.

This is illustrated in Appendix III, Figure 1. It shows how the economies of scale, combined with technical change, improved human skills and associated externalities lead to higher returns to capital in rich countries – or at least enable them to avoid a decline in returns to capital despite an increase in supply. Once the importance of technology, including human skills and learning-by-doing, is recognised as a prime mover of growth and profitability, it is easy to see why capital does not always move to poor, migrant-sending countries where it is scarce, and labour cost is low, but rather tends to be concentrated in rich and dynamic economies.

This also largely explains why most of the foreign direct investment that went to developing regions in recent years was confined to a handful of countries – countries that, in addition to having attractions of low-cost labour and internal markets, have actively followed a dynamic policy of upgrading their technology, infrastructure and human capital, while simultaneously liberalising their economies and providing a conducive foreign investment environment.

It is not that capital does not move at all to poor or less dynamic countries. Because of the enormous inter-country differences in factor proportions and given, in the case of some countries, their special attractions due to abundant petroleum reserves, virgin forests and rich mineral deposits, capital does move to labour-surplus countries but only up to a point, as shown in Appendix II, Figure 2.

From all indications there is a strong positive correlation between inflows of foreign direct investment, economic growth and reduced emigration pressure. Whether the relationship is causal, coincidental or consequential, it is striking that several countries such as Chile, Malaysia, Singapore, Taiwan, China, and Thailand have concurrently witnessed broad-based economic growth, inward foreign direct investment flows and reduced emigration pressure. While foreign direct investment may stimulate some new streams of migration, it is hardly likely to be a main cause for irregular migration.[27]

In designing a comprehensive strategy for combatting irregular migration, the issue of foreign direct investment cannot be left aside. It is particularly important for reducing irregular migration among those who move in search of better opportunities abroad. Clearly, the migrant-sending countries themselves play the primary role in creating conditions necessary to attract foreign direct investment, consistent with their national development objectives. Given that the sources of foreign direct investment are mostly in the private sector, there are limits to what the governments of the source countries can do to increase the inflows of investment into migrant-sending countries. Yet the role of government policy measures in encouraging the private sector to invest in migrant-producing countries has more than marginal potential.

A detailed discussion of such measures is beyond the scope of this study. Suffice it to note briefly that these measures could range from removal or relaxation of restrictions on outward investment to active fiscal and financial incentives including tax concessions, financial assistance for investment, and effective information and promotion services. These can also include trade-related preferences in industrial country markets to encourage direct investment flows to developing countries; holding of minority shares in projects in developing countries; and providing funds in support of joint ventures or loans and credits to stimulate corporate investment in developing countries. Of particular importance are the bilateral and multilateral agreements guaranteeing fair and equitable treatment of foreign investors and covering certain political and economic risks, such as inconvertibility of local currency for dividend remittances, expropriation and loss due to civil strife.

It is not that nothing along these lines has been done. On the contrary, a number of industrial countries, and several regional and international institutions such as the European Union and the World Bank, have already been engaged in a number of these various activities, although the range and scope of the measures vary both between countries and between institutions. What needs to be noted, however, is that few of the poor countries, which are also

---

[27] This however does not exclude the possibility that when the pressure for irregular migration already exists in a country, the direction of the flows may be positively influenced by the external links established through foreign direct investment. For instance, outward investment from the Taiwan Province of China may have encouraged inflows of irregular migrants from countries that have been major recipients of its FDI. In 1990, the majority of Taiwan's foreign (mostly irregular) workers, estimated at between 100,000 and 200,000, were from Malaysia, the Philippines and Thailand – the countries which also had large FDI inflows from China. The fact that Taiwan attracted the irregular migrants mainly from these countries rather than from other neighbouring countries, including those with much lower wages, can be attributed to the impact of FDI flows on the direction of irregular migration. See Joseph Lee, 'Capital and labour mobility in Taiwan', in Gustav Ranis, *Taiwan: From Developing to Mature Economy* (1992); and Ching-Lung Tsay, 'Clandestine workers migration to Taiwan', Paper presented to the Conference to international migration Flows and foreign Investment in Asia., Tokyo, September 1991, (mimeo).

actual or potential sources of irregular migration, have been able to benefit from the existing measures. From the perspective of prevention of irregular migration, it is important that the measures be expanded and adapted to meet the specific needs and conditions of these countries. This applies particularly to possible new multilateral initiatives, notably in the WTO, on foreign direct investment flows. Poor countries may fail to benefit from freer movement of foreign investment unless it is accompanied by measures to safeguard their economic and social interests during the transition. Equally important are measures to help them overcome the existing structural constraints and thus attain a threshold of development which, as discussed above, is essential both for attracting such investment and for ensuring its sound and effective use.

Private capital flows Many of the major structural deficiencies that inhibit FDI inflows into poor, migrant-sending countries also account for their inability to have access to the private capital market on a stable and predictable basis. In several developing economies, as in Mexico before the peso devaluation in 1994, increased flows of such funds have only added to the volatility of the stock markets and fuelled greed and corruption of the affluent. And yet, given the right policy environment and a sound regulatory framework, developing countries, which now have a share of no more than 10 per cent of world market capitalization, can have access to significantly increased private capital flows, with the possibility of turning them into a positive force of stable economic growth. As a recent report of the World Bank noted, structural forces such as the ageing of the population in industrial countries and the resulting pressure for reform in pension schemes, alongside the growing integration of the developing countries, can be a powerful force to help sustain private capital flows to these countries at record levels in the future.[28]

Debt relief Many of the world's poorest economies which are also burdened with heavy external debt are actual or potential sources of irregular migration. At the end of 1994, 41 of these countries had a total external debt of $200 billion, representing more than 220 per cent of the individual countries' exports. Should these economies slip further, there could be added pressures for both survival and opportunity-seeking migration, and in the absence of opportunities for legal entry, many of them will turn to irregular channels. Clearly, for these countries the first step to take in order to avoid a deepening of the existing poverty and economic stagnation is to reorient and revamp their domestic development policies.

However, efforts by these countries alone may not be enough. This is because in addition to the direct cost of debt servicing, these countries also tend to suffer from several major handicaps associated with their indebtedness. These

---

[28] World Bank, *Private Capital Flows to Developing Countries: The Road to Financial Integration*, Washington DC, 1997.

handicaps inhibit future economic growth and thus create a vicious circle. Foreign direct investment, for example, continues to be shy because of the fear of future debt crises. Domestic investors are likely to be held back in the belief that their profits will be highly taxed to pay back the foreign creditors, and the country's scarce financial and technical resources are often tied up in a seemingly endless series of refinancing and rescheduling negotiations with foreign donors. Further public spending on external debt servicing reduces social spending, reinforcing poverty and deprivation among the low-income groups.

An internal World Bank document prepared in 1995 indicated that up to 23 of the 41 countries would face difficulties to bring down their debt burden to manageable levels even under the most optimistic assumptions of economic growth. More recent World Bank studies show that some eight of the 41 countries will be unable to reach sustainable debt burdens in less than 10 years even if all anticipated policy reforms, export growth and rescheduling of bilateral debts take place. A further 12 or so countries will find it difficult to reach the sustainable levels of debt in less than five years.

These analyses underscore the critical importance of outside help in reducing the debt burden of these countries. And given that their debts are owed to the bilateral (68 per cent), multilateral (20 per cent) and private sources (11 per cent), any such help should embrace both bilateral and multilateral action. The seriousness of the situation has now led the World Bank and the IMF to work on a programme of debt sustainability for highly indebted countries. Debt sustainability is defined as a ratio of debt service to exports of 20–25 per cent and a present value of all claims not exceeding 200–250 per cent of exports. After considerable debate and discussions, an agreement was reached in September 1996 to launch a debt relief initiative (Heavily Indebted Poor Country Debt Initiative) at an estimated cost of $5.3 to 7.7 billion over a decade. The essence of the programme is to provide poor countries with unsustainable debt burden and which demonstrate a record of sound economic policies and management to a sustainable level within six years. Some twenty countries, (several of which face high emigration pressures) are likely to benefit under the present scheme.

The agreement is a major breakthrough in providing debt relief by pooling multilateral and bilateral resources together. This, however, does not mean that the scheme has been free from all criticisms. In particular, the extent of proposed relief and the criteria for determining eligibility have been the subject of critical comment: the scheme has been called by some as being "too little, too late".[29] In the case of Mozambique, for instance, it has been estimated that

---

[29] Andrew Simms of London-based Christian Aid, quoted in *Financial Times*, London, 26 September 1996. Similar criticism was voiced by Mr. Kenneth Clarke, the United Kingdom Chancellor of the Exchequer, who expressed the view that debt must be reduced to a "clearly, and not just barely, sustainable level" and that relief must be offered "in a realistic time table", *Financial Times*, 1 October 1996.

the country will pay about three times as much in terms of debt service costs in 2004 when it would qualify for relief under the scheme. There is certainly a strong case for linking debt forgiveness, debt rescheduling and sound economic management, but the application of such a policy raises a set of complex issues, a detailed discussion of which cannot be undertaken within the scope of the present study. The important point to note in the present context is that in a significant number of debt-ridden countries a comprehensive and long-term solution to irregular migration cannot be isolated from the problem of reducing their debt hang over.

The wide-ranging economic measures discussed in this section have policy implications that extend beyond the issue of irregular migration and management of international migration in general. It will therefore be unrealistic to assume that countries, whether sending or receiving, would base their broad economic, including trade and investment, policies on migration-related considerations alone. However, a greater awareness of the manner in which these economic policies affect migration should help governments in ensuring that concerns over irregular migration be fully taken into account in designing national and international policies relating to trade, investment, aid and debt relief.

Political and human rights aspects of the strategy

The countries that force people to migrate for political reasons (many of whom may not qualify for, or may not otherwise find an asylum) should be encouraged and enabled to maintain or restore fundamental human rights, including minority rights, so that people need not seek protection outside their own countries. International pressure and persuasion should also be used so that the countries respect territorial integrity and sovereignty of states, foster democratic values and adopt measures in support of peace and reconciliation. The states should be encouraged to use the guidelines provided in various international instruments on human and minority rights and refugee and humanitarian law in enacting or strengthening national legislation on these subjects. In CIS countries, which make up one of the most vulnerable areas (discussed in Chapter 2), a beginning has been made to bring ethno-political tensions under control, while promoting the recognition of human and minority rights. The comprehensive *Programme of Action*, adopted by the CIS conference on migration and refugees[30] (Geneva, May 1996), contains a litany of measures to ensure the protection of human rights and facilitate the implementation of international humanitarian law. They deal *inter alia* with measures to prevent communal tension and internal disorder from escalating and resulting in human rights abuses, violent crimes and population displacements. This is to be achieved

---

[30] *Programme of Action*. op. cit.

through preventive diplomacy, early warning, building of democratic institutions and peaceful settlement of conflicts. The sponsoring organizations – UNHCR, IOM and OSCE – are to cooperate with the CIS countries in implementing the action programme, each acting in its own field of competence.

It is true that the action programme is basically a declaration of intent, and lacks specific targets and commitments. Much therefore depends on how and to what extent the CIS states are prepared to translate the objectives and intent into action. There is little doubt, however, that the conference has proved to be a very constructive and timely initiative, holding promise for the future. Although the conditions vary widely between regions, similar initiatives in other unstable and conflict-prone regions and areas, notably in Africa, should prove useful in spurring collective action.

Environmental aspects

The two-way links between environmental degradation and ecological disasters, on the one hand, and disorderly and irregular mass migration, on the other – are now slowly receiving attention, but they are yet to be fully factored into the relevant public policies. Few countries can boast of adequate emergency preparedness and contingency planning against possible massive and disorderly movements that may be caused by environmental factors. One important reason for this may well be the lack of adequate or precise predictive value of the current knowledge about these linkages.

Even so, there is considerable scope for applying existing knowledge and technological potential to prevent severe disaster situations that could lead to massive and disorderly population movements. Policies need to be developed to enhance environmental awareness and sensitise the public in order to reduce the risks of material and technological disasters and minimise the consequences of such disasters. Plans must be on hand for mobilising inputs that may be required for protection and assistance in the case of such disasters, for identifying structures to be set up and procedures to be followed, and for locating the sources of supplies. The assistance of the United Nations Department of Humanitarian Affairs (or the competent UN unit in the event of its reorganisation) could be useful in planning and organising such assistance programmes.

The *Programme of Action*, adopted by the 1996 CIS conference, acknowledges that states bear responsibility to eliminate the consequences of environmental degradation and disaster and recommends that environmental norms be brought in line with international standards, and that the safety of all nuclear and chemical installations be effectively insured. These basic principles are no doubt valid also for other regions, and the case for intensification of national and international efforts to ensure their effective application remains strong. At the international level, there is scope for closer collaboration between the United Nations Environment Programme (UNEP) and agencies like the

IOM and UNHCR to develop a concerted and comprehensive approach to environmentally-induced population movements, both internal and external.

5.3. Use of external aid

Aid can be used more effectively to reduce irregular migration than has been done so far. Financial and technical aid can of course be of value in enhancing the capacity of the concerned receiving countries (both developing and in transition) in enforcing border control, surveillance and punitive measures (discussed below). As concerns development-related aid, it can play an important role in strengthening the preventive action by focusing on the root causes, both political and economic, in the sending countries.[31] For example, in allocating development funds to specific projects, more emphasis can be laid on strengthening basic institutions and structures that can foster and sustain democratic values, improve societal governance and promote respect for human and minority rights. Aid donors and recipients can be more circumspect in identifying the emerging sources of political and ethnic tensions and using the aid resources to attenuate them. Closer attention can be given to enhancement of migration management capacity through development of sound migration structures and legislation.

Likewise, on the economic front, development aid can be more carefully targeted on areas of high emigration pressure and on groups of people who are the potential candidates for irregular migration. There also exists a wide scope for using aid resources, both technical and financial, in support of macro-economic, demographic, and environmental policies as well as those concerned with trade and foreign investment (some of which are mentioned in this Chapter) that are likely to have an important effect on reducing pressures for emigration, especially that of an irregular nature. But this can only be translated into action if the aid donors and recipients are prepared to link migration and refugee issues to development cooperation activities within a coherent framework. Several governments, notably the Netherlands and Sweden, have recently indicated an interest in such a coordinated policy approach. However, so far real progress has proved to be slow. In general, migration and refugee-related assistance continues to have only tangential links with the mainstream aid activities of donor and recipient countries alike.

5.4. Legal and institutional measures

A country is in no position to carry out effectively the various specific measures mentioned in the preceding two sections unless it has a clearly defined policy

---

[31] See in this connection, W.R. Böhning and M-.L. Schloeter-Paredes, *Aid in Place of Migration?*, ILO, Geneva, 1994. Bimal Ghosh, 'Migration-development linkages: Some specific issues and practical policy measures', *International Migration*, Vol. XXX, No. 3/4, 1992, pp. 445–448.

on migration, including irregular migration, supported by a sound and coherent legal and institutional framework. Border control and punitive measures, for example, have little meaning unless the national legislation explicitly stipulates the conditions of entry, stay, employment and exit of foreigners and also the rights and obligations applicable to them. Enforcement of visa rules can become arbitrary if the regulations concerning the issuance of visas and their renewal are not clear. Effective measures against irregular employment of foreigners cannot be undertaken if the conditions governing such employment are not properly articulated. In short, punitive, remedial and preventive measures against irregular migration are often closely interwoven with the legal (and as discussed later in this section, institutional) framework.

Migration legislation and structures

National legislation on irregular migration should draw on, and be consistent with, international norms and standards reviewed in Chapter 4. A detailed discussion on the scope and content of model legislation relevant to irregular migration is outside the purview of the present study. However, a number of important points that deserve special attention in such legislation have already been noted in the discussion on specific matters such as anti-trafficking measures, employer and carrier sanctions, regularisation and expulsion.

The absence of a sound legal framework not only inhibits effective punitive and preventive measures against irregular migration, but it can itself be a source of irregularity or illegality in migratory movements in two ways. As discussed in Chapters 1 and 2, when migration legislation of a country fails to take account of its internal labour and demographic needs and conditions and the external pressures from different sources in a realistic manner, it becomes difficult to secure compliance with its provisions. It has also been noted that when the legislation is ambiguous, incomplete or otherwise deficient there is the risk that the migrants or those concerned with their transport, residence or employment may involuntarily do things which the authorities may consider illegal or irregular. Aside from the already existing lacuna in the legal system, problems of ambiguity and inconsistency may arise following introduction of new laws.

Much of what has been said above also applies to the institutional framework. In the absence of an efficient migration structure and mechanism, a country cannot be expected to ensure the safety of its borders and deal effectively with the various ramifications of irregular migration. A well-organised migration structure, including a high-level coordination mechanism, capable of interacting effectively with various government agencies concerned, and coordinating all official policies which have an actual or potential impact on migration, is essential for developing coherent migration policies and legislation, including those dealing with irregular migration. It is equally important that the coordinating body enjoys the confidence and cooperation of migrants' associations and other non-governmental organisations concerned. The coordination mechanism has a particularly significant role to play in connection with the formulation and implementation of the various medium and long-term preventive measures mentioned in this Chapter. The main reason for this is that these measures cut across different policy areas and competencies of various government agencies, which makes policy coordination both important and at the same time difficult.

An adequate number of border officials, well trained and adequately equipped, is clearly necessary to enforce checks and maintain surveillance at borders in an effective and humane manner; especially so since the methods used by irregular migrants, particularly traffickers, are becoming more and more sophisticated. Staff at border crossing points need to have up-to-date information on high risk groups, travel documents and visa regulations, and the necessary training and devices to detect the falsification of documents in a way that is efficient, expeditious and non-discriminatory. Appropriate procedures must be elaborated and the staff must be suitably trained to deal with cases of detention and expulsion at the border. Given the close links between asylum seeking and irregular migration as discussed in Chapter 1 and 2, it is important that appropriate mechanisms exist to handle asylum applications in keeping with the country's refugee status determination procedures.

National migration structures must also include suitable mechanisms for emergency preparedness and contingency planning to ensure quick and effective responses to emergencies and thus avoid large-scale population movements, including disorderly and irregular external migration.

Training is important for strengthening institutional capacities needed to deal with all aspects of irregular migration. In devoting attention to the training of the border police and other officials directly concerned with the enforcement of regulations, governments must not be oblivious of the fact that development of skills and expertise is also important in various areas of short and long-term action, including emergency preparedness, contingency planning and management of migratory pressures.

As with migration legislation, institutional improvements are important for adequate enforcement of punitive and preventive measures against irregular migration. In many cases, institutional deficiencies – such as the absence of, or difficult access to, passport and visa issuing offices, cumbersome, time-consuming and costly procedures and corruption among officials – can themselves contribute to irregular migration by encouraging migrants to avoid the official agencies and procedures and take recourse to irregular channels (discussed in Chapter 2). Removal of these deficiencies should be given a high priority in the fight against irregular migration.

Migration information system

A sound and efficient information system is an essential part of the institutional arrangements needed to combat irregular migration. It has been noted that irregular migration is increasingly organised by trafficking syndicates, using multi-country networks and sophisticated equipment and communication systems. Access to such communication and information systems enables them to change the routes, destinations, hideouts and means of transport with exceptional manoeuvrability and if necessary at short notice. The situation makes it particularly important for the members of the border police force of the potential destination country to share information not only among themselves but also with their counterparts in the transit and, if possible, sending countries to track the actual and anticipated movements of traffickers. As the experiences of countries of Southern Europe – and more recently those of Central and Eastern Europe – have revealed, such exchanges are feasible only when there exists a well developed information system with access to modern computer and telecommunication facilities.

The importance of a sound information and communication system does not lie only in its supportive role in relation to border control and punitive measures. In common with various other constituents of the institutional framework, improvement in the information system can also make a direct contribution to combatting irregular migration by removing some of its basic causes. Discussion in Chapter 2 has shown that in many cases irregular migration may result from lack of information of the regulatory conditions governing the migrant's entry, residence and/or employment in the destination country, rather than from a deliberate defiance of those conditions. It has also been noted that a significant proportion of migrants, including the trafficked ones, are induced or duped to join the irregular flow as a result of misleading information and propaganda or false promises by the traffickers and other intermediaries. It is important to prevent such false publicity or propaganda by making it a punishable offence under national laws, as is done in many countries, consistent with international norms. But this is not enough. Positive measures must also be taken to disseminate reliable, objective and up-to-date information about the regulatory conditions governing migratory movements and the consequences of irregular entry, residence or employment in a foreign country. By informing the potential irregular migrant of the pointlessness of his/her action when for example job opportunities are scarce and housing situations are difficult in the destination country, and by alerting them about the risks involved in moving through irregular channels, it is possible to prevent much of the current irregular movements. It is also one of the best ways to counteract false propaganda by traffickers and intermediaries.

Disseminating information on international and regional norms concerning protection of human and minority rights, fundamental freedoms and international humanitarian laws, and sensitising the public about their values can contribute to the prevention of political and civil strife and violent conflicts, thereby decreasing the pressure for disruptive and irregular migration that often follows. The potential of a well-designed information programme in promoting basic human and minority rights and democratic values, and thus relieving one of the potent causes of unregulated migration still remains to be fully recognised and effectively tapped.

Another aspect of the preventive role of the information system concerns early warning about possible pressures for population movements, regular and irregular, resulting from new or sudden developments such as social and economic upheavals and distress, communal and ethnic tensions and strife, environmental degradation, technological hazards and other human emergencies. Migration services should maintain close cooperation with the early warning mechanisms in these various areas to collect, analyse and disseminate the relevant information in order to prevent or attenuate the situations through timely action. Capacity building for carrying out early warning functions relating to possible sources and patterns of irregular migration could be invaluable both for the potential receiving and source countries. Close cooperation with neighbouring countries through sub-regional and regional arrangements should be particularly useful in achieving this objective.

In order to enhance the credibility and usefulness of the programme, information must be precise, reliable and up-to-date. Alongside bilateral and regional cooperation, the involvement of non-governmental organisations at both local and national levels and the support, as appropriate, of international organisations such as the IOM, the ILO and UNHCR would contribute to the credibility and impact of the information programme. Cooperation with regional organisations such as the Council of Europe and the OSCE could be valuable in diffusing information concerning human and minority rights. Finally, non-governmental organisations like the International Red Cross and Red Crescent movement can play a particularly useful role with regard to the dissemination of information on humanitarian laws and standards.

5.5. Better management of international migration

The discussion in this Chapter, as foreshadowed at the beginning, has unveiled the critical importance of a coherent and comprehensive strategy to combat irregular migration. It does not provide a blueprint of such a strategy, but focuses on a number of its most important constituent elements which deserve special attention. The discussion has also revealed that in a broad sense irregular migration is a disorderly and defiant form of movement of people across countries – a manifestation of the failures and deficiencies of existing migration policies, laws and institutions. Underlying these failures there are often deep-rooted economic, political and environmental causes. Not surprisingly, many of the measures mentioned in the Chapter are as important for fighting irregular migration as for ensuring a better management of international movements of people. The two are closely inter-linked.

International migration involves both benefits and costs. In avoiding uncontrolled migration and fighting irregular movements, the positive benefits that, on balance, many countries have derived in the past from migration and can continue to derive from it must not be lost sight of. But designing a policy of orderly and regular migration, aimed at maximising the benefits and minimising the costs for both sending and receiving societies and the migrants themselves, is not an easy task. It calls for a delicate balance of many conflicting and converging interests within the national society; and since migration by its very nature is an inter-country process with increasingly important global dimensions, it warrants close and continuing cooperation between sending, receiving and transit countries at the bilateral, regional and international levels. As nations move fast into a 'New Global Age', a coherent and internationally harmonised migration regime needs to be urgently designed to foster and facilitate such action.[32] This will also serve as a most potent means of reducing the mounting pressure for irregular migration and fighting the manifold problems it entails.

[32] For the main features of such a regime, see Bimal Ghosh, 'Movements of People: The search for a new international regime', *Issues in Global Governance*, Kluwer Law International, 1995. London, the Hague and Boston (in cooperation with the Commission on Global Governance) pp. 405–424. Further work is now underway in this area under the auspices of the IOM, and with the financial support of the Swedish and Dutch Governments. The term 'A New Global Age' is borrowed from the OECD publication *Towards a New Global Age*, Paris, 1997.

APPENDIX I

Development and migration nexus: Does development reduce migration?

It is now part of the conventional wisdom that development has a J-curve effect on migration – first more and then less migration. The transitional period of high migration is sometimes called the 'migration hump[1]'. A labour-surplus country thus needs to cross the migration hump through development before emigration pressure can be expected to decline. The 1990 US Commission for the *Study of International Migration and Cooperative Development*,[2] for example, strongly argued that economic development was the only effective means of reducing pressure for migration, including irregular migration, while asserting that economic development in the short-term stimulates migration. The Commission also stated that it takes many years – even generations – for sustained growth to achieve the desired effect.

Clearly, more light needs to be shed on the nature of the interactive process between development and migration, the different variables that influence the process and the time element involved. Unless this is done, the paradigm put forward by the Commission, however useful, will continue to leave policy makers in a political dilemma.

Why does economic development initially stimulate migration? The main reasons are that development brings changes in social institutions, family relationships and the way of life; it encourages spatial mobility and creates new aspirations. While these rising expectations may not be immediately matched, development enhances the ability of people to move, both financially and otherwise. The consequence is a net increase in out-migration.

Figure 1a is a simplified model to capture the effects of economic development on migration. The rising AA curve shows that, generally, as a labour-surplus country attains a certain level of development, the ability of potential migrants to move increases. Emigration from the country reaches a high point at E^1 where the demand (in terms of need and propensity) for emigration (D^1) meets the AA curve. However, as development makes headway, the demand

---

[1] Philip Martin, *Trade and Migration: NAFTA and Agriculture Institute for International Economics*, Washington D.C. 1995.

[2] Commission for the Study of International Migration and Cooperative Economic Development, Unauthorized Migration: An Economic Development Response, Washington D.C. July 1990.

Fig. 1. Effects of economic development on emigration.

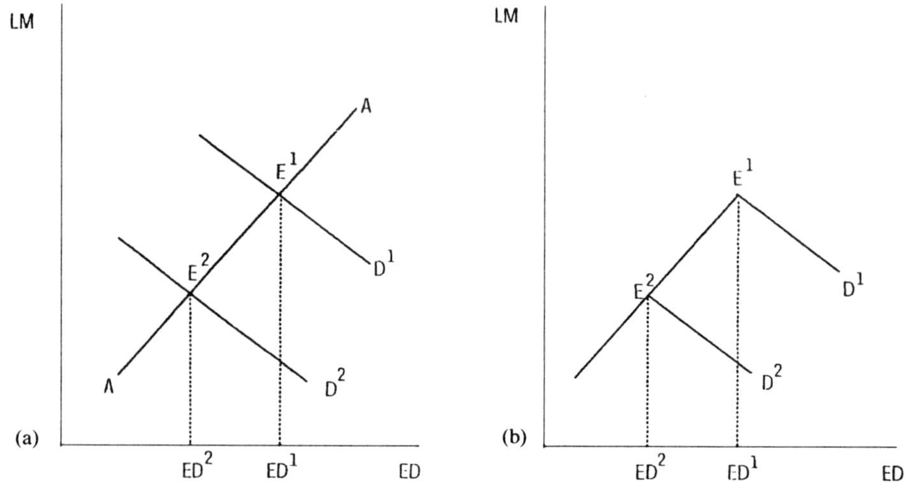

LM = Level of migration. ED = Level of economic development. D^1 = Demand for emigration (driven by unemployment, opportunity-seeking, etc.). D^2 = Demand for emigration with migration-reducing development. A = Ability to migrate as a function of economic development (increase in income or financial capacity). Does not take into account factors such as entry possibilities in potential countries of destination. E^1 = Maximum level of migration with demand D^1. E^2 = Maximum level of migration with demand D^2.

for emigration continues to fall and becomes the constraining factor beyond ED^1 (Figure 1b). When further development takes place on a sustained basis, and people become more optimistic about the future of the domestic economy, the demand for emigration tends to fall at a faster rate than that of the increase in the ability to migrate. As this happens, there could be a decline in migration, and the stage is set for what is sometimes called the 'migration transition' to be effective.

What is the time frame for this transition to take hold? It is true that in Western and Northern Europe, as exemplified by the past experiences especially of Great Britain, Germany, and Sweden, the change-over from emigration to immigration countries was the result of economic development sustained over several generations.

But, is the nature of the process immutable or the time horizon sacrosanct? Newly industrialising economies in East Asia – Singapore, Malaysia and more recently the Republic of Korea and even Thailand – have brought emigration under control in less than 15 years and in some cases in only 10 years. The story of the erstwhile emigration countries of Southern Europe is not much different. In the Caribbean, the migration transition occurred quickly in several economies such as the Bahamas, the Cayman islands and the US Virgin Islands in the wake of accelerated expansion of tourism and off-shore banking activities.

In some instances the swing has been too sharp, the problem of high emigration pressure being replaced by that of excessive immigration.

Admittedly, the contextual circumstances in which the transition took place in all these countries were not exactly the same; but the situation clearly shows that the time element is far from constant in the change-over process.

In fact, the time dimension in the migration transition is not an independent variable: it is simultaneously correlated to (i) the pattern and characteristics of development and (ii) the principal causes and types of migratory flows. A disaggregated, rather than an over-arching, view of both migration and development makes it easier to capture how the time element interacts with them.

Figure 1 shows how the pattern of economic development affects the level of migration (although it does not differentiate between different types or causes of migratory flows). If, for example, the pattern of development is of a migration-reducing nature (e.g. broad-based development with a focus on both employment creation and dynamic economic growth), then the over-all demand for emigration at any given level of development is likely to be lower, as illustrated by D^2, with E^2 as the peak point of emigration.

But the impact of development on emigration depends not just on the pattern and strategy of development, but also on the main types or principal causes of migration. A broad distinction between 'survival migration' and 'opportunity-seeking migration' provides a useful analytical tool in this connection. As explained in Chapter 2, even a high level of development can for a long time co-exist with considerable pressure for survival migration (driven by poverty, unemployment and a sense of relative deprivation) if it pays scant attention to job creation or aggravates income inequality. Conversely, development based on low-wage, low-cost export strategies that fail to encourage technological upgrading of the economy and create high-wage jobs may continue to induce opportunity-seeking migrants to look for better jobs and opportunities abroad, as exemplified by large-scale migration among the Caribbean middle class people in the past.

When development is broad-based and at the same time geared to dynamic economic growth and better income distribution, generating a new optimism among the potential migrants that tomorrow will be a better day, the demand for emigration, be it driven by poverty and unemployment or opportunity seeking, tends to fall more quickly, and the migration transition is likely to take place within a relatively short period of time, as seems to have happened in East Asia.

This, however, does not imply that development can be a full substitute for economic migration. As long as inter-country income disparities and economic divergence exist, there will always be some migratory movements in search of better opportunities. Development will continue to help this process as it brings new opportunities through closer integration of the economies of labour-surplus countries with the global economic system. These development-induced new flows will go hand in hand with the increased flows of trade and investment and inter-penetration of markets. As already discussed in Chapter 2, for these opportunity-seeking migrants, the move however is more a matter of choice than of economic compulsion. They are apt to move only to the extent that the anticipated gains outweigh the perceived costs and risks and they would normally avoid seeking entry through irregular channels. In other words, these movements will need to be seen as a part of the structural characteristics of economic globalisation.

What happens if the process of development is reversed?

Answering the question is another way of discerning the relationship between development and migration. There is little doubt that if the economies of the labour-surplus countries fail to move forward or, worse still, slide back in the future, the pressure for emigration will sharply increase, involving both survival and opportunity-seeking migrants. Unplanned and unwanted, the movements of survival migrants are likely to be disruptive at both ends of the flow, further straining the relationship between the countries of origin and destination. Even if many of them fail to reach the destination country, the build up of such enormous migration pressure will be a source of instability both in the home country and abroad. An additional disturbing aspect of the scenario under conditions of economic stagnation is that that even the opportunity-seeking migrants may feel compelled to seek entry into destination countries through the irregular channel (the distinction between the two flows will be blurred). The combined effect will lead to a sharp increase in migrant trafficking.

Figure 2 encapsulates the migration effects of alternative rates and patterns of development. The curve *MC* shows the moderately increasing migratory pressure under an existing rate and pattern of development. The sharply rising curve *MP* shows the build-up of enormous emigration potential in the case of economic stagnation. The migration trend under broad-based and dynamic economic development is indicated on curve *MD*, with *C* as the point of maximum migration. It shows that while such development may moderately increase migration in the short term, the increase is likely to be insignificant, compared to the vast potential for migration under conditions of economic stagnation. The distance between *MD* and *MP* shows the amount of potential migration avoided.

The discussion may now be summed up. First, over time and on balance, economic development tends to reduce emigration pressures in a labour-surplus country, although in the short term it may encourage some new streams of migration. Second, the time period needed for the migration transition to take place is far from constant; it is closely and simultaneously correlated to the pattern and strategy of development and the predominant causes and types of flows. Third, development-induced new streams of migration mostly relate to the search for better opportunities, increasingly linked to economic globalisation. These opportunity seeking migrants find easier social acceptance in the

Fig. 2. Migration under alternative patterns and rates of economic development.

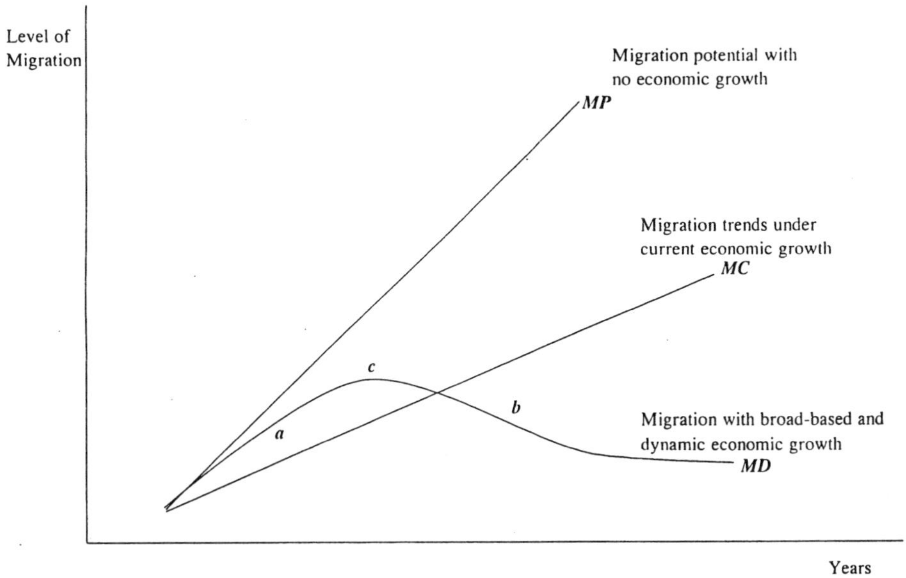

a Additional migration due to increased ability to migrate (mainly opportunity-seeking migration). *b* Reduced incentive to migrate due to broad-based economic growth in sending country. *c* Point of maximal migration.

receiving society, and hardly seek entry through irregular channels. Fourth, in the absence of economic development, the volume of pressure for migration will be overwhelming, the nature of the flows will tend to be disruptive and disorderly at both ends, and irregular migration, especially in the form of trafficking, will be further encouraged.

APPENDIX II

Unmet labour demand, immigration restrictions and irregular migration: How the process works

Figure 1 below is a simplified illustration of how under conditions of unmet labour demand (receiving country) and continuing labour supply (sending country) immigration restrictions lead to irregular migration.

In the absence of any restrictions on migration, demand is given by *DD*, supply by *SS*, and the terms of employment and the number of migrants employed are given by T^* and Q^* respectively.

A quota in the amount Q_1, together with a minimum wage for legal migrants T_1, leaves unsatisfied labour demand and labour supply. There is thus an incentive for migrants to work illegally, and for employers to hire them within the limits of Q^*-Q_1 and under terms lower than T_1. The exact volume of irregular migration (and the related terms of employment) would then depend on contextual circumstances, notably, the financial and non-financial costs of

Fig. 1.

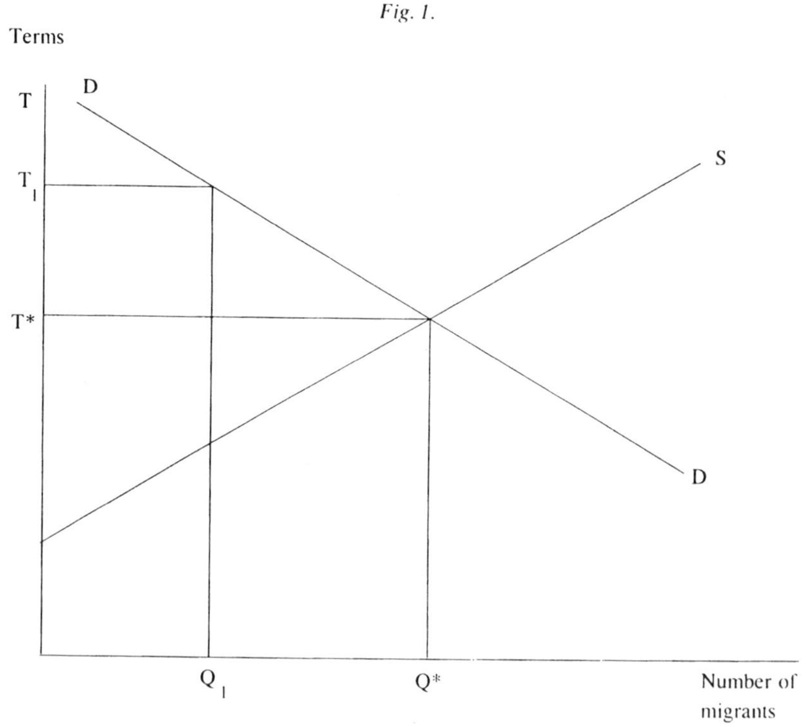

hiring workers illegaly due, for example, to employer sanctions, which would lower the demand for irregular workers. In practice, sanctions against irregular workers might also reduce their potential supply. These likely effects on demand and supply are ignored in the present simplified model; also ignored are the effects of segmentation of the labour market into formal and informal sectors.

APPENDIX III

Capital flows and rates of return: why investment gravitates to rich and dynamic economies

Under neo-classical theories, capital should move from capital-abundant countries to capital-short, poor countries. In reality, however, capital tends to gravitate to rich and dynamic economies and is generally shy to flow into capital-short countries. The following two figures explain the reasons underlying this seemingly paradoxically situation.

Figure 1 shows that higher efficiency and superior production function of labour in rich and dynamic economies, combined with technological change

Fig. 1.

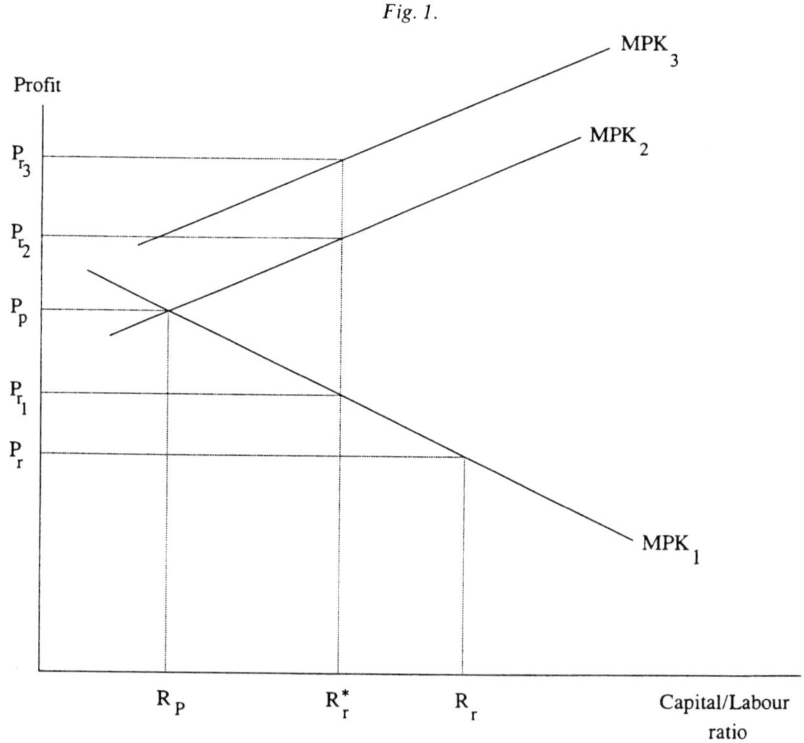

Source: Keith Griffin and A.R. Khan, UNDP, 1992.

Fig. 2.

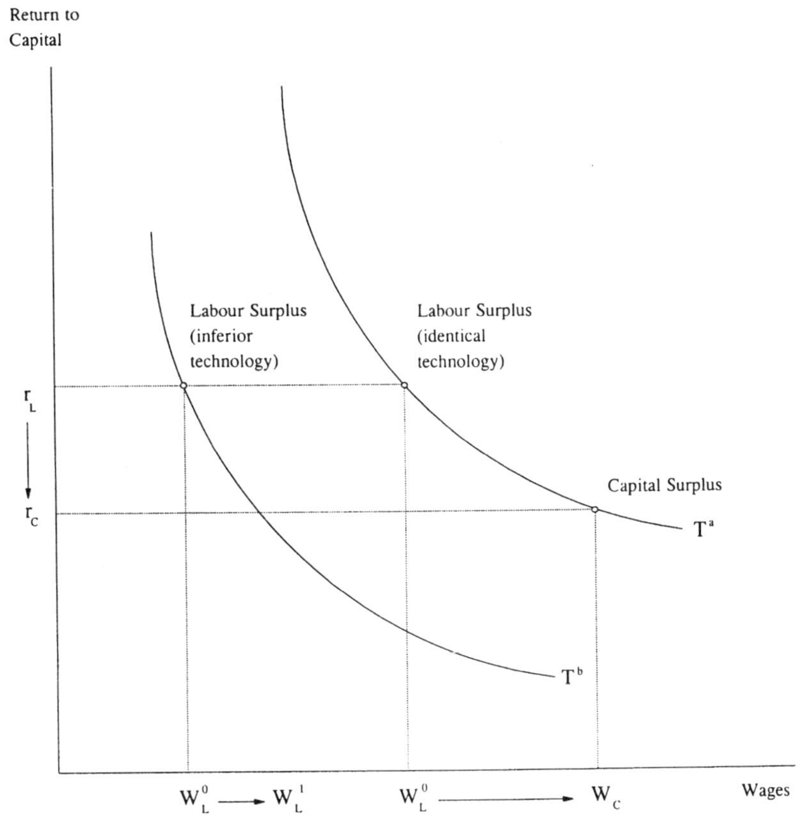

and associated externalities, enable the rich and dynamic economies to continue to benefit from higher returns to capital, creating an important gap in the profit rates of these countries and those that are poor or less dynamic and innovative. Capital thus tends to gravitate to the former.

In the above figure the rate of return to capital or profit (P) is measured on the vertical axis and the capital–labour ratio (R) on the horizontal axis. On the neo-classical assumption of symmetrical production function of labour in both rich and poor countries and a diminishing marginal product of capital (MPK_1), the profit rates in poor countries (P_p) are higher than those in rich countries (P_r). However, if the capital–labour ratios in rich countries are calculated by measuring labour in the same efficiency units as poor countries, the differences in the capital–labour ratios and profit rates will be much smaller between the two groups of countries. The profit rate (return to capital) is shown to rise to Pr_1, with a capital–labour ratio of $R*r$. When increasing (instead of diminishing) returns to capital in rich countries is taken into account, the marginal product of capital rises to MPK_2, and the rates of return (Pr_2) exceed those in poor countries. Finally, continuing technical change and associated externalities in rich and dynamic economies serve to raise the marginal product of capital further to MPK_3 and the rates of return to capital move furthest up to Pr_3, creating an important gap in the profit rates of the two groups of countries.

In a related presentation, Figure 2 explains that although capital moves from capital-rich to labour-abundant countries because of the attraction of low wages (and other possible advantages), the process is likely to stop short of closing the wage gaps between the two groups of countries. Superior technology ensures a higher rate of return to capital in rich and dynamic economies. The movement of capital from the latter to labour-abundant countries stops at the point where returns to capital are equalized, even if the wage gap is not fully closed.

According to neoclassical theories, countries with relatively abundant labour and scarce capital will have a high rate of return to capital but low wages. If the Capital-Surplus countries (*CS*) and Labour-Surplus countries (*LS*) have the same technology (T^a) then initially the rate of return to capital is higher in *LS* than in *CS*; as capital flows from *CS* to *LS* it lowers the marginal product of capital and (thus return to capital) raises the marginal product of labour (and thus wages) in *LS*. Eventually *LS* wages, W_L rise to their *CS* counterpart W_C; while the rates of return to capital get equalised as well. If the *LS* has inferior technology (T^b), however, the process of capital flows from *CS* to *LS* will not succeed in fully closing the gap between *LS* and *CS* wages; wages in the *LS* will rise from W_L^0 to W_L^1 but at that point the returns to capital are equal and no further capital flows will take place. In order for capital flows to equalise the levels of wages both regions need to have the same technology as well.

BIBLIOGRAPHY

Aderanti Adepoju, 'International Migration in Africa South of the Sahara', *International Migration Today*, Vol. 1, UNESCO and University of Western Australia, 1988.

Aderanti Adepoju, 'Expulsion of Illegals from Nigeria: Round Two', *Migration World*, Vol. 14, No. 5, 1986.

Aderanti Adepoju, 'Undocumented Migration in Africa: Trends and Policies, *International Migration*, Vol. XXI, No. 2, 1983.

Agence France Presse, 14 February 1996.

Akomako-Sarfoh J., 'The effects of the expulsion of migrant workers on Ghana's economy, with particular reference to the cocoa industry' in: S. Amin (ed.) *Modern Migration in West Africa*, Oxford University Press, London, 1974.

Reginald Appleyard, 'International Migration in East Asia', *International Migration*, Vol. XXXI, No. 2/3, 1993.

Solon Ardittis (ed.), *The Politics of East-West Migration*, Macmillan Press, London, 1994.

Michael Baker and Dwayne Benjamin, 'The receipt of transfer payments by immigrants in Canada', Working Paper, University of Toronto, 1993 (mimeo).

R. Barrow and X, Sala-i-Martin, 'Convergence across States and regions', unpublished manuscript, Harvard University, 1991.

BBC summary of World Broadcasts: 25 April 1994, 23 February, and 29 March 1995.

F.D. Bean, E.E. Telles and B.L. Lowell 'Undocumented migration to the United States Perception and evidence', *Population and Development Review*, Vol. 13, No. 4, December 1987.

G. Bertinetto, 'International Regulations on Illegal Migration', *International Migration*, Vol. XXI, No. 2, 1983.

Jochen Blaschke, 'Gates of immigration into the Federal Republic of Germany', *International Migration*, Vol. XXX, No. 2/3, 1993.

W.R. Böhning and M-.L. Schloeter-Paredes, *Aid in Place of Migration?*, ILO, Geneva, 1994.

W.R. Böhning, 'Integration and immigration pressures in Western Europe' in *International Labour Review*, Vol. 30, No. 4, 1991.

W.R. Böhning, 'Regularising the irregular', *International Migration*, Vol. XXI, No. 2, 1983.

George J. Borjas, 'The Economics of Migration', *Journal of Economic Literature*, Vol. 23, December 1994.

George Borjas, 'Self-selection and the Earnings of Immigrants', *The American Economic Review*, September 1987.

Vernon M. Briggs Jr., 'International Migration and Labour Mobility: The Receiving Countries' in Julien van den Broeck (ed.) *The Economics of Labour Migration*, Edward Elgar, Cheltenham, UK, Brookfield,USA, 1996.

Budapest Group, 'Harmonization of Legislation to Combat Trafficking in Aliens', paper prepared for the third meeting of the Budapest Group (set up by the Budapest Conference of Ministers to Prevent Uncontrolled migration) Zurich, September 1995.

Budapest Group, 'Overview of the mandate and activities of the Expert Group and of its recommendations', Doc. BG3/5, Zurich, September 1995 (mimeo).

Jorge A. Bustamante, *Undocumented migration: A theoretical-methodological framework*, OECD, Paris, 1993.

Gilian B.Caldwell, *The Sex Trade: From Russia With Love: A Project of the Investigative Network*, Washington DC, 1995 (mimeo).

Barry Chiswick, *An Analysis of Economic Progress and Impacts of Immigrants*, Final Report to the US Department of Labour, Washington DC, 1980.

Commission for the Study of International Migration and Cooperative Economic Development, Unauthorized Migration: An Economic Development Response, Washington D.C. July 1990.

Commission of the European Communities, *Commission Communication to the Council and the European Parliament on Immigration*, Sec. 91, 1855 Final, Brussels, 23 October 1991.

Bruno Contini, 'The Second Economy in Italy' in: Vito Tanzi (ed.), *The Underground Economy in the United States and Abroad*, D.C. Heathe and Co., Boston, 1982.

Corriere della Sera, 20 August, 1993, 30 November 1995, and 18 January 1996.

Council of Europe Parliamentary Assembly, *Traffickers and Employers of Clandestine Migrants*,· January, 1993 (Restricted document AS/PR (44) 26).

Daily Labour Report, 21 September 1994.

The Daily Telegraph, 1 November 1990.

Gregory DeFreitas, 'The Impact of Immigration on Low-Wage Workers', 1986 (mimeo).

De Volkstat, 5 October 1995.

Christian Dustmann, 'Earnings Adjustment of Temporary Migrants', *Journal of Population Economics*, 1993.

The Economist, (London): 1–7 April, 5–11 August, and 8–15 December 1995, 1–7 March 1997.

Economic Commission for Europe, '*International migration in the ECE region: Contemporary critical aspects*', paper presented at the Expert Group Meeting on Population Distribution and Migration, New York, United Nations, (mimeo), 1994.

W. Elkan, 'Labour migration from Botswana, Lesotho and Swaziland', in: W. M. J. Van Binsbergen and H.A. Melnik (eds.), *Migration and the Transformation of the Modern African Society*, Leiden, 1978.

El Pais: 18 March, 15 and 23 April, 3 and 29 September, 1991; 16 February, 20 and 22 July 1993; 4 January, 7 September 1994 and 25 April 1997.

European Union, *Resolution* (78) 44, 26 October 1978.

Expresso, 15 August 1992.

Federal Ministry of the Interior, 'Survey of the policy and law regarding aliens in the Federal Republic of Germany', 1991 and 1993.

Financial Times, (London): 21 October, 1994; 27 March, 13 April, 20 October 1995; 8 February, 14 February, 17 April, 20/21 April, 27–28 April, 3 May, 1 August, 26 September, and 1 October, 1996.

Michael Fix and Jeff Passel, *Immigration and Immigrants: Setting the Record Straight*, The Urban Institute, Washington DC, May 1994.

Frankfurter Rundschau, 8 August 1991, 12 April 1997.

John R. Fraser, 'Illegal Immigration in the United States and the Limits of Sanctions Against Employers' in: *Migration and Development: New Partnerships for Cooperation*, OECD, Paris, 1994.

M. Fukushima, *Immigrant Asian Workers and Japan: The Reality I Discovered at 'HELP'*, 1991.

Anthony Gar-on Yeh, *Foreign Labour in Hong Kong: Trends, Impacts and Implications*, OECD, Paris, 1990.

J.P. Garson and Y. Moulier, 'Clandestine immigrants and their regularisation in France: 1981–82', Geneva, ILO, May 1982 (mimeo).

Bimal Ghosh, *Gains from Global Linkages: Trade in Services and Movements of Persons*, Macmillan Press, London, St. Martin's Press, New York, 1997.

Bimal Ghosh, *Uncontrolled Immigration into Small Countries*, Paper prepared for the International Organization for Migration, Geneva, 1996 (mimeo).

Bimal Ghosh, 'Movements of People: The Search for a New International Regime' in: *Issues in Global Governance*, Kluwer Law International, London, The Hague and Boston, 1995.

Bimal Ghosh, 'Economic migration and the sending countries', Paper presented to the 15th conference of the Belgian-Dutch Association for Post-Keynsian Economics, University of Antwerp, October 1994.

Bimal Ghosh, 'The Future of East-West Migration' in: Solon Ardittis (ed.), *The Politics of East West Migration*, Macmillan Press, London, 1994.

Bimal Ghosh 'International population movements and global governance: A select list of key issues', Geneva, 1993 (mimeo).

Bimal Ghosh, 'Migration, Trade and International Co-operation: Do the Interlinkages Work?', *International Migration*, Vol. XXX, No. 3/4, 1992.

Bimal Ghosh 'Migratory Movements from Central and Eastern European Countries to Western Europe' in: *People on the Move: New Migration Flows in Europe*, Council of Europe, Strasbourg, 1992.

Bimal Ghosh, 'Migration-development linkages: Some specific issues and practical policy measures', *International Migration*, Vol. XXX, No. 3/4, 1992.

Bimal Ghosh, 'Trends in International Migration: the European Perspective', *The Courier*, No. 129, September-October, 1991.

M. Grantover, 'Small is beautiful: Labour markets and establishment', *American Sociological Review*', 49(3), 1984.

Keith Griffin and A.R. Khan, *Globalization and the Developing World: An Essay on the International Dimensions of Development in the Post-Cold War Era*, Human Development Report Office, UNDP, New York, 1992.

The Guardian, 14 June 1995.

M. Hasenau, 'Setting Norms in the United Nations System: the Draft Convention on the Protection of Rights of All Migrant Workers and Their Families in Relation to ILO Standards on Migrant Workers, *International Migration*, Vol. XXVIII, No. 2, June 1990.

Bernard Hockman and Guy Karsenty, 'Economic development and relative specialization in service', *Development Policy Review*, 10 September 1992.

Donald Huddle, *The Net Costs of Immigration: The Facts, the Trends and Their Critics*, Carrying Capacity Network, Washington DC, 1996.

Donald Huddle, *The Net Costs of Immigration to California*, Rice University, Houston, 1993.

Andrea Ichino, *The Economic Impact of Immigration on the Host Country*, Unpublished paper, Bocconoi University, Milan, Italy, 1992.

The Independent, 16 May 1992.

Inter-Governmental Consultation (IGC), *Illegal Aliens: A Preliminary Study*, Geneva, 1995.

Inter-Governmental Consultation (IGC), 'Summary Description of Legislation of Aliens Trafficking', Secretariat of the Inter-governmental Consultations on Asylum, Refugee and Migration Policies in Europe, North America and Australia, Geneva, December 1995.

Inter-Governmental Consultation, IGC Work Plan for 1995, *Illegal Aliens*, Geneva, 14 October 1994.

Interpreter Releases – report and analysis of immigration and nationality law, Vol. 74, No. 7, 11, 24, 24 February, 24 March, and 30 June 1997.

International Herald Tribune (Paris): 7 September 1993; 4 April 1995, 13 February, 7 April, 21 May 1997.

ILO, S. Weintrraub and S. Diaz Briquet, 'The use of foreign aid for reducing incentives to emigrate from Central America', in W.R. Böhning and M.L. Schloeter-Parades, *Aid in Place of Migration*, Geneva, 1994.

ILO, *The Dilemma of the Informal Sector*, Geneva, 1991.

IMF, *World Economic Outlook*, Washington DC, 1996.

IOM, *Trafficking in Migrants*, (Quarterly Bulletin): March, December 1996; March, June 1997.

IOM, '*Trafficking of Women To Countries of the Western European Union: Characteristics, Trends and Policy Issues*', Geneva, 1996.

IOM, *Chinese Migrants in Central and Eastern Europe: The Cases of the Czech Republic, Hungary and Romania*, Geneva, September 1995.

IOM, Migration Information Programme, *Trafficking and Prostitution: The Growing Exploitation of Migrant Women from Central and Eastern Europe*, Geneva, 1995.

IOM, 'International Response to Trafficking in Migrants and the Safeguarding of Migrant Rights', Geneva, 1994.

IOM, Migration Information Programme, *Transit Migration in Ukraine*, Geneva, August 1994.

IOM, Migration Information Programme, *Transit Migration in the Russian Federation*, Geneva, July 1994.

IOM, Migration Information Programme, *Transit Migration in Poland*, Geneva, April 1994.

IOM/The Refugee Policy Group (RPG), *Migration and Environment*, Geneva and Washington DC, June 1992.
International Policy Council on Agriculture, Food and Trade, *Sugar Policy in the Post Uruguay Round Era*, Washington DC, 1996.
Inter-Press Service, 17 March 1994.
Japan Economic Newswire, 15 May 1994.
Jiji Press Ticker Service, 16 May 1994.
Journal de Geneve, 5 December 1995.
Journal Officiel, 26 June 1996.
Kang, S.D., 'Globalization of the labour market also in South Korea?', February 1996.
Saburo Kawai, 'Japan and International Migration: Situation and Issues', *International Migration*, Vol. XXXI, No. 2/3, 1993.
P. Krugman, 'Does Third World growth hurt First World prosperity?', *Harvard Business Review*, July-August 1994.
La Libre Belgique: 17,19/20 and 22 January 1991; 10 February 1993.
Richard Layard et al., *East West Migration: The Alternatives*, The MIT Press, Cambridge, Mass. USA; London, England, 1992.
R. Layard, S. Nickell and R. Jackman, *Unemployment: Macro-economic Performance and the Labour Market*, Oxford University Press, New York, 1991.
Joseph Lee, 'Capital and labour mobility in Taiwan' in: Gustav Ranis, *Taiwan: From Developing to Mature Economy*, 1992.
Le Monde: 24 April 1992; 1 March, 16 November 1995.
Le Soir: 18,23,24 January 1991; 10 February 1993.
Liberation: 22 October, 1992; 29 November, 5 December, 1995.
Lin Lean Lim and Nana Oishi, *International Labour Migration of Asian Women: Distinctive Characteristics and Policy Concerns*, 1996 (mimeo).
Reinhard Lohrmann, 'Irregular Migration: An Emerging Issue in Developing Countries', in: Reginald Appleyard, *The Impact of International Migration On Developing Countries*, OECD, Paris, 1989.
Juan Luis Londono, *Poverty, Inequality, and Human Capital Development in Latin America, 1950–2025*, World Bank, Washington DC, 1996.
Robert Lucas Jr., 'Why doesn't capital flow from rich to poor countries?', *American Economic Review*, May 1990.
A. Macheret, *L'immigration etranger en Suisse al'heure de l'integration europeenne*, Georg, Geneva, 1969.
Raisul Awal Mahmood, 'Clandestine Foreign Workers and Domestic Labour Market: Process of Integration and Implications.' Paper presented to the IOM/UNFPA Policy Workshop on Emigration Dynamics in South Asia, Geneva, September 1996 (mimeo).
Philip Martin, 'Guest Workers' Policies: An International Survey', 1995 (mimeo).
Philip Martin and Elizabeth Midgley, 'Immigration to the United States: Journey to an Uncertain Destination', *Population Bulletin*, Vol. 49, No. 2, Washington DC, September 1994.
Migration News: Vol. 1, No. 3–5, 9 April-June, October 1994; Vol. 3, No. 1,2,7,8, January, February, July, August, 1996; Vol. 4, No. 1, 2, 4,5, 7, January, February, April, May, July 1997.
Migration News Sheet, February, April, May, September, November 1991; January, June, November, December 1992; September 1993; January, February, July, November 1994; January, March, May, November 1995; February, March, May, September 1996, May, July 1997.
The Mixed Economic Progress, Rand Corporation, Santa Monica, July 1996.
National Research Council, *The New Americans: Economic, Demographic and Fiscal Effects of Immigration*, Washington DC, 1997.
New Straits Times, 18 March 1994.
New York Times: 23 February and 16 September 1994.
David North and Marian F. Houston, *The Characteristics and Role of Illegal Aliens in the US Labour Market: An Explanatory Study*, Washington, DC, Linton and Company, 1976.

OECD, *Towards a New Global Age*, Paris, 1997.
OECD, 'Irregular immigration in Italy', Note by the Secretariat, Paris, 5 June 1995 (mimeo).
OECD, 'Migration Trends in Some Asian Countries', Paris, 1993, (mimeo).
OECD, *Trends in International Migration* (SOPEMI) Paris, 1990, 1992, 1993, 1997.
Padoa-Schioppa (ed.), *Mismatch and Labour Mobility*, Cambridge University Press, 1991.
Marta Peletier, 'Regularisation and Obligations of Unauthorized Immigrants in the Receiving Countries. Protection of the Fundamental Rights of Unauthorized Immigrants', *International Migration*, Vol. XXI, No. 2, 1983.
A. Pelligrino, 'Colombian migration in Venezuela', in: R. Appleyard (ed.), *The Impact of International Migration on Developing Countries*, OECD, Paris, 1989.
A. Portes and S. Sassen-Koob, 'Making it underground: Comparative material on the informal sector in Western market economies', *American Journal of Sociology*, 93(1), 1987.
Presidents' Commission, 1951.
Prognos, *The Development of the EC Labour Market*, Basel, 1989.
Sharon Russell, K. Jackobsen and W.D. Stanley, *International Migration and Development in Sub-Saharan Africa*, World Bank Discussion Papers, Africa Technical Department Series, Washington DC, 1990.
San Francisco Chronicle, 23 June 1993.
Christoph Schmidt, 'The Earnings Dynamics of Immigrant Labour', Universität Munchen, Discussion Paper, No. 92–28, 1992.
I.J. Seccombe and R.I. Lawless, 'State intervention and the International Labour Market', in: R. Appleyard (ed.), *The Impact of International Migration on Developing Countries*, Paris, OECD, 1989.
Select Commission on Immigration and Refugee Policy, *US Immigration Policy and the National Interest* (Final Report), Washington DC, US Government Printing Office, 1981.
Roger Mark Selya, 'Illegal Migration in Taiwan: A Preliminary Overview', *International Migration Review*, Vol. 26, Fall 1992.
Julian Simon, *Immigration: The Demographic and Economic Facts*, Cato Institute, Washington DC, 1995.
Julian Simon, *The Economic Consequences of Immigration*, Basil Blackwell, Oxford, 1989.
S. Spencer, 'Illegal migrant laborers in Japan', *International Migration Review*, Vol. 26, No. 3, 1992.
Der Spiegel, No. 49, 1995.
P. Stalker, *The Work of Strangers: A. Survey of International Labour Migration*, ILO, Geneva, 1994.
Der Stand, 2 January 1996.
The Straits Times, 14 March 1994.
Süddeutsche Zeitung: 8 June, 25 November, 1994; 16 May 1995.
Swedish Ministry of Labour, *A Comprehensive Refugee and Immigration Policy*, Stockholm, 1990.
F.D. Taylor, 'Undocumented Mexican immigrants and the earnings of workers in the United States', *Demography*, Vol. 23, No. 1, February 1988.
J.E. Taylor, *Micro Economy-wide Models for Migration and Policy Analysis: An Application to Rural Mexico*, OECD, Paris, 1995.
Ching-Lung Tsay, 'Clandestine workers migration to Taiwan', Paper presented to the Conference on International Migration Flows and Foreign Investment in Asia, Tokyo, September, 1991 (mimeo).
United Nations, Economic and Social Council, Commission of Human Rights, 'Measures to improve the situation and ensure the human rights and dignity of all migrant workers', E/CN.4/1997/65, 16 December 1996.
United Nations, *World Population Monitoring 1997*, New York, 1996, (Draft).
United Nations, *Review of Population Trends, Policies and Programmes*, Economic and Social Council, E/CN.9/1995/2, 17 January 1995.
United Nations, 'Update on the CIREFCA Process', United Nations General Assembly, Executive Committee of the High Commissioner's Programme, Forty-third session, A/AC.96/INF.176, 21 September 1991.

United Nations, *International Migration Policies and Programmes*, Population Studies, No. 80, New York, 1982.
UNCTAD/IOM, *Foreign Direct Investment, Trade and Migration*, Current Studies Series No. 29, United Nations, Geneva, 1996.
UNCTAD, *World Investment Report 1995*, United Nations, Geneva and New York, 1996.
UNCTAD, documents submitted to the Commodities Committee, Geneva, 1995.
UNCTAD 'A preliminary analysis of the results of the Uruguay Round and their effects on the trading prospects of developing countries: report by the UNCTAD secretariat' 10 June 1994, United Nations document No. TD/B/WG.413.
UNCTAD, 'Note on international trade and poverty alleviation', June, 1994 (mimeo).
UNCTAD, *Trade and Development Report 1991*, United Nations publication, Geneva, 1991.
UNDP, *Human Development Report 1992, 1994, 1995, 1996 and 1997*, Oxford University Press, New York, 1993, 1994, 1996, 1997.
UNDP, Central Evaluation Office, 'UNDP/UNRO Cooperation: An Evaluation', December 1989.
United Nations Economic Commission for Europe, *International Migration Bulletin*, No. 7, United Nations, Geneva, November 1995.
UNHCR/IOM/RPG, International Symposium on 'Environmentally-induced Population Displacements and Environmental Impacts Resulting from Mass Migrations', Geneva, 21–24 April 1996.
UNHCR/IOM, CIS Conference on Refugees and Migrants, 'Programme of Action', CISCONF/1996/PA/5., 20 May 1996.
UNHCR/IOM 'Joint Operational Strategy in the Countries of the Commonwealth of Independent States, Years 1996–2000', CISCONF/1996/CRP/2/Rev, 23 May 1996.
UNHCR, *The CIS Conference on Refugees and Migrants*, European series, Vol. 2, No. 1, January 1996.
United Nations International Research and Training Institute for the Advancement of Women, *The Migration of Women*, Santo Domingo, 1994.
United Press International (UPI), 18 June 1996.
US Commission on Immigration Reform, *US Immigration Policy: Restoring Credibility*, Washington DC, 1994.
US Department of Labor 'The relationship between the Immigration Reform and Control Act of 1986 and Labour Standards: An exploratory essay', Washington DC, 1990.
US General Accounting Office, *Report to the Congress: Immigration Reform: Employer Sanctions and the Question of Discrimination*, Washington DC, March 1990.
R. Utuza, *Population Redistribution Mechanisms as Related to Various Forms of Development in Population Distribution Policies in Development Planning*, United Nations, New York, 1981.
M. Villapondo et al, *A Study of the Socio-Economic Impact of Illegal Aliens, County of San Diego*, Human Resources Agency, San Diego, CA., 1977.
Wall Street Journal, 9 September 1994.
Robert Warren, *Estimates of the Undocumented Immigrant Population Residing in the United States, by Country of Origin, and State of Residence: October, 1992*, INS Statistics Division, Washington DC, 1993.
Washington Post, 28 December 1995.
The Washington Times, 3 November 1995.
Sidney Weintraub and Gilberto Cardenas, 'The Use of Public Services by Undocumented Aliens in Texas', Policy Research Project Report, Lyndon Johnson School of Public Affairs, University of Texas, Austin, 1984.
Linda Weiss, 'Explaining the Underground Economy: State and Social Structure, *The British Journal of Sociology*,Vol. 38, 1987.
P. Wickramsekara, 'Recent trends in temporary labour migration in Asia'. Paper presented to the seminar on Migration and the Labour Market in Asia in the year 2000, Tokyo, January 1995.
Jonas Widgren, 'Multilateral Co-operation To Combat Trafficking In Migrants and The Role of International Organizations', ICMPD, Vienna, 1994.

Jonas Widgren, 'Movements of Refugees and Asylum-seekers: Recent Trends In A Comparative Perspective', OECD, Paris, 1991.
World Bank, *Private Capital Flows to Developing Countries: The Road to Financial Integration*, Washington DC, 1997.
World Bank, *Poverty Reduction and the World Bank: Progress and challenges in the 1990s*, Washington DC, 1996.
World Bank, *Taking Action to Reduce Poverty in Sub-Saharan Africa*, Washington, DC, 1996.
World Bank, *World Bank Development Report 1995 and 1996*, Washington DC, 1996 and 1997.
Pan Yotopoulos, 'The World Distribution of Income: Some Estimates', *Pakistan Journal of Economics*, 1976.
Klaus Zimmermann, 'European Migration: Push and Pull', paper presented at the World Bank's Conference on Development Economics, April 1994.

INDEX

Italic page numbers refer to tables, figures or boxes.

Refugees and Human Rights

1. P. Kourula: *Broadening the Edges.* Refugee Definition and International Protection Revisited. 1997 ISBN HB 90-411-0480-1
PB 90-411-0481-X
2. B. Ghosh: *Huddled Masses and Uncertain Shores.* Insights into Irregular Migration. 1998 ISBN 90-411-0531-X

KLUWER ACADEMIC PUBLISHERS – DORDRECHT / BOSTON / LONDON